Inside the Pakistan Army

A Woman's Experience on the Frontline of the War on Terror

Inside the Pakistan Army

A Woman's Experience on the Frontline of the War on Terror

Carey Schofield

Biteback Publishing
London

PENTAGON SECURITY
INTERNATIONAL
AN IMPRINT OF PENTAGON PRESS

Inside the Pakistan Army / Carey Schofield

ISBN 978-81-8274-563-6

First Indian Edition 2011

First published in Great Britain in 2011 by **Biteback Publishing Ltd, Westminster Tower, 3 Albert Embankment, London**. This edition published in arrangement.

Published in India by
PENTAGON SECURITY INTERNATIONAL
An Imprint of
PENTAGON PRESS
206, Peacock Lane, Shahpur Jat
New Delhi-110049

Printed at
Aegean Offset Printers, Greater Noida, U.P.

Contents

Acknowledgements

It has been a great privilege to be able to study the Pakistan Army for the last few years. I am truly grateful for all the support and encouragement that the Army has given me during this time.

I would like to record my gratitude to General Pervez Musharraf and to General Ashfaq Parvez Kayani, the Chiefs of Army Staff while I was working on this book, and to the very many other officers and soldiers who gave generously their time and their insights.

I owe particular thanks to the Inter-Services Public Relations Directorate, under Major General Shaukat Sultan, then Major General Waheed Arshad (now Lieutenant General), and finally under Major General Athar Abbas, for patience and consideration above and beyond the call of duty.

Outside the Army, I would like to record my gratitude and affection for Afzal Khan and his family, whose kindness and hospitality never failed. There were tough times during my research, and I would not have been able to cope without the support of Afzal, his daughter, Zishan Afzal Khan (Mouse), and their extended family. Nothing negative that I say about civilians could ever apply to them. Within this family I also owe a particular debt of gratitude to Dr Humayun Khan.

Among those who have helped me in England I would like to record my thanks to Hew Strachan, Ian Talbot, Ian McLeod, Shama Husain and Claodete and Patrick Galea.

Michael Smith has helped and supported me throughout my work on the Pakistan Army: I cannot repay his kindness.

Lastly, Biteback Publishing has shown astonishing forbearance during the writing, editing and production of this book. James Stephens and Katy Scholes have been towers of strength, and without Sam Carter's sleepless nights you would not now be reading this. I thank them all.

Carey Schofield, London 2011

N
AFGHANISTAN
North West
Frontier
Nowshera
Abbotabad
Peshawar
Cherat
ISLAMABAD
Rawalpindi
Chakwal
Kharian
Gujranwala
Faislabad
Lahore
Punjab
Okara
Multan
Muzaffargarh
Quetta
Sibi
ISLAMIC
REPUBLIC
of
IRAN
Nasirabad
Baluchistan
Larkana
Sindh
INDIA
Gwadar
Hyderabad
Karachi
ARABIAN
SEA
International Boundary
State Boundary
National Capital
State Capital
Cities
Districts
Towns

NORTHERN AREAS
OF PAKISTAN
GILGIT
CHITRAL
AFGHANISTAN
SWAT
KOHISTAN
DIR
SHANGLA
KASHMIR
BATTAGRAM
BAJAUR
MALAKAND P.A.
MOHMAND
BUNER
MANSEHRA
KABUL
MARDAN
CHARSADDA
ABBOTTABAD
SWABI
HARIPUR
PESHAWAR
NOWSHERA
KHYBER
ORAKZAI
KURRAM
HANGU
KOHAT
ISLAMABAD
N. WAZIRISTAN
KARAK
MIRAMSHAH
DATTA KHEL
BANNU
PUNJAB
LAKKI MARWAT
S. WAZIRISTAN
PAKISTAN
TANK
WANA
DERA ISMAIL KHAN
FATA
Khyber-Pakhtunkwa
Miles
0 25 50 100

1

The Question of the Pakistan Army

When President Barack Obama walked into the East Room at the White House and announced that Osama bin Laden had been tracked to a house in Pakistan and killed by US Navy Seals, who left taking his body with them, the Pakistan Army was faced with the gravest crisis in its 64-year history. The American operation had been successfully completed before the Pakistan Army, intelligence services or government knew what was happening.

That morning, 2 May 2011, General Ashfaq Parvaz Kayani, the Chief of Army Staff, stood exposed before the world as either incompetent or complicit in harbouring a mass murderer. Admiral Mullen, Chairman of the Joint Chiefs of Staff, had telephoned Kayani at 03.00 (Pakistan time), a couple of hours after the killing, to give him the news.

Pakistanis were appalled. The violation of sovereignty was the truly traumatic aspect of the whole thing for most people: American troops could, it was now clear, carry out an operation on Pakistani soil, far away from the Afghan border, with complete impunity. In Abbottabad, home to the Pakistan Military Academy and the regimental centres of two of the country's most prestigious regiments, the US Army could land helicopters, while others hovered nearby, and a bloody operation ensue, without anyone in the armed forces being aware that anything was going on.

The Pakistan Army's relationship with the US military was thrown into question. The Pakistan–US relationship as a whole was equally uncertain after the raid.

In fact, the Pakistan Army has never been entirely trusted by the West. Its role in the war against terror has often been seen to be as ambiguous as it has been central. Has the Army's notorious ISI (Inter-Services Intelligence Directorate) continued to support its long-term allies amongst the Taliban, with or without the tacit consent of the head of state? Have elements in the Army siphoned off aid given them by the Americans to support the very forces it was supposed to be used to suppress? How strenuous or even sincere has the Army ever been in its attempts to round up Taliban fighters fleeing from NATO forces across its borders? To what extent has every element in the military machine been under the control of the head of state? The Pakistan Army has been dogged by these questions. Despite the protestations of successive Army chiefs, Western officials have continued to brief journalists about the double dealing of Pakistan's Armed Forces and the intelligence directorates.

Whatever its misgivings about the loyalties of the Pakistan Army, however, the United States has had no choice but to rely on it in this war. Without the support of President Pervez Musharraf, the US-led war in Afghanistan would have been an even more perilous undertaking.

This dependence has compelled it to overlook Pakistan's central responsibility for the world's worst case of nuclear proliferation. Pakistan developed its capacity in response to the nuclear threat from India, but this technology has been sold to North Korea, Iran and Libya at least – and perhaps to other states too. Was the largesse that this brought kept solely by the infamous Dr A. Q. Khan, the so-called 'father of the Islamic bomb', or was it shared by a wider circle?

Many of Pakistan's own intellectuals accuse the Army of being more interested in making money than in defending the state. They describe the military as parasitical, insisting that it grabs the best land – both agricultural and commercial – for its senior officers, monopolises large areas of the country's economy and seizes the most lucrative state contracts for companies that it runs. They argue that the ills that beset Pakistan are the result of a corrupt and predatory Army.

Although the country's chattering classes enjoy attacking the military, the working man always took a certain pride in the Army. Following the killing of Osama bin Laden feeling against the Army spread into the middle and lower classes, which had until then been generally been supportive of the Army. The people of Pakistan were appalled by the Army's apparent incompetence; they felt betrayed. After the events of 2 May 2011 the Army's relationship with its own people was ruptured.

In the days and weeks that followed Lt General Ahmad Shuja Pasha, the Director General of the Inter-Services Intelligence Directorate – the famous ISI – bore the brunt of public criticism. A marathon session in the National Assembly – held in camera but widely reported afterwards – was an unprecedented humiliation for the ISI; the Director General was subjected to prolonged hostile and even mocking questioning. An observer described how 'Kayani watched – only leaving the hall for the occasional cigarette – while his subordinate was torn limb from limb'. General Shuja Pasha lost his temper during the questioning and publicly offered to resign.

General Kayani's stock within the Army plummeted to an all-time low. He had lost respect when he accepted an extension of three years in his post as Chief of Army Staff: he had promised to respect the institution of the Army above everything else, and to attend to the welfare of the troops. But by overstaying his welcome, his own officers felt, he undermined the institution, wrecking the proper rotation and giving it a chief who was becoming much older than most of the three-star generals. General Kayani's Pakistan Army number is 12850, but his lieutenant generals' PA numbers tend to begin with 16. Furthermore, over the years Kayani's own activities had come under the spotlight. When he took over as Chief he was respected for his efforts to improve the housing provided for NCOs and soldiers. Now, general officers pointed out, it was clear that the most spectacular and expensive improvements had been to his own residence, Army House, where he intended to spend another two years and more.

After the killing of bin Laden General Kayani held a series of 'town hall' meetings in key garrison cities. According to officers who were present (captains and majors) the questions were tough and the attitude towards the Chief verging on insolent.

Senior serving and retired officers began to say that the mood towards the Army's senior leadership – from within the Army as well as from troublesome civilians – was worse than at any time since 1971–2, when the Army was blamed for the loss of East Pakistan. Civilians distinguished between the soldiers and young officers who were dying in the war against terrorism, and for whom they had sympathy and respect – and the top brass, whom they saw as – at best – spoilt and incompetent. From different corners of the country, and from men of varying ages and ranks, the message was the same. Public opprobrium was so intense that trust between the armed forces and civilians seemed to have disappeared.

As the country was engulfed in an apparently relentless wave of terrorist attacks, contempt for the military grew. A prolonged assault on PNS Mehran, a naval base in the southern port city of Karachi, killed sixteen people including ten soldiers. The public was shocked by the savage terrorist attack, but people were also angered that lapses in security had allowed the carnage, at a time when the whole country was braced for violence in retaliation for the killing of Osama bin Laden.

Pakistan is poor and beset by social ills. Overwhelmingly the most serious of these is the fact that the legal system does not work. The police are not effective. The courts are corrupt and incompetent. There is simply no justice. People are patriotic, but disillusioned with the state. This was the direct cause of the Swat uprising, and has contributed to the strength of the Taliban elsewhere in Pakistan. It has also undermined attempts to counter militancy in the country. When the Army has captured terrorists and handed them over for trial, they have not been convicted, even for heinous crimes.

Militant extremism has grown drastically over the last decade. The threat is everywhere, and generally ignored. When the Taliban moved from Swat into neighbouring Buner in April 2009, headlines across the world – and in Pakistan – screamed that the Taliban were only sixty miles from Islamabad. They were missing the point. Extremists with violent views – call them Taliban or what you will – were already in Islamabad. Servants in the houses of the rich all seemed to have brothers, sons, cousins connected to mosques that were known to be hotbeds of violence.

It is not hard for a visitor to see the close connections between ordinary people and the extremists. A driver I knew, who worked for one of the biggest hotels in Islamabad, had a sister who had been in the Red Mosque. He was a bright young man, hardworking and enterprising, always dressed in shirt and trousers (rather than the loose local shalwar kameez) even in the height of the summer's heat. There were two things he liked talking about. The first was how he could find a better-paid job, preferably abroad. The second was his sympathy for the Taliban, especially when they came under attack. He spoke in a neat, brisk way and his conversation was punctuated with 'Madam' every few words. But as he drove – fast and straight, never looking at me in the mirror – and spoke so politely he was, in fact, expressing his support for al Qaeda and Taliban attacks in Pakistan and Afghanistan and abroad.

Questions surrounding these issues face anyone who is trying to understand the Pakistan Army. I have spent seven years studying this institution, and frequently despaired of reaching the truth. The Pakistan Army gave me greater access than they had ever afforded any outsider,

Pakistani or foreign. I travelled all over the country to visit military units and training establishments. In the autumn of 2005, at the suggestion of the Army, one of the military tailors in Rawalpindi made a uniform for me. I had extended discussions with General Musharraf – and travelled with him on a number of occasions – and with his principal staff officers. I visited the ISI headquarters repeatedly over the years and have known the last four men to hold the post of Director General of the ISI. For months on end I lived in Pakistan, and was constantly visiting and talking to and lunching with serving and retired officers. I came to understand their morals and manners, to know how they felt about the key issues facing them. But, the better I got to know the Army, the more bewildered I became. I found it hard to reconcile what I knew of the institution with its reputation at home and abroad, or, indeed, with what its officers sometimes said about it. The officers I met believed, above all, in safeguarding Pakistan. Like professional soldiers everywhere they believed in stability and order. Some were noticeably pious, others avowedly liberal, and many more were quietly professional and tolerant. The vast majority were hardworking, intelligent people whose views could not easily be categorised. They were united in their patriotism and their loyalty to the Army.

In the Army, at least, discourse is reasoned. Military men listen to each other and argue logically and courteously. The civilian world outside the cantonments is wild and violent: unreason rules, and shrill voices harangue mindlessly.

Throughout my time with the Pakistan Army the 1971 war, which led to the loss of half the country (when East Pakistan became the new, independent state of Bangladesh) was the elephant in the room, the extraordinary issue that (almost) no one mentioned. Yet the experience of that conflict scarred Pakistan's officers for decades.

Three successive chiefs had a major influence on my view of the Army. General Jehangir Karamat, General Pervez Musharraf and General Ashfaq Parvez Kayani each embodied different aspects of the Army and of the country.

But there were others. In no particular order, I think of the unimpeachable Imtiaz Hussain; glamorous Hamid Rab Nawaz; outgoing Safdar Hussain; scrupulous Khalid Shameem Wynne; clever and kind Ahmad Shuja Pasha; darkly brilliant Nadim Ijaz; indefatigable Sallahuddin Satti; neat Tariq Majid; honourable Hamid Khan; guileless Javed Alam;

principled Masood Aslam; gutsy Alam Khattak, gentle Munir Hafiez and his thoughtful cousin Mahmud Durrani; wryly humorous Shaukat Sultan; endearing Ahsan Saleem Hayat; uncompromising and enlightened Waheed Arshad; and the rather grand Ahsan Azhar Hayat.

Faisal Alavi contributed a lot to this book. He talked a great deal and he loved writing, so sent long emails – from which I have quoted at length – in reply to my questions. He spoke to me, in 2008, of his belief that he might be murdered. I have never known whether or not there any truth in what he feared. I have, however, felt some responsibility to tell his story.

All these people helped to shape my vision of the Army. But hundreds of other conversations with officers of every rank and with their soldiers have taught me what I know about the Army. I have been on the frontline in the war against terror. I have visited units on the border with Afghanistan, whose soldiers are fighting in perilous conditions in North and South Waziristan; I spent time with the troops in the old princely state of Swat and in the tribal region of Bajaur, places where the Army has been shocked by the strength of the insurgents; I have been to Quetta, a calm old British Indian Army cantonment in Balochistan where the twin perils of a spillover of Taliban fighters from Afghanistan and virulent nationalism are ever present; I have been to Kashmir, the area so close to the hearts of the Pakistan Army, and for which so much blood has been spilt; I have visited Pakistan's Special Forces at their mountain headquarters in Cherat and at their Tarbela base; and I have visited the Pakistan Army's corps headquarters, including those facing the country's geographically vulnerable eastern border.

The most crucial facts to know about the Pakistan Army are these:

The Army is over 550,000 strong, with a further 304,000 paramilitary troops including the Frontier Corps and Rangers.

In 2010 Pakistan's defence budget was $5.2 billion.

The Indian Army is 1,129,900 strong, with a further 1,300,586 paramilitary troops.

India's defence budget was $38.4 billion.

(From *The Military Balance 2011*, published by London's International Institute for Strategic Studies.)

The Pakistan Army is desperately over-stretched. One-third of its strength is tied up in counter-insurgency operations on the western border, one-third is deployed on the eastern border. The remaining third is preparing to go on operations. It can not sustain this level of commitment indefinitely.

It is worth pointing out that Pakistan Army troops are still deployed on the Siachen Glacier. A ceasefire has been in effect since 2003, but the conflict has not been resolved.

2

The Place of the Army in Pakistan

Pakistan has been created and its security and defence is now your responsibility. I want them to be the best soldiers in the world, so that no one can cast an evil eye on Pakistan, and if he does we shall fight him to the end until either he throws us into the Arabian Sea or we drown in the Indian Ocean.

(The *Quaid* speaking to the Guard Commander in Peshawar, March 1948. *The Pakistan Army: 1947–49*, Major General Shaukat Riza.)

Pakistan has a population of 185 million, making it the sixth most populous country on earth. It has borders with the two most populous, China and India. With the latter it has had three major wars (1947, 1965 and 1971), and the still unresolved Siachen Glacier conflict (1984–) in Kashmir. In 1999 there was the Kargil conflict, also in Kashmir, and a precarious standoff in 2001–2. India, not surprisingly, overshadows the Pakistan Army's thinking.

Pakistan is a federal republic with four provinces: Punjab, Sindh, Balochistan and Khyber Pakhtunkhwa (until recently called the North West Frontier Province). Punjab is the most significant of these, standing in some ways in relation to the country as England does to Britain. It has the largest population (more than half of all Pakistanis live in Punjab) and is often resented by the other provinces for dominating public life, for complacency and for assuming that its interests are those of the country at large. Punjabis are accused of snobbery and of a certain flat-footedness: there is a sense that they don't get the jokes that the others are making about them. The Army is often accused of being Punjabi dominated, although it is making great efforts to broaden its recruiting base. Its name derives from the Persian *panj-ab*, 'five rivers', referring to the five rivers (Jhelum, Chenab, Ravi, Beas and Sutlej) that flow across Punjab into the Indus.

Sindh, to the south, derives its name from the Indus; home to an ancient civilisation, it has been known by the same name since the seventh century BC, at least, when the Assyrians called it Sinda. Sindh has the second largest population and includes Karachi, Pakistan's largest city and main financial centre. If the Punjabis are compared to the English, then the Sindhis must be the Welsh, with a strong cultural tradition, a track record for producing some of the greatest orators in the country's history, an enthusiastic style of religion and a knack of annoying the dominant nationality.

Balochistan, to the west, is the largest of Pakistan's provinces. It covers over 40 per cent of the country, but it is home to only 5 per cent of its people, including a large Pashtun population. Its main city is Quetta, home to the Army's Command and Staff College and a corps headquarters, and an important port is being developed at Gwadar. Balochistan is rich in mineral resources including copper, gas and gold, but powerful landlords control most of the wealth. The people are generally poor. There has been a simmering insurgency in Balochistan, fuelled by these landlords, ever since the creation of Pakistan. If the Punjabis are the English, and the Sindhis the Welsh, the Baloch, away to the west, are the Irish. Admired, often actually liked, they are nevertheless felt to be unpredictable. There is always the possibility of real trouble from that quarter.

Khyber Pakhtunkhwa, in the north-west, is the stronghold of Pakistan's Pashtun population. Much of the province is mountainous, but it also includes lush valleys and valuable farmland. The province has had to cope with a vast but fluctuating population of Afghan refugees for much of the last thirty years; after concerted efforts at repatriation the number is probably now down to about a million. Terrorism and the fear of terrorism have had a destructive effect on the economy and on society over the last decade. But the Pashtun are resilient. Using my model of the British Isles, the Pashtun are undeniably the Scots: a slightly dour northern people renowned for their liking for money, who nevertheless have a wild romantic strain and while complaining about the dominance of their southern neighbour manage to be very well represented in public life, including the armed forces.

In addition to the four provinces in Pakistan, there are the Federally Administered Tribal Areas (FATA). These areas, straddling the border with Afghanistan, were never placed under regular administration by the British. They were inaccessible, and the Pashtun tribespeople troublesome, so a system was evolved whereby the tribes ran their own affairs but their potential for violence (especially towards the British) was contained by tribal gatherings (*jirgas*), selected tribal leaders (*maliks*) and political agents, British officials of the Indian Civil Service representing the government locally. The law in the FATA was the 1901 Frontier Crimes Regulations, based on collective punishment of the tribes when any of their members stepped out of line. Until the last few years it appeared that this system, anachronistic and anomalous though it was, worked. Governments of Pakistan always had more urgent issues to deal with than rationalising the status of the Tribal Areas, so the FATA remained since 1947 virtually untouched by federal hand. There are seven Tribal Agencies in FATA. From north to south these are: Bajaur, Mohmand, Khyber, Orakzai, Kurram, North Waziristan, and South Waziristan. There are also six small areas called the Frontier Regions (FR): FR Bannu, FR Dera Ismail Khan, FR Kohat, FR Lakki Marwat, FR Peshawar and FR Tank. These are administered by a civil servant in the adjoining district that the FR is called after. FR Bannu is thus administered by Bannu District, which is a settled area (in other words, not part of FATA).

There are also a number of Provincially Administered Tribal Areas (PATA), whose status is similar to that of the FATA, except that they fall under the Provincial Governor rather than the federal government. PATA in Khyber Pakhtunkhwa include the formerly independent princely states of Chitral, Dir and Swat.

Azad Jammu and Kashmir, usually referred to simply as Azad Kashmir (Free Kashmir) is part of the former princely state of Jammu and Kashmir, the disputed territory that has defined Pakistan's relationship with India ever since 1947. It is a self-governing state under Pakistan.

Gilgit-Baltistan, in the far north-east of Pakistan, was also part of the state of Jammu and Kashmir. This territory was known as the Northern Areas until 2009.

The four provinces of Pakistan, plus Kashmir, apparently correspond to five nationalities: Punjabis, Sindhis, Baloch, Pashtun and Kashmiris. The four major provinces all have mixed populations, however, and there is an almost infinite number of smaller identities within these larger divisions. The Pashtun divide into tribes and sub-tribes, the Punjabis into tribes and *qaums* (clans) and they speak a number of languages including Seraiki, Hindko and Dogri.

But there is another major community in Pakistan. This is the mohajirs, the migrants who moved from India at the time of partition or since. These Urdu-speakers, as they are frequently called, who form about ten per cent of the population, are in many ways the backbone of Pakistan. They are well educated and hardworking, and unfettered by the tribal rivalries and old quarrels that absorb so much energy elsewhere in the country.

Pakistan's three key cities are Islamabad, Lahore and Karachi. They represent the country's abiding interests. Islamabad is the capital, a small modern city where everything revolves around government. With Rawalpindi, home of the Army's General Headquarters, a stone's throw away, this is the seat of power.

Lahore, on the other hand, is an old Mughal centre, courtly, decaying beautifully, full of whispered intrigue, parties, scandals, snobbery. This place is about social life.

Karachi, the largest city in Pakistan, is said to have a population of twenty million, half of them Urdu-speaking mohajirs. There are also large Pashtun and Punjabi communities here. Less than 10 per cent of Karachiites are Sindhis. The city is riven with ethnic violence and political feuding. But life – and commerce – go on and people ignore the troubles and the growing poverty and the trivial obsessions of other cities. In the metropolis, business is business.

The Army looks east, constantly, to its traditional enemy. It looks north, anxiously, to Afghanistan. But it also looks west, to Iran. Pakistan's border with Iran is the only one that is not disputed. Although Iran's current instability is a source of concern, many Pakistanis will argue that their country is bound to its western neighbour by older links than those connecting it with the rest of south Asia. Although the Mughal and British rulers brought most of south Asia into one dominion, large areas of what is now Pakistan were once ruled by Persia. Sindh and Punjab were part of the Achaemenid Empire, seven thousand years ago, and Balochistan was ruled by the Sassanids. The Urdu language derives its alphabet and much of its vocabulary from Persian. The words of the Qaumi Tarana, Pakistan's rousing national anthem, are written in a highly Persianised Urdu. At a reception at the Presidency on 14 August (marking Independence Day), a senior officer told me, with evident satisfaction, that its entire vocabulary was either Persian or Arabic. He was pleased that the national hymn was uncontaminated by words of Sanskrit origin.

Ever since Pakistan was created in 1947, the Army has been its most powerful institution. The death of the country's founder, Muhammad Ali Jinnah, a year after independence, and the assassination of his successor in 1951, left the country rudderless and increased the importance of the Army. So it has a high profile in the country, for historical reasons. Not only has it governed for almost half of the country's history, but it has provided arguably the most competent and benign governments the country has known, as the political and intellectual elites (they, in their turn, infantilised by long periods of military rule) have demonstrated their irresponsibility and inability to solve the country's problems. Even in periods of civilian rule, the Army has been seen to be the crucial power-broking institution. Politicians in Pakistan believe that they have to reckon with what the generals will tolerate.

The argument that the Army is the only thing that really works in Pakistan is one of the most commonly stated facts about the country. Even the Army's critics frequently repeat it. It is not the whole truth; the better bits of the Civil Service of Pakistan, including the Foreign Service, work as well as most others. Notwithstanding these exceptions, there is a lot of truth in the assertion that the Army is the only thing that works in the country.

Pakistan's judicial system has – for decades – been a byword for corruption and incompetence. Years before President Musharraf sacked Chief Justice Iftikhar Chaudry I was told, ruefully, 'In England you hire a lawyer. Here it's much simpler: you hire the judge.' It was not a joke, just a self-deprecating observation of a type that Pakistanis are rather good at. The police force is little better. Policemen are generally assumed to be incompetent and brutal. They are certainly poorly paid, badly equipped and schooled in the knowledge that anyone with a bit of money will be able to buy himself out of trouble (unless he is up against somebody more powerful) and that no one will thank a policeman for pursuing the facts rather than listening to advice. Senior police officers have high social status and are seen at all the best parties. These men are from the Police Service of Pakistan, recruited centrally and deputed to the provinces. They are described, by an Ambassador I know, as 'very corrupt and also inefficient'.

The Army functions. It exists in every province; it meets every morning. It can cope with the unexpected and it upholds standards of behaviour that military people in other countries would recognise.

The Pakistan Army is, in many ways, like other national armies. All depend on order and discipline, on a strong *esprit de corps* and on a culture that will sustain individuals and the institution alike during times of hardship. The Pakistan Army looks like the British Army, or at least it looks like the British Army used to look. The regimental system, the structure, the terminology and the argot all come mostly from its forebear, the (British) Indian Army. But it has evolved, since 1947, into a unique organism, partly indigenous and partly Western.

Over the six decades since independence and partition from India, the Pakistan Army has had to confront numerous threats. The worst was in 1971, when an uprising in East Pakistan and war with India led to the loss of half the country. The Army was humiliated, reviled by its own people. Insurgency in Balochistan, from 1973 to 1978, again endangered the integrity of the state. Neither side held back when it came to brutality. In the last decade the Pakistan Army has faced its most intractable enemy, in the frontline of global terror. The state's territory may not be threatened, but continual low-level violence, punctuated by the shock of dramatic acts of terror, such as the bombings in public places, attacks on Army and police personnel and high-profile assassinations, takes its toll. The Army has debated how to handle the terrorist threat, as any professional fighting force would. Army officers endlessly agitate over the relative importance of dialogue, of development, of the consistent use of sufficient military force and of effective coordination between the military and civilian authorities.

All the time, riven through the Army's thinking and its debates is the influence of religion. The Army preserves its past, and takes great interest in the history of its old units. Drawing on the glories of originally British regiments and Islamic warrior traditions, the Army has developed a morality and style of its own. Much as they love the inherited titles and the battle honours, some men in uniform seem to feel that an Islamic military ethos should be fundamentally different from its Western counterpart. The legacy of the East India Company and the Raj may be colourful but it is also pompous humbug. A Muslim serving in the Pakistan Army is bound to wonder whether the Army of the Islamic Republic should not embody a cleaner and more masculine virtue.

The Pakistan Army is large: well over half a million strong, not counting paramilitary forces. The reserve forces (retired officers and men who left the Army within the last eight years) add another half million to the strength. Despite the dangers and the political controversies that the Army has faced, there has never been a shortage of people wanting to join Pakistan's armed forces. Although the constitution provides for conscription, it has never been necessary to draft men.

There is barely a family that has not had someone in uniform; even in the most apparently unmilitary families, there is almost always a grandfather or a cousin or an uncle who was in one of the services.

Images of the Army are written into the collective memory of the country. The names and deeds of the heroes of the 1965 war with India are familiar to everyone of a certain age in Pakistan. The anthems of that time stir feelings of patriotism and nostalgia even in those who are too young to remember 1965.

Whenever there is a natural disaster, a flood or earthquake, or a big rail accident, troops will be called in to help. Pakistan's geographical situation, and its often inadequate infrastructure, mean that such disasters occur frequently. The floods of the summer of 2010 were the greatest catastrophe in the nation's history, but virtually every year some residential areas are flooded.

The Corps Commanders, the lieutenant generals who command the nine geographically based corps, are public figures. The Corps Commanders Conference, where they all meet together with the Chief of Army Staff and the eight Principal Staff Officers and heads of the Army's directorates (Military Operations, Military Intelligence, Inter-Services Public Relations), are always reported in the media. The fashionable salons of Islamabad are abuzz with stories about what has been said at these gatherings. In their air-conditioned drawing rooms the generally idle rich talk knowingly about what is happening behind the scenes. They wear expensive Western clothes and speak English... and the less they know the more they talk. The Corps Commanders Conferences are not seen to be internal Army affairs. Many Pakistanis are convinced that the country's political course is decided at these meetings.

The Army lives mostly in calm and leafy cantonments, where – typically – low white buildings line broad avenues. Some of the forty or so cantonments are 'open', really just sectors of major cities such as Lahore or Karachi. Houses in these well-planned areas are much sought after by civilians. Not only are they safer than other parts of the cities, due to Army security, but water, sanitation and other services are more reliable. Other cantonments are 'closed', self-contained towns that outsiders cannot enter without permission. The housing provided for the Army is generally clean and functional, but it is not luxurious. Junior to middle-ranking officers might well live more comfortably if they were civilians. They would earn significantly more if they had jobs in industry. But the cantts, as they are known, are soothing oases of cleanliness and rational urban planning. Moving between the Army and the civilian worlds, the message is clear: the Army runs things, even towns, better than the civilians. The gap between the two has fuelled the allegation that the Army has creamed off national resources for itself. It does not help, in this instance, that the cantonments were started by the British after the Mutiny in 1857, when it seemed prudent to remove troops from city centres. The Army is sometimes seen as the natural successor to the Raj, assuming as if by right the role of protector of the nation; the cantonments certainly have the air of colonial rule.

Men at Their Best

A man's life changes forever when he joins the Army. From now on he belongs to the military. He will never shake off – and nor would he want to – the training instilled in him. Whenever two soldiers, of whatever rank, walk side by side they naturally fall into step. Formal harmony is created at once.

It is hard for those outside the Army to understand why soldiers want to accept a way of life that imposes such discipline and restrictions. Submission to higher authority sits uneasily with modern life, even in a country such as Pakistan where almost everyone bows to the dictates of faith. The virtues prized by the Army – loyalty, self-sacrifice, duty, honour – seem anachronistic in the grasping and cynical twenty-first century. The idea of delegating power over oneself for the sake of the greater good is laughable to the Pakistani elite.

But the Army dignifies its personnel. Even the newest *jawan* (soldier, literally 'young') has his rights as well as his duties, giving him a status that he would be unlikely to find in the world outside. The way he ought to conduct himself is laid down, as is the way he should behave towards his superiors. Throughout his Army service, he will know what he ought to be doing at any moment. The knowledge that he is at the bottom of the command structure is less significant than the fact that he has joined an honourable institution that will look after him. Not only is soldiering a noble calling, but the Army will now look after his parents as well as his wife and children. The Army takes far better care of its personnel than most other employers in Pakistan, institutional or individual.

Ordinary soldiers understand the Army's failings. They bear the brunt, after all. It is clear, when they talk, however, that they revere the institution and that they serve it with unstinting loyalty. The *jawans*, modest though they may be, never forget one important fact: they are the backbone of this Army.

Conditions in the Army are tough. Pakistan's climate is unforgiving and soldiers face constant hostility from the sun and from freezing cold. Even without combat operations, the Army is in constant danger from the terrain.

Lt General Safdar, Commander XI Corps in Peshawar, told me that when he was commanding a brigade in the Northern Areas he used to send vehicles out, daily, to pick bodies out of ravines. He was clearly exaggerating, but not much.

Although the Army's presence is seen throughout the country – and felt whenever there is a disaster or a political crisis – it remains a world apart. One of its slogans, 'men at their best', sums up its attitude towards its own. It is proudly elitist, confident that its selection process identifies the fittest and most dedicated and grooms them into effective leaders.

The idea of 'how we do things' is very powerful in the Pakistan Army. This notion involves standard operating procedures, prescriptions and accepted ways of doing things. At its suffocatingly petty worst it is a maddeningly self-satisfied approach that stifles initiative and innovation and brooks no argument. The 'how we do things' yardstick is often very funny, with the Army almost parodying itself in its obdurate conservatism. But this way of looking at the world and assessing possible courses of action is an intrinsic strength of the Army. Convention is hallowed and previous commanders and long dead subedars are commemorated. The Army's way of doing things may be rigid, but it is tried and tested. It is crucial to the Army's understanding of its own identity.

Loyalty to the institution overrides everything else. Among themselves, officers will debate the effectiveness of current operations as they endlessly reassess history. They are interested in the Army to the point of obsession, and they are disturbed by any failings it may have They will argue about personalities and politics, swop stories of absurdities and criticise GHQ, but none of this indicates any ambivalence about the Army. Officers will almost invariably rein in their own doubts for the greater good of the institution. They have no doubt that the Army is more than the sum of its parts and that, whatever its foibles, its wisdom usually prevails.

Factions have not emerged in the Army. Men with very different ways of life and attitudes to key issues serve shoulder to shoulder. It is possible to identify groups in the Army, but – surprisingly – these are not based on social background or religious fervour. The links that bind military men together tend to come from service and regimental loyalty and friendships born through working together. Strange groups of people remain friends for years, because they have served in the same place, surviving danger, having fun, bringing up their families together, coping with the loss of comrades.

This is the source of the Pakistan Army's power. Its strength does not derive from its weaponry but from its institutional culture. Officers and men alike know what the Army stands for and they subscribe to its values. They like the military ideals of service and selfless sacrifice. They submit to discipline, and they do so most willingly, wanting to be part of the Army they revere.

But the Army is changing, and it is changing faster than the rest of the country. In its early years the Pakistan Army was officered by the sons of landed families and successful professionals; the country's prominent families all had someone in the Army. Young men entering Pakistan's Military Academy nowadays tend to come from less affluent backgrounds.

For the old-timers, the privileged sons of the elite, there was not only a feeling of entitlement but also a sense that anything was possible. In the old men, who served in the early days of Pakistan, you can still see the panache and detect the readiness for adventure that characterised the country's first soldiers.

After independence in 1947 the soldiers continued to resemble their forebears. The Pakistan Army went on enlisting men mainly from the British Empire's favourite recruiting grounds in Punjab. The dependable tribes that the Raj had relied on – Awans, Janjuas, Sattis and Gujjars – formed the backbone of the growing Pakistan Army. Successive regimes realised, however, that Pakistan could not afford to allow any group to feel that the Army was 'other'. President Musharraf's government, in particular, wanted to open the Army up to people who did not come from established Army families.

Other major armies have undergone similar changes. But in Western

Europe social changes have affected them more slowly than the rest of society. In Pakistan the reverse has been true. In a country that remains, in the expression used by Pakistanis themselves, largely 'feudal', the Army has provided one of the few avenues to the top for an able but penniless man. This is a country where it is hard for a young person without connections to break into any well-paid job, let alone any of the professions. But the Army is porous, open to talent: the current Chief of Army Staff, General Kayani, is the son of a non-commissioned officer.

Beset by Enemies

Never far from the surface, in the Pakistan Army, is the sense that the country is beset by enemies and that there are spies everywhere. There is a feeling that Pakistan has always been engaged in an existential struggle and that it remains imperilled from many quarters.

Bharat – the Sanskrit for India – is the ever present threat. Officers and men speculate endlessly on Indian intentions and capabilities. India, most men in uniform believe, is implacably hostile to the country's existence and intent upon absorbing Pakistan's territories into its own republic. Hindustan opposed partition, and – as Pakistanis constantly recall – snatched Kashmir against the will of the people. In the 1965 war, also fought over Kashmir, the Indian Army reached the outskirts of Lahore. In 1971 India supported Bengali separatists and contributed to the breakup of the country.

Quite apart from its military aggression, Pakistanis point out, the Indian national anthem itself refers possessively to Sindh in its second line: 'Thy name rouses the hearts of the Punjab, Sindh, Gujurat and Maratha'. The words of the anthem were written by Tagore in 1911, but it nevertheless seems odd that the national hymn of India should assume its dominance over Sindh, which is entirely Pakistani territory. The threat from the east has dominated the Army's thinking from the day of its birth. Although some Pakistani generals and diplomats now believe that peaceful coexistence with India is possible and crucially important for Pakistan, others remain deeply suspicious of Hindustani motivation. Pakistani thinking on Afghanistan is governed by the conviction that the Indians are plotting to encircle them.

The United States' intentions are an even greater concern for many senior officers. The Americans have been crucial allies since the 1950s. They have poured money into Pakistan. A great many senior officers of the Pakistan Army have undergone training in the US at some stage in their careers. Yet the Americans are profoundly feared by many Pakistan Army officers, who are convinced that the United States wants Pakistan to fragment; they believe that the Americans are unwilling to allow a strategically placed nuclear-armed Muslim state to survive intact, and they adduce Western attitudes to Palestine and in the war in Iraq as evidence of deeply rooted anti-Islamic bias. Military people are not alone in believing that India and the US are both committed to the destruction of Pakistan. These views are widely held in Pakistan, even among Western-educated elites.

In view of these concerns it is not surprising that the Pakistan Army is obsessively security conscious. 'Unlicensed contact with foreigners' is forbidden, to the great embarrassment of officers who have enjoyed hospitality abroad. Successive generations have chafed at regulations that prevent them returning the kindness they encountered attending courses in the US, UK, China and elsewhere. The ban goes against the grain for Pakistanis, a people for whom hospitality is bound up with self-respect. But the procedures that an officer has to go through in order to get Military Intelligence sanction for contact are tedious and intrusive. Officers frequently feel that it is simply easier not to attract attention by asking permission. A few brave souls see their foreign acquaintances without licence. Others ignore friendly approaches from old friends, and cringe with shame when they recall how well they were treated on their travels. These regulations do not cover family members who live abroad but officers complain that it is unclear exactly which contacts are covered. In a country where almost everyone has relations abroad, particularly in Britain and North America, and where there is such extensive interaction with other militaries, the taboo on contact with foreigners is bewildering. It only makes sense in context: in its sixty years Pakistan has been dogged by serious security concerns. Even when the Army was not actively engaged in operations, there was political tension with India. The obsession with secrecy was undoubtedly heightened through covert activities during the Soviet war in Afghanistan and then in Indian-controlled Kashmir. Clandestine operations against powerful adversaries, planned and executed by the intelligence agencies, depended for their success on subterfuge, secrecy and deniability. This created habits in the Army and ISI that are often said to characterise these organisations today.

Parallel concerns about security have lead the Military Intelligence (MI) Directorate to take a profound interest in exactly what officers are up to. The character of the MI directorate depends to some extent upon the character of its Director-General (DG). Some DGs are said to have used their powers lightly, to provide tactical intelligence and maintain security within the Army. General Nadeem Taj and General Muhammad Asif are well thought of in the Army. Other former DGs have different reputations and their legacies linger in the Army's collective consciousness. Who drinks, whose marriage is unhappy, who has connections to politicians or powerful businessmen: all of these things may be of interest to the MI. 408 Intelligence Battalion records what is going on throughout the Army and can make its presence felt in a way that many in the Army consider counter-productive. It has been accused of creating an atmosphere of mistrust, and generating anxiety among the officer corps. The feeling that it is easy to put a foot wrong and blight one's career leads men to avoid risk of any sort. It can also undermine relationships within units if officers fear that their colleagues' gossip, even if it is not malign, may reach the wrong ears. This approach is not even good for security, the MI's critics say. The hysteria about secrecy blurs the distinction between important material and simple information that need not be restricted. It also creates barriers between the military and the rest of society that damage the Army's standing.

It is frustrating to see an Army that is so impressive and which works so closely with Western armies that (except in one or two important but arcane areas) it can have no real secrets, making itself appear hostile and even occasionally ridiculous. It is worth pointing out, though, that intrusive surveillance, leading to an almost total lack of privacy, is a routine feature of Pakistani family life. Extended families and close-knit circles of friends and acquaintances, stretching over several generations, give people the security and support that have disappeared from many Western communities. The price to be paid for this is that everyone always knows what everyone else is doing. Loss of reputation is a serious matter, and the fear of this instils caution.

Faith

Think not of those who are slain in Allah's way as dead. Nay, they live, finding their sustenance in the presence of their Lord; they rejoice in the bounty

> *provided by Allah. And with regard to those left behind, who have not yet joined them (in their bliss), the (martyr's) glory in the fact that on them is no fear, nor have they (cause to) grieve.* Quran: Surah 3. 169–70

The civilising values of Islam permeate the Army. The presence of the faith is tangible, manifest in the language that people use even when they are not talking about religion. The qualities that Army officers seem to admire – honesty, loyalty, frugality, modesty, contentment, dignity, respect – are characteristically Islamic ideals. Evidence of the faith is everywhere in the Army, from time set aside for prayer five times a day (in accordance with the requirements of the religion), to the provision of a prayer-suit to every gentleman cadet at the Pakistan Military Academy; from the *qibbla* (arrow sign pointing to Mecca) in most offices to the slogans encouraging soldiers to fight in the way of Allah. *Jummah* (Friday) prayers are an important event in units when everyone gathers together, regardless of rank. At the beginning of official or semi-official events short passages from the Koran are often sung. Funerals, all too many of them nowadays for young men killed in the line of duty, are simple, as Islam prescribes. There is no complicated requiem ritual; the mourners gather in an open place and pray standing in straight lines, fortified by the calm dignity of the community at prayer as well as by hope. All these things attest to a faith that ennobles and enlightens, and that is simply taken for granted most of the time. It seems entirely natural, within the Army, that the flawed are nurtured and the exuberant guided.

Religion was one of the issues that interested me most in my time with the Pakistan Army. There were constant allegations, in the world's media, about Islamist penetration of the armed forces. The Army was aware of cases where soldiers or officers had been radicalised and was determined to prevent this happening again. So I looked, all the time, for opportunities to talk about religion. Some were shy about this, as Army officers anywhere might be. Others chatted away happily. One of the officers working in the Inter-Services Public Relations Directorate was rather obsessive about religion. He made a lot of religious jokes that I struggled to understand. One day he told me that he had bought his mother a pair of shoes, for which she had been very grateful: 'It's all right, Ama, I said. The Prophet, peace be upon him, said that Heaven is under our mother's feet.' He giggled cheerfully at this witticism. He used to talk about the end of the world a lot, and shop like there was no tomorrow.

Religion is a powerful motivating force in the Pakistan Army. The country was created on the basis of religion, and it is therefore clear to any patriotic Pakistani that its interests are Allah's interests. The certainty that God is on their side has long motivated Christian armies, after all. Faith that their cause is right and that, if it comes to it, the Almighty will reward those who die fighting for him, gives soldiers courage.

Although religion is woven into the fabric of everyday Army life, it is not the done thing to talk about the details. In my travels with the Pakistan Army away from Rawalpindi I normally interviewed senior officers alone, without anyone sitting in on the conversation. One day, however, Major General Shaukat Sultan (the Director General of Inter-Services Public Relations) accompanied me to a meeting with a three-star general. The conversation was fine, until we got onto the subject of religion, when our host said that he was a Shia and began to explain some of the differences between Shias and Sunnis. I could see that General Shaukat Sultan was uncomfortable, and then angry, although I had the impression that he liked the man in question. Afterwards, as we walked down the wooden corridor leading to the way out, he explained his irritation: 'He should not have talked to you about being a Shia. Within the Army we are simply Muslims. We pray together, we all go to the mosques in the units. There is no such thing as Shia, no Sunni inside the Army.' I knew General Shaukat Sultan well, and considered him to be of a most equable disposition. I therefore realised that this issue must be something about which he cared deeply. It makes sense: the unity of the Army is vital. The institution must take precedence over sects of any sort.

The Army is intensely aware of the threat of extremism penetrating the ranks, and tries to ensure that soldiers are inoculated against radicalism through constant exposure to sound religious education and informed debate. A captain from the artillery explained to me that he had been taught, at the Pakistan Military Academy, to examine his conscience in the light of various surahs (chapters) of the Koran. He still carried a notebook with him, containing details of this exercise, and although he was bashful about it, he produced the notebook.

Surah 2, the longest chapter in the Koran, deals with various issues, including encouragement to embrace Islam, the prohibition on charging interest on loans and a famous passage (the best-known verse in the Quran) of the power of God.

Based on this chapter, the captain told me, there was a list of questions that a man should ask himself. It went like this:

> Ayah (verse) 42: Have I tried to cover the truth with falsehood?
> Ayah 44: Have I been enjoining right conduct on others and forgetting to practise it myself?
> Ayah 177: Have I been patient through adversity and crisis?
> Ayah 263: Have I been using kind words?

And so on.

He was clearly interested in his religion. This training had not been compulsory, he said, but he was grateful for it.

None of this was the language – nor the approach – of extremism.

The Islamic calendar interested me. In Pakistan the state runs, like most of the rest of the world, on the Western Gregorian calendar. But there's another rhythm to life in Pakistan, an entirely separate way of marking time. Both ways keep going, stridently uncoordinated. The Islamic calendar has twelve months, each of thirty days: every year the Islamic calendar moves backwards by about five days in relation to the Gregorian calendar.

During a long road journey in the north of Pakistan I asked a brigadier about the months of the Islamic year. He was a religious man, tall and lean with a small beard and an intense interest in the world.

The first month of the year, the brigadier told me as we drove along a rocky mountain road, is *Muharram* (derived from the word *haram*, 'forbidden'), a period of great significance to Shia Muslims in particular. The 10th of *Muharram* is *Ashura* ('tenth day'), when the Shia remember the killing of Imam Husain – the grandson of the Prophet Muhammad – his family and others at the battle of Kerbala (680 AD). Mourning processions are held in places where there is a large Shia population, led by a riderless white horse. Talk of a procession conjures images of calm progress, but these were notorious for their passion and even violence.

I did not need to ask whether he was Shia or Sunni; his distaste was clear. 'Men and boys parade, stripped to the waist, singing and chanting. They slash at their backs using chains with razor blades, or knives, until their flesh is raw, with blood pouring down their legs. They are bewailing that they were not at Kerbala to save Husain and his companions.' The bearded brigadier commented that the security forces – police, Army and paramilitary – are always on the alert for sectarian attacks at the time. On the same day, the 10th of *Muharram*, Sunni Muslims celebrate Moses's victory in Egypt, freeing the Israelites from captivity.

The second month is *Safar*, 'empty', so called because after the month of *Muharram* was over, everyone went off to war leaving their houses empty. Soldiers were sometimes superstitious about this month, the brigadier said, considering it unlucky. No matter how often they were told that this sort of thinking was irrational and un-Islamic, some clung to the idea.

Rabi al-Awwal, 'the beginning of spring', includes the birthday of the Prophet, and is followed by *Rabi al Sani*, 'the second spring'. It is confusing that the names of several months correspond to seasons, when the calendar rotates so that the months may occur in spring, summer, autumn or winter. The kindly brigadier said that, in his opinion, it was good to be reminded of the time of the second Caliph, Umar, when the months were named. *Jamadi al Awwal*, 'the first freeze', and *Jamadi us Sani*, 'the second freeze', follow. The seventh month, *Rajab* 'respect', is a sacred month named after a river in Paradise, whiter than milk and sweeter than honey. Anyone who has fasted during this month, even for one day, will be able to drink from this river. Another holy month follows. *Sha'baan* means 'to spread out or distribute'. The brigadier told me that the night of the 15th of this month is believed to be the time when Allah determines the fate of every human being – including who shall die – for the coming year, and it is spent by many Muslims in prayer and in reading the Quran. On this night, Allah descends to the lowest of the heavens, nearest to the earth, and asks, 'Is there no one asking forgiveness, that I may forgive them? Is there no one asking sustenance that I might sustain them?' Prayers offered on this night will, it is said, be answered. My companion liked talking about this, I thought. The language and the concepts were comfortable and familiar. But every few minutes he would say 'you don't have to believe this', or 'this thing is not important in Islam'.

Ramazan (or Ramadan as it is called elsewhere in the Islamic world), 'scorched', is the most sacred month of the year. All able-bodied Muslims are expected to fast between sunrise and sunset, no matter how long the hours of daylight may be.

The next month, the brigadier told me, was *Shawaal*, 'raised', and was traditionally another holy month during which the faithful make up any days of fasting that they had missed during *Ramazan*.

Ziqqad, meaning 'the month of truce', is the eleventh month and also considered holy. *Zil-hajj*, 'the month of pilgrimage', is the final month. It is during this month that the Haj, the pilgrimage to Mecca that all Muslims should make once during their lives, takes place. The month ends with the great feast of Baqr Eid, the Festival of Sacrifice, celebrating the mercy of Allah that allowed Abraham to sacrifice an animal rather than his son. Families buy an animal in the weeks leading up to Eid and kill it – or have it butchered – on the morning of the festival.

This drive, with the brigadier instructing me and talking easily about religion and soldiering as well as the weather and the rather worrying state of the road, confirmed in me a thought I had had before. It was not possible to categorise people's views on religion, partly because Islam pervades the Army and Pakistani life in general. Everyone had a particular set of attitudes, convictions, reservations, which cannot be summarised in a single scale running from moderation to extremism.

The Legends

Like all fighting forces, the Pakistan Army is fortified by its stories. Tales of the battles fought and the deeds achieved, told and retold to successive generations, take on greater meaning with the passing of time, transformed into legends that inspire and sustain the men. The essential truth remains, but the tale takes on an importance beyond the bare facts. Out of the confusion of the battlefield, where the distinction between life and death seems so arbitrary, a clearer picture emerges where actions have significance and courage succeeds.

Despite the benefits that come with Army service, the medical care, the education, the sense of dignity for all, Army life is hard and dangerous and the Army's legends seem to justify the demands it makes of its soldiers.

The fundamental issues of human existence – life and death, order and chaos – are the essence of Army life. Drill and routine training may fill most of a soldier's time, but the point of it all is to be able to fight when called upon to do so. Military people are constantly preparing themselves for the tests that may lie ahead. Tales of bravery and endurance inspire succeeding generations who see themselves as the heirs, in unbroken lineage, of their heroes. Recounting the stories of the fallen also comforts those who are left behind. The loss of a man to a stray bullet or an improvised explosive device is given significance through reverential telling. In venerating the memory of the dead, the Army attests to the dignity of the living. Courage, achievement and luck – implying divine support – are commemorated.

There is massive involvement with the idea of death in the Pakistan Army. Self-sacrifice is an obsession. Soldiers dying in battle, or killed in training are revered as *shaheeds*, martyrs (literally, witnesses), considered to have died for the religion. A Christian or a Sikh soldier would be as much a martyr as a Muslim, nevertheless, and officers and men seem surprised that this could be questioned. Battle-scarred veterans and new *jawans* alike tell of young men who gave their lives during operations and who went to their graves with their wounds still bleeding in proof of their martyrdom.

The idea of martyrdom is much more widely used in Islam than in Christian thinking. Anyone who has died in a plague, in a fire or a traffic accident, or by drowning, and any woman who has died in childbirth are considered martyrs. To a Christian, used to the idea that martyrdom defines those who have been killed for their faith, the idea that victims of an earthquake can be so described is almost blasphemous. But most people in the Army seem to believe that a soldier who has laid down his life for his country will be more greatly honoured in Paradise than someone who has died in an accident. The title *shaheed* comforts the family of a martyr, and the Army friends of a man killed in battle frequently express their envy of the honour bestowed on him, as well as sorrow. Death in action redefines a man's whole existence. Martyred, his life takes on retrospective significance and his family and friends are considered to be blessed by his sacrifice. Despite this, the Army's losses over the last few years have taken their toll. As well as expressing the traditional sentiments, young officers these days, hearing of the loss of yet another of their acquaintances, will talk of the waste and will express anger.

For Valour

The Pakistan Army is very, very sparing with its most honoured awards. The 'attaboys', the non-operational awards and campaign medals are dished out pretty freely. A soldier or officer who does his job well can expect to be given a number of medals for long, meritorious or distinguished service. The *Tamgha-i-Khidmat* (Medal of Service) Class III is given to NCOs and soldiers, Class II to junior commissioned officers, and so on, up to the *Sitara-i-Imtiaz* (Star of Excellence) for colonels and above, and the *Hilal-i-Imtiaz* (Crescent of Excellence) for major generals and above.

The highest honour that Pakistan can bestow upon a soldier is the *Nishan-i-Haider*, the Emblem of Haider. *Haider*, meaning 'lion', is a title of Hazrat Ali, the cousin and son-in-law of the Prophet Muhammad. Ali was a distinguished warrior, revered for his courage, and also for his learning, faith, honesty, loyalty to the Prophet and magnanimity towards defeated enemies.

The *Nishan-i-Haider* is given to those of any rank 'who have performed acts of greatest heroism or most conspicuous courage in circumstances of extreme danger and have shown bravery of the highest order or devotion to the country, in the presence of the enemy on land, at sea or in the air...'

The men who have been awarded the *Nishan-i-Haider* are venerated for their sacrifice. Their faces are familiar to anyone who takes the most cursory interest in Pakistan's history or its Army. In Rawalpindi a row of murals portraying their images lines a stretch of The Mall (one of the city's main thoroughfares) near to the Army's General Headquarters.

The *Nishan-i-Haider* has been awarded only eleven times in over sixty years, never to a living man. In principle it could be awarded to someone who has not laid down his life, but it is hard to imagine the circumstances in which this might happen. By contrast, Britain's Victoria Cross – the highest military decoration – has been awarded 1,356 times since it was instituted in 1856.

These are the men who have received the *Nishan-i-Haider*:

Captain Muhammad Sarwar Shaheed (1910–27 July 1948) 2 Punjab Regiment.

Major Tufail Muhammad Shaheed (1914–7 August 1958) 16 Punjab Regiment.

Major Raja Aziz Bhatti Shaheed (1938–10 September 1965) Punjab Regiment.

Major Muhammad Akram Shaheed (1938–1971) Frontier Force.

Pilot Officer Rashid Minhas Shaheed (Air Force) (1951–20 August 1971) Pakistan Air Force.

Major Shabbir Sharif Shaheed (1943–6 December 1971) 6 Frontier Force.

Jawan Sowar Muhammad Hussain Shaheed (1949–10 December 1971) Driver.

Lance Naik Muhammad Mahfuz Shaheed (1944–17 December 1971) Sipahi.

Captain Karnal Sher Khan Shaheed (1970–5 July 1999) 27 Sindh/NLI.

Havaldar Lalak Jan Shaheed (1967–7 July 1999) Northern Light Infantry.

Naik Saif Ali Janjua Shaheed (25 April 1922–26 April 1948) (was awarded *Hilal-e-Kashmir* – an equivalent to *Nishan-i-Haider*).

3

How the Pakistan Army Got to Be Where It Is Today

The Pakistan Army, like any other great institution, has its own view of the events that have shaped it. Its narrative is a powerful interpretation of the past, possibly more coherent than that of the state itself, which is constantly prey to confused and competing interpretations. People argue about every historical issue – to the extent that it often feels as though there is no solid ground on which to build the nation's story. The Army, however, is fairly clear about how it got to be where it is today.

Islam is not only the basis of the country's identity and the source of much of Pakistani culture, for Pakistan's soldiers it is also a defining aspect of the profession of arms. The faith is often said to owe more to the power of the sword than any of the other great world religions, and the myth of the great Muslim warriors – from the Prophet Muhammad himself onwards – remains a potent inspiration for the Pakistan Army.

The Army does not believe that might is invariably right. But soldiering proved its worth with Muslim armies sweeping across the Arabian Peninsula and north Africa and into central and south Asia in the decades after the death of the Prophet Muhammad. Military men are not merely upholding the values of their civilization, defending the lands of the faithful; they may also spread the word of God.

It is clear that the first Muslims reached parts of what is now Pakistan soon after the death of the Prophet Muhammad (632 AD). In 644 AD, the second Caliph, Umar, sent an expedition to Sindh ('the Land of the Indus') during his campaign to conquer the Persian Empire. Punjabi officers gleefully recall the report that reached the Caliph from Makran (in Sindh):

> O Commander of the faithful!
>
> It's a land where the plains are stony; Where water is scanty; Where the fruits are unsavoury; Where men are known for treachery; Where

> plenty is unknown; Where virtue is held of little account; And where evil is dominant; A large army is less for there; And a less army is useless there; The land beyond it is even worse.

The Caliph listened to his envoy, and decided not to attempt to conquer the lands beyond Makran.

In 711 the seventeen-year-old Muhammad bin Qasim led a punitive expedition, launched at the behest of the Governor of Iraq, to avenge pirate raids on Arab ships. With an initial force of 6,000 Syrian cavalrymen he subdued large tracts of territory, and Sindh and southern Punjab were brought loosely under Arab control. The conquerors stopped short of wholesale forcible conversion of the population to Islam, but these lands were at least brought into the *Ummah*: the Community of the Believers. Succeeding waves of Muslim conquerors from the north (Afghans, Persians and central Asians) seem to have been more interested in power than in winning souls. But they made converts too. The allure of Islam, its vigour, its cultural sophistication and worldly power must have been strong. Furthermore, the new faith was open to all and offered the poorest Hindus redemption from caste slavery.

People argue about the relative influence of armed invaders and the wandering mystics. Many claim that it was gentle Sufi preachers who won hearts and minds, rather than the conquering armies. The Sufis' pietistic faith meshed easily with the pluralistic practices of the Hindus, the argument goes. Their vision, lacking the intellectual austerity of the Arabs, attracted thousands of disciples, many of whom embraced Islam. Sufi thinking and practices certainly influenced the spiritual landscape of south Asia. Pakistan is littered with the well-tended shrines of Sufi saints, to the disapproval of more austere Muslims, and many devout Pakistanis claim to be drawn to Sufism. In some rural areas Islamic beliefs and practices are still said to be seriously polluted by strains of Hindu thinking and observance.

Although Islam was strongest in the south, missionaries were at work elsewhere.

In the eleventh century new Muslim invaders arrived, and Mahmud of Ghazni, 'the sword of Islam', pounded the Punjab with raids every other year for a quarter of a century. Zealously he smashed idols, looted temples and converted Hindus by the sword. His dynasty, the Ghaznavids, was followed by other conquerors, and in 1206 the Mamluk (martial slave) Qutb-ud-din Aybak proclaimed himself Sultan in Delhi, transforming northern India into *Dar-ul-Islam* (Land of Submission) rather than *Dar-ul-Harb* (Land of War). The system of martial slavery was an important institution in eastern Islam, offering intelligent, brave and loyal Turkish soldiers tremendous opportunities, and institutionalised the concept of a glamorous and gifted military and political elite.

By 1290 there were Muslim rulers in much of India and by the end of the sixteenth century the Mughal empire dominated the subcontinent. The Mughal rulers of the seventeenth century became universal symbols of power and wealth, luxury and ferocity. Their courts reflected the emergence of a new Muslim civilisation, synthesising Persian, Indian and Central Asian manners and styles. An idealised memory of the age of the great Mughals remains an important myth in Pakistan today. Indian trade with the rest of the world increased, partly due to the presence of Portuguese, Dutch, British and French trading interests at different ports throughout the subcontinent.

Queen Elizabeth I granted monopoly English trading rights in 1600 to a small merchant group, the East India Company, who first arrived in the port of Surat in 1608. The dialogue with the British was first opened up by the Mughal Emperor Nooruddin Muhammed Jahangir, who offered them the unique privilege to trade and establish factories at the port. In a letter to King James I, Emperor Jahangir wrote:

> ... I have given my general command to all the kingdoms and ports of my dominions to receive all the merchants of the English nation as the subjects of my friend; that in what place so ever they choose to live, they may have free liberty without any restraint; and at what port so ever they shall arrive, that neither Portugal nor any other shall dare to molest their quiet; and in what city so ever they shall have residence...

By 1640 the company had a permanent presence in south Asia, trading under Mughal concessions, progressively exploiting local rivalries, seizing influence and profiteering.

By 1765, eight years after the military defeat of Siraj ud-Daulah at the Battle of Plassey, the British were collecting taxes on behalf of Mir Jaffar, the Mughal governor they had installed in Bengal, and taking their share of the revenue. From this base they expanded the service of lending a mercenary force to a local potentate and so gained a foothold in Madras and then in the region around Bombay. Several servants of the company, the best known of whom are Robert Clive and Warren Hastings, became inordinately rich through this practice, the first step in colonial domination. Parliament – committed to free trade – eventually objected to the East India Company's trading and now revenue-collecting monopoly, and by 1833 measures had been taken to curb and regulate these rights. The trading rights were rescinded and the company was charged with administering and gathering taxes as its main source of revenue from the patchwork of territories it had conquered throughout India.

The rapid expansion of British rule after the conquest of Bengal in 1757 was the cause of deep resentment amongst the native rulers and population. Apart from its own imported regiments most of the East India Company's army was made of native mercenaries who fought on behalf of the new colonial power. Several petty material issues, such as an ordnance denying pensions to new recruits, were causing unrest in this native army. The final straw was the introduction of a new rifle – the Pattern 1853 Enfield – whose cartridges were rumoured to be greased with pig and cow fat. The native soldiers, the sepoys, were expected to bite the cartridges to access their powder and shot. The troops began to resist orders to do this: to the Muslim sepoys pigs were unclean and the Hindus considered the cow sacred. Mutiny broke out at Barrackpore in the east and spread to the rest of India. The native kings, aggrieved and fearful of the recent edict of the Governor General, Lord Dalhousie, that in the absence of a direct male heir their kingdoms would lapse to British administration, joined the revolt. The rising was the greatest military challenge the Company had seen. It has become known in India and Pakistan as the First War of Independence. However, by 1858 this uprising had been suppressed by the East India Company and the native troops that remained loyal to it. This brought to an end the Mughal Empire. Bahadur Shah Zafar, the last powerless puppet Emperor, was formally deposed by the British and exiled to Burma.

The fall of the Mughal Empire meant the end of the privileged status of Muslims in India. No longer the nominal – if fairly powerless – ruling element, the Muslims were now mistrusted by the British and susceptible to the jealousy of the Hindu masses who had resented the often aggressive, if not oppressive, Mughal rule. The political, social and economic structure of India was reordered and Islamic style abandoned. The Muslims lost their empire and felt themselves politically vulnerable. Many feared for their identity.

Two crucial factors distinguished the lands that were to become (West) Pakistan from the rest of what was then India. First, these territories were brought into the British Empire later than the rest of the subcontinent. When General Napier conquered Sindh in 1843 the British had been controlling other parts of India for ninety years. Punjab (including much of what is now Khyber Pakhtunkhwa) was not annexed until 1849. There was less time, before the British finally left in 1947, for representative institutions to develop. So the more autocratic style of early colonial rule – the so-called 'Punjab School' of horseback governance advocated by John Lawrence, based on rough and ready justice delivered in local languages by men who were largely free from bureaucratic supervision – lasted longer here than in the rest of India.

The second issue that distinguished this area was its strategic importance. In the second half of the nineteenth century the British were obsessed by the Russian threat. The Russian Empire – I was told by a retired Pakistani officer – moved eastwards at the rate of fifty square miles a day for about a hundred years. The British were convinced that the Tsars had set their sights on India. Afghanistan was all that lay between the two great powers. This was the period of the Great Game, a strategic rivalry which lasted almost one hundred years. This rivalry between the two powers also forms the background to Rudyard Kipling's *Kim*, perhaps the greatest spy novel ever written.

The British never managed to exercise more than a fairly loose control over the tribal regions of the North West Frontier – the area bordering Afghanistan to the north-west, with Baltistan to the north-east and still-divisive Kashmir to the east. They were often met with fierce resistance from the Pashtun nationalists and Afghans, as in the case of the Massacre of Elphinstone's Army (1842) when around 16,000 soldiers and civilians were killed as the East India Company retreated from Kabul to Jalalabad. This massacre is to this day one of the largest single defeats ever sustained by the British Army. Following it, they took a different tack, exploiting local tribal and religious differences to set up artificial borders and installing chosen leaders in the newly created regions in an attempt to keep order and divert hostilities away from the British.

In the main, the tribes were allowed to govern themselves, provided British people or property were not attacked, in which case punitive measures would be taken against the tribe as a whole. Even fifty years after it had notionally been brought into the British Empire, it remained a pretty lawless region. Here, for example, Lucas White King, then an Assistant Commissioner, is writing to his fiancée back home of a journey through one of the wilder parts of the district (D. I. Khan) of which he was the civilian in charge:

> I am encamped on the border of my District within 18 miles of the 'Takht-i-Suleiman' (11,500 ft). I am trying to see what diplomacy will do to bring these wild tribes to reason before hostilities commence. I have so far succeeded in detaching one important tribe and hope to interview their leading man today but I hear another tribe is on the warpath and this makes me very anxious. The troops do not arrive here till 28th and if any attack on the villages were made, I should be blamed. You can have no idea... what brutes these Afghans are! You cannot trust their word for a single hour. *25 October 1890, Camp Chaudhuran, Derah Is. Khan*

Lucas White King probably looked like a typical sahib to the Indians, a high-flying Indian Civil Service officer whose father, Henry, also served the Empire and ended his career as Deputy Surgeon General in Madras. Eighty years later, however, Lucas's son told me that Henry King had been a man of strong Fenian sympathies who refused to stand for the National Anthem at official functions.

Henry King was warned that his family would be thrown down a well during the 1857 Mutiny, as British families elsewhere had been. He was not unnerved. Lucas, a generation on, faced greater danger in his service of the Queen.

> I got orders to ... meet him [the General] in the heart of Kidderzai country. Next day we started at daybreak ... & went on with 2 guns, a few sabres, & about 300 men. When we got to the narrowest part of the pass a halt was ordered to get the men together. When we were all in the wildest confusion, mules & horses plunging about trying to get up a terrific ascent, the enemy began to fire on us from both sides of the

> Hepib which is very narrow here with beetling cliffs 500 ft high on each side. We managed to get through without any loss, wonderful to say.... When we got out into more firm ground a party in front began firing at us and here one poor [devil] was shot dead. We then brought up the guns and the enemy fled....We expected that they would fire at us during the night but I suppose they were too cowed to do anything.... When I came to the ordnance guard I found our 2 guns trained on the village ready to fire. I promptly forbade them firing as the village was full of women & children, and as far as I could tell the men had not fired at us. The gunmen were of course awfully disgusted but the General acted on my suggestion... *8 November 1890, Shirani Field Force Camp, Shirani Hills.*
>
> All the Kidderzai chiefs are now in prison except one who has bolted. I don't think that there will be any more trouble but the settlement will take some time and I don't expect to be in Derah for a month or so....
>
> I have got 5 of the men who fired at us in... I threatened to burn their villages if they were not given up. They are 'prisoners of war' & nothing very terrible will be done to them although our military 'fire eaters' are very anxious to blow them from the guns! One of them had a Russian D.B. gun with the name 'Postuklof' engraved on the block. I wonder what the history of the gun is! The poor people here are very frightened and have taken refuge in the hills in great numbers. I made an expedition up one of their valleys the other day & hope I succeeded in reassuring them....In the valley beyond martial law is in vogue & the people are fired at whenever they show their faces! I won't allow this in my jurisdiction. *12 November 1890, Camp Karan Kizai, Shirani Field Force.*

This was a fairly characteristic episode from the period. Pakistani officials tell me that little has changed now, even to the methods of maintaining order, the Russian guns and making the tribes give up troublemakers by threatening to burn down their villages.

As a result of events such as these, and its strategic importance, the area was, in effect, militarised. Military imperatives outweighed commercial considerations, and the landscape came to be dotted with British cantonments and forts. In the Punjab – the Raj's favourite military recruiting ground after the 1857 uprising, when the British felt they had to reduce the strength of the Bengali soldiers – a strong relationship developed between the local people and the Army. The area had been ravaged by war and famine during the eighteenth century. Although the Sikh Wars, which eventually brought the Punjab into the British Empire, were bloody, Punjabis rapidly became the backbone of the Army. Soldiering for the British offered some sort of security and dignity to the peasantry. Landowners also sent their sons into the Army. The British needed dependable soldiers and they rewarded those that served them well. Their policy of recruiting from the 'martial races' brought Sikh Jats and Hindu Dogras into the military, as well as Muslim Punjabi Rajputs. Punjabis, less than 10 per cent of the population of British India, eventually made up more than half of the Army. The focus of the Indian soldiers was loyalty to the regiment and the honour – the *izzat* – of their *biraderi* (literally, their brotherhood, but really their community).

Although the British were recruiting local people as soldiers and commissioning them as junior commissioned officers (a category intended to bridge the gap between the Indian soldiers and British officers) 'Indianisation' of the Army took some time. There was still a belief among many in the British Army that it would be unsuitable to induct Indian officers. In this context Shuja Nawaz, the Pakistani-American writer and commentator, highlights the attitude of General Wilcocks, who commanded the Indian forces in Europe during World War I: 'He considered the Indian innately inferior to the British, with the latter being able to command and the former only able to follow.'

But the need for more officers to command the Army in India was undeniable, and it was becoming politically difficult to resist the idea of commissioning Indians. In 1912 the Prince of Wales Royal Indian Military College was set up to educate the sons of noble Indian families and to prepare cadets to be sent to train as officers at Sandhurst. Iskander Mirza, later to be President of Pakistan, was among the first Indian Sandhurst graduates. Initially, the few Indian officers who were given the King's commission were sent only to eight specially selected units. There was political pressure to increase the proportion of Indian officers, however, and the British Empire needed ever more officers. So the Indian Military Academy opened its doors in 1932, admitting forty young men twice a year. As their number increased, the position of the Indian officers became easier. Army life was comfortable then, for Indian as well as for British officers. A civilian friend whose father served in the Indian Army before independence describes a privileged existence:

> These old British army and civilian settlements were built away from the bazaars and crowded alleys of the Hindu and Mughal-built cities. Our neighbours were inevitably other officers and their families with the rank and name of the occupier proclaimed on a wooden board outside the gate.
>
> The cantonment thus developed into a European town in India, whose main house type was the bungalow. The first British settlement in India was in Fort William in Calcutta and following that when the houses were replicated in Bombay and Lahore, the population referred to them as 'Banglas', the 'Bengali constructions', anglicised into 'bungalows'.

The bungalow's design evolved as a type over a hundred years. The model for the cantonment bungalow was a combination of the detached rural Bengal house, sitting in its compound, and the British suburban villa. The fusion of these two types led to a building form which would later become an enduring symbol of the Raj.

> The bungalows imitated the Graeco-Roman style with columns holding up porches in which Aba's car and occasionally an army jeep would be parked. The drawing room and the bedroom, which led away to the dining room at the back, all had high ceilings and almost always a ventilator window with a wooden frame and a rope wound round a pulley to open this frame on hinges to let hot air out or cold air in.
>
> The dining room would connect by a covered passageway to the kitchen, which was always an outhouse, and beyond it the sheds for coal and wood and beyond those, at the back of the compound, the servants' quarters.

Rudyard Kipling wrote a series of stories called *The Smith Administration* in which the civil servant Smith lived surrounded by a retinue – a whole community – of attendants with ranks and hierarchies and religious differences and caste contentions. Kipling used this administration, housed in the cantonment bungalow, as a metaphor for Empire itself. My elderly friend's description of the Army town recalls Kipling's insight:

> The cantonment came to divide itself into a hierarchy of streets with different sizes of houses. We all knew where the brigadiers and the one or sometimes two generals in that cantonment lived as they would have

> larger houses, sentries outside them and a flag pole which was ceremonially attended to. Captains, majors and colonels were not entitled to these.

Army life was not only comfortable. Some Army families, at least, seem to have enjoyed a sense of entitlement that amounted to a feeling of superiority:

> Having been born and brought up in the Army, I suppose I took on some of its assumptions. Civilians were always other, mullahs were by and large trouble, traders had to be watched carefully for cheating and greed. Even capitalists, businessmen who shared the cantonment clubs with us, were slightly suspect. Civil servants were, somewhat like us, upright servants of order.

The officer's son looked back fondly on the world of his youth:

> I have gone a different way, but I can still feel a nostalgia for the simplicity and honesty of that cantonment existence. It lacked a lot. There was no talk of art or literature. Architecture was mosques and forts and tombs. History was what the text books said, a good school was one run on academic and military lines. There was no real snobbery. Soldiers were soldiers. Officers, *jawans*, all – though they had to, while they occupied it – knew their rank and operated within it. There was never any thought of the inequality of men and women – they had their roles and their functions and that was how God and the Army wanted it.

By the early twentieth century the British realised that they had to do something to answer Indian demands for self-government. In 1906 a newly elected Liberal government announced its intention to introduce reforms that would give greater power to the Indians. These measures, introduced under the Indian Councils Act, were not going to come into force until 1909, but their announcement focused minds on the question of what it meant to be a Muslim and an Indian. Hindus were seen to be richer and more powerful than the Muslims, with a far larger commercial and professional class. Even more to the point, 75 per cent of the population was Hindu. In the decades after the 1857 uprising, some Muslim intellectuals – under the leadership of the scholar and educational reformer Sir Syed Ahmed Khan – had argued that loyalty to the crown was a better long-term strategy for India's Muslims than democratic self-government, as demanded by the Indian National Congress, the political party at the forefront of the struggle for independence in India.

Clearly the Muslim minority faced the danger of permanent political exclusion under majority rule, so collaboration with the established autocratic Raj seemed to promise a greater share of office and influence than mass democracy. Once the new reforms were in the offing, however, this was no longer a feasible policy. So the All-India Muslim League was set up in 1906 by Muslim notables to protect the interests of the Muslims within the new electoral systems. The Viceroy – Lord Minto – agreed to the request for a separate Muslim electorate (which was introduced in 1909), effectively accepting the argument that India's Muslims constituted a separate interest group, if not yet quite a separate nation. This was a defining moment for the Muslims of south Asia, although the concept of a separate homeland only slowly emerged.

Mohammed Ali Jinnah, the Bombay lawyer – whose singleminded determination was to lead eventually to the creation of Pakistan – disapproved of the agreement with Lord Minto. He disliked the feudal flavour of deals done by unelected aristocrats behind closed doors. In the early years of his political career, Mr Jinnah was a prominent advocate of Muslim–Hindu unity. He was for many years a member of both the Congress and the Muslim League and was the architect of the landmark 1916 Lucknow Pact between the two organisations. This agreement changed the Muslim League's orientation. It was no longer to be concerned with the struggle for the rights of the Muslims under British rule, but was to fight for Indian self-government. Mr Jinnah's vision of the south Asian Muslim nation developed with the passage of time.

Roderick Matthews, a south Asian historian, describes the evolution of his thinking:

> Jinnah maintained a consistent line throughout his career in terms of protecting the interest of India's Muslims. In order to guarantee that Muslims would share equally in the benefits of self-government and

> economic development, he tried to make deals with the Congress to ensure that the Hindu majority would play fair by the Muslim minority. He therefore brought forward proposals in 1916, 1927 and 1929 which provided for either separate electorates or constitutional safeguards; Congress rejected or ignored these initiatives. But once he had failed to receive assurances at either the London Round Table Conferences (1930–33), or through negotiations with Congress in 1935, and after Congress had refused to allow Muslim League members into provincial governments in 1937, Jinnah finally decided that security for Muslims was only attainable under separate political arrangements.

In the Lahore Resolution of 1940 Mohammed Ali Jinnah demanded a separate Muslim state:

> Mussulmans are not a Minority. The Mussulmans are a nation by any definition... The Hindus and Muslims belong to two different religious philosophies, social customs, literatures... indeed, they belong to two different civilizations which are based mainly on conflicting ideas and conceptions.

In order to garner support from different elements of the Islamic community, he kept his argument intentionally vague, and avoided stating explicitly that it was his view that Muslims should look to partition to safeguard their interests. Many in India were Muslim in little but name, but would be persuaded to come around to the idea of a Muslim state, independent of India – if at all – for fear of communal violence. Even in Punjab there were those who thought the creation of a Muslim homeland unnecessary. The *Jamiat-e-Ulema-e-Hind*, a leading Islamic body and influential political party, went so far as to say that it was un-Islamic. But Mr Jinnah's vision prevailed.

Although he envisaged a secular state as the homeland for south Asia's Muslims, there was from the outset a feeling in some quarters that Jinnah's mission was divinely guided, an elderly Pakistani widow told me. The *Quaid* – or leader – seemed to be like Moses, she said, forging for his people a way to freedom in their own land. Pakistan, carved at impossible speed along arbitrary lines on the map and with its two wings divided by a thousand miles of alien territory was, despite all its frailties, God's country.

The most severe weakness that beset the new nation was its uncertain military viability. This was discussed in senior British military and ministerial circles from 1946, giving serious cause for concern. The proposed Pakistan stood to inherit all the 'hot' borders of British India but with only about 20 per cent of the military assets. Britain had no interest in creating a weak state in such a strategically important area.

One way to get round this problem was to ensure that Pakistan stayed in the Commonwealth and therefore qualified for military aid. Mr Jinnah was happy to give informal assurances that the new country would seek Commonwealth membership, and the British used his undertaking as a lever to get India to stay in the Commonwealth too. Jawaharlal Nehru could not have tolerated a situation in which Britain was rendering economic and military assistance to Pakistan – as a dominion – but had no similar obligation to India. At one point Lord Mountbatten hinted to the Congress Party that Karachi would become the principal British naval base in south Asia if India refused to accept dominion status. India duly came into the Commonwealth at independence.

This served British global interests very well, but there was a further evident difficulty. Without the rich areas of east Punjab and west Bengal, the British knew that military affairs were bound to take a disproportionate place within the economy of Pakistan. They used this prospect to try to scare Mr Jinnah into agreeing to enter a federal Indian union with a central defence structure. The gambit failed, and he decided to take the new country anyway. But as foreseen, the burden of defence and security became unduly heavy for the new state, ensuring that military affairs took centre stage.

Pakistan came into being on 14 August 1947. W. H. Auden satirised the scandalously ill-planned process of Partition:

> ... He got down to work, to the task of settling the fate
> Of millions. The maps at his disposal were out of date
> And the Census Returns almost certainly incorrect,
> But there was no time to check them, no time to inspect
> Contested areas. The weather was frightfully hot...

'He' in this poem was Sir Cyril Radcliffe, whose Boundary Commission decided the borders of the new countries.

On 15 August Pakistan became independent. The new nation rejoiced, but its people were to suffer for decades to come from the chaotic manner in which the subcontinent had been divided. Incomparably more blood was shed in the random slaughter of the summer of 1947 than in all Pakistan's wars since. A million people – many more, by some estimates – died in the communal violence that accompanied partition and independence.

It was grim. Suddenly, communities that had lived peacefully together attacked each other mercilessly. No one in the affected areas was safe. Kamal Matinuddin, who was to become a lieutenant general in the Pakistan Army, was an officer cadet at the Indian Military Academy in Dehradun in the summer of 1947. Almost fifty years later he recalled that there had been about forty-five Muslim cadets at that time, eight or nine of them Punjabi. Matinuddin himself came from Lucknow in Uttar Pradesh. 'All of us chose to go to Pakistan. The creation of Pakistan created such a spirit, we all wanted to go.' The idea had been that the cadets should finish their training and then go to Pakistan. But by October, with communal violence spreading, the British Commandant of the academy announced that it was unsafe for the Muslim cadets to stay. There was a camp of about ten thousand Sikh and Hindu refugees barely half a mile away from the academy. Brigadier Barltrop, the Commandant,

> called us to assemble one night, and said: 'I can no longer guarantee your safety. You will leave before first light.' So we had six or seven hours in which to pack, pay our canteen bills, write to our parents, collect our laundry from the dhobi and so on. It was not considered safe to drive through East Punjab, so we flew to Lahore in a transport aircraft.

There was, however, nowhere for the officer cadets to go. Kamal Matinuddin and his fellows were sent to field regiments until the Army had somewhere to finish training them.

There were forty-six military training establishments in pre-partition India; only seven were in what was to become Pakistan. The most useful of these were the Royal Indian Army Service Corps School at Kakul and the Staff College at Quetta. Pakistani veterans recall that the Indians stripped – in so far as they could – even these institutions. Yahya Khan, then a major, decreed that an armed batman should sleep in the Staff College library to prevent the books being removed. 'Was this correct?' an elderly man mused recently. 'I'm not sure. But he saved the Staff College library, and we remember him for that.' The apparently unfair division of Indian military assets led to burning resentment among Pakistan's armed forces. 'They inherited the apparatus of government; we started out sitting on orange-boxes.'

The Pakistan Military Academy was established at Kakul, on the premises of the old Indian Army Service Corps School. Iqbal Shafi, who later retired as a brigadier, passed out in the first course from the newly formed academy. He recalled that there was not even a bell to mark the change of lessons. So a bugle call was used instead. Brigadier Ingall, the first commandant of the new academy, later recalled in his memoirs (*The Last of the Bengal Lancers*) how he scrambled around looking for equipment:

> I had heard that the Pakistan Government had decided not to post any troops in tribal territory; this new policy meant the closure of two military posts, at Razmak and Wana, each of which housed a complete brigade group with officers' clubs and all the usual facilities. I wrote to the two brigade commanders ... asking that they donate to the Academy all furniture, furnishings, crockery – in fact anything they no longer needed. Their response was magnificent: lorry-load after lorry-load arrived at Kakul; we now had adequate equipment to furnish all our messes.

Pakistan was threatened from the start. In the summer of 1947, as partition and independence were taking place, the Hindu Maharajah of the Muslim-majority state of Jammu and Kashmir seemed unable to decide between Pakistan and India. Many Pashtun tribesmen – native to Afghanistan and the North West Frontier Province – had been active in the Muslim League, supporting the establishment of an independent state for Muslims. In October that year, in response to reports that the Muslims were being massacred there, the tribesmen moved into Kashmir.

Indian troops arrived in Kashmir as the indecisive Maharajah acceded to India. Many Pakistanis – and others – believe that the Maharajah acted under duress. Most of the population did not want to join India. However, Kashmir's leading politician, Sheikh Abdullah, was in favour and Jawaharlal Nehru, India's first Prime Minister, was of Kashmiri ancestry and wanted the territory. Lord Mountbatten backed the move. Pakistanis felt that the famously beautiful territory of Kashmir was being stolen from them. Their new country was being damaged by an external foe, and the rest of the world did not care. The loss of territory and of assets (including the headwaters of the vital Indus and Jhelum rivers) was a great blow to the young nation.

Passion over the injustice of Kashmir has ever since been central to Pakistani identity. Grievances over the partition of Punjab and Bengal, and the loss of Kashmir, were fuelled by the sense that India, richer and more powerful, could with impunity seize what rightfully belonged to Pakistan. Disparate people, many of them migrants, were thrown together in August 1947 with little in common except for the fact that they were (mostly Muslim) south Asians living, by chance or by choice, outside Hindu India. Anger over the fate of Kashmir, the most painful issue of all throughout Pakistan's existence, was one of the issues that bound the nation together. For the Army, the plight of the Kashmiris is still an intensely emotional issue. Many officers believe, however, that some agreement over Kashmir now has to be reached; they are concerned that India's position is growing stronger, as its economic power increases.

Fighting in Kashmir continued, with irregulars pitted against Indian troops until May 1948, when the Pakistan Army was deployed. This war set former comrades against each other. Many Muslim Indian Army officers had agonised over whether to move to Pakistan. Those who left, embracing their comrades as they departed, assumed that the division between the two countries could not be too deep. Some left property, assuming that they would be able to return to it. The UN imposed a truce at the beginning of 1949, and called for a plebiscite to be held to determine the future of Kashmir. A line was drawn, giving Pakistan control of the western part of Kashmir, known since then (to Pakistanis and those who sympathise with their position) as *Azad* – 'free' – Kashmir, and some other small areas. India retained two-thirds of the disputed territory.

The Gilgit Rebellion

The episode of Major William Brown, the Commandant of the paramilitary Gilgit Scouts, illustrates the chaos of partition, but, unlike so many of the 1947 partition stories, this one had a happy ending. The Gilgit Agency – the mountainous northern area where the British Empire, China and Afghanistan met – had been leased by the British from the Maharajah of Kashmir and was treated as part of British India, administered by a political agent responsible to Delhi. The 24-year-old major faced a moral dilemma:

> Are we going to support the Kashmir regime as we are duty-bound to do? Surely we shall be acting against our own democratic sentiments, which could never agree with the hundred thousand Muslim inhabitants of the Gilgit province being forced against their wills to become members of the Indian Union. Or shall we actively join and naturally lead the revolution in favour of Pakistan which will undoubtedly take place? Or shall we take the coward's way out by sitting back and watching the entertainment from a neutral point of view?

William Brown resolved to commit an act of high treason against his own King-Emperor and on 4 November 1947 he raised the flag of Pakistan over the Scouts' lines in Gilgit.

Brown knew that the odds were against him getting through this intact. He did not know whether the government of Pakistan would even support the move. The local Governor, Brigadier Ghansara Singh, refused to hold a referendum to decide the future of Gilgit. Major Brown had him arrested and placed in protective custody, along with troops loyal to him.

There was constant threat of Indian invasion. The Islamic Republic of Gilgit was proclaimed with Raja Shah Rais Khan (member of the local ruling dynasty) as its president. The flag of the new republic was raised over the governor's mansion and the new government claimed the area of Gilgit-Baltistan, several princely states, Kargil and Ladakh as its territory, with the aim of joining the Dominion of Pakistan. The republic came to an end on 16 November 1947 with the arrival of Pakistan's representative, Sardar Mohammad Alam, who took the area into Pakistani possession.

A rioting mob turned on minorities and destroyed the Gilgit bazaar. Mullahs preached jihad and there were attempts to incite mutiny and civil war. Nevertheless, with the help of his loyal Scouts, of Mohammed Alam – and of several games of polo – William Brown succeeded in leading an almost bloodless revolution. He held the province together, made it an integral part of Pakistan and spared it the decades of conflict endured by Kashmir.

William Brown was then, in his own words, 'removed from this vital corner of the world at a time when I was most needed, because I was proving an embarrassment to the British Government'. Major

Brown's role in securing the area for Pakistan was finally acknowledged by President Pervez Musharraf, who awarded him the title *Sitara-e-Pakistan* posthumously in 1994. The award was received by his widow, Margaret.

Early Days

From the beginning, it was not just the military threat to Pakistan that made the Army such a crucial institution in the state.

The death of Mr Jinnah barely a year after independence, and the assassination of Liaquat Ali Khan in 1951, set a tone of violence and inadequate political leadership. 'Pakistan had no leadership,' an elegant retired brigadier told me at his house in Rawalpindi.

> But in the Army there was, obviously, leadership. Personal example, honesty and punctuality were all part of the Army's way of doing things. The Army was the only credible and dependable institution in the country. The Indians thought that, without resources and without a political class, Pakistan would fail. They thought that we would come running back to them in a few months.

Pakistan survived, of course, but its governments were a mess during its first decade. As the state of Pakistan had been cobbled together during the chaotic months of mid-1947, there had been no opportunity to decide how the new Muslim state, with its eccentric geography, would operate. There was one obvious flaw in the young democracy: the majority of the population lived in East Pakistan, but West Pakistanis would not tolerate a government dominated by Bengalis. The One Unit policy, introduced in 1956, was an attempt to evade this issue by merging the four provinces and the Tribal Areas of West Pakistan into one unit, intended to balance the populus East. The measure was presented as an administrative reform that would cut expenditure and reduce provincial local rivalries.

Anxiety about the restive Bengalis was a major reason for the long delay in agreeing a constitution: the West Wing was not at all keen to enfranchise the East. The Government of India Act 1935, a framework designed for colonial rule, remained the constitutional model for nine years. In 1956 the squabbling politicians managed to adopt a constitution.

The Dominion of Pakistan became a republic, and Iskander Mirza, the last Governor General, became the first President.

Meanwhile the Army had grown from its uncertain start. Inherited structures and discipline were the framework within which highly motivated officers and men had turned it into a competent force. Two years after becoming President, Iskander Mirza abrogated the constitution and declared martial law. He appointed the Army's Commander-in-Chief, General Ayub Khan, as Martial Law Administrator. Just three weeks later Ayub sent Iskander packing and declared himself President.

General Ayub Khan's bloodless coup was justified by citing that, given the years of chaos and corruption, the Army promised a 'sound, solid and strong nation'. He began by delivering growth and increased prosperity, helped by considerable economic assistance from the USA and Great Britain following two beneficial defence treaties. He also initiated, in 1961, the work of creating a new capital, as Karachi was too far away from Army General Headquarters in Rawalpindi. The new city of Islamabad was built just ten miles from Rawalpindi.

Zulfiqar Ali Bhutto, Ayub Khan's Foreign Minister, was resolutely anti-Indian and encouraged him to adopt an aggressive policy. Following moves by the US to supply arms to India during its war with China, Bhutto also instigated a change in foreign policy, which until now had been almost entirely pro-Western. He advised Ayub to build diplomatic ties with China in addition to the long-standing links with the USA, to strengthen Pakistan's position. In 1963 this policy shift culminated in the Sino-Pakistan Agreement, whereby China and Pakistan established a border agreement. China ceded approximately 750 square miles of land and Pakistan acknowledged the sovereignty of China over large parts of northern Kashmir. The pact is still not recognised by India, which disputes the legality of negotiating sovereignty over the disputed lands.

War with India, 1965

Pakistan was at this time becoming increasingly concerned by India's procrastination over the plebiscite that the UN had called for in 1949. By 1965, buoyed by the supply of equipment from the US, the Pakistan Army believed that it was strong enough to solve the dispute with India over Kashmir by force. It was encouraged by India's weak showing in its war with China in 1962 – the main pretext for which was disputed borders in the Himalayan region. 'We thought we could beat the Indians. We tried.

We did not totally succeed,' a retired officer commented. 'But we did not fail either,' he added, grinning. A successful little war against India early in 1965 for control of the Rann of Kutch (a barren region in the Indian state of Gujurat) emboldened the Pakistani Army. Three hundred and fifty square miles of Indian territory was awarded to Pakistan by an international tribunal in June. Pakistan had claimed ten times as much land, but the verdict was cheering nevertheless. At this point Operation Gibraltar was conceived. Civil unrest was growing in Indian-occupied Kashmir, and Pakistan had become aware of what it saw as aggressive troop movements. Both Ayub Khan and Zulfiqar Ali Bhutto supported a plan, to be executed by the Pakistan Army, which involved a covert breach of the ceasefire line in Kashmir with the intention of encouraging an uprising of the Muslim majority in Kasmir. The plan, though considered well conceived, was a failure. In the final analysis, the Pakistanis had underestimated the Indian Army. Following the Sino-Indian war just a couple of years previously, the Indian Army was, admittedly, in a state of flux, as was perhaps demonstrated by the Rann of Kutch episode. The infiltrators were detected quickly and handed over to the local authorities. It did not take long to find that they were Pakistanis and that many were from the Army itself. The Indian Army moved to secure the border immediately, most of the infiltrating forces were captured and counter-attacks were launched across the ceasefire line by India, sparking the September War.

The conflict was no longer confined to Kashmir. On 6 September the Indian army launched a major attack across the border towards Lahore.

The War resulted in thousands of lives lost and no clear winner. The Indian Army managed to capture the strategically important Haji Pir Pass in Pakistani-occupied Kashmir. The pass connects Uri with Poonch in Indian-occupied Jammu and Kashmir – and was probably the route taken by many of the Pakistani Army's infiltrating forces in the failed Gibraltar operation. Despite the hostility, there were still personal connections between the two armies. The writer Aatish Taseer recalls his Indian grandfather's account of this time: 'The men knew each other, and at the end of the day when the fighting stopped, they would call to each other. He was proud of the Pakistani prisoner-of-war from his old cavalry regiment [Probyn's Horse] who refused to surrender to the infantry, and immediately dispatched an artillery unit to give him the honourable surrender he demanded.'

Following UN intervention a ceasefire was reached five weeks after the war began and the following year the Tashkent Declaration – which was hoped to be a resolution for lasting peace – stipulated that the warring nations had to pull back to pre-conflict positions. The Pakistan Army regained the Haji Pir Pass but it was punch-drunk, blaming weaponry, lack of ammunition and lack of US support for its inability to seize victory. Pakistan achieved some notable successes during this seventeen-day war, however.

Ayub Khan's position was significantly undermined by the military failings. Zulfiqar Ali Bhutto resigned as a result of the Tashkent Declaration, which was unpopular in Pakistan since it did not address the question of a settlement in Kashmir. On resigning, Bhutto rode a wave of popularity, giving political speeches across Pakistan. In 1967 in Lahore, he officially founded the Pakistan People's Party (PPP). Now ailing, and beset by public protest, Ayub Khan resigned in favour of General Yahya Khan – his lieutenant – on 25 March 1969.

Another General

The job that General Yahya Khan inherited was not an easy one. He promised free, fair elections based on adult franchise within one year. But moving Pakistan towards democracy was complicated; as usual, the question was what should be done about the East Wing. The wars of 1965 had added to the strains between the two parts of the country. The issue of Kashmir was of less emotional significance to the Bengalis than it was to the Pashtun, the Punjabis and the Sindhis, and the war had highlighted the isolation of the East: only a single, not very well equipped infantry division infantry division was stationed there. It was not surprising that the Bengalis began to talk about their need for a separate defence capability. The war had also demonstrated that the Pakistan Army was not invincible, and the point was not lost on the separatists.

The general made his own life more difficult by alienating the civil service of Pakistan at the beginning of his time in office. Professor Ian Talbot has described this:

> Martial Law Regulation no. 58 established a system of accountability for civil servants, who could be dismissed for inefficiency, corruption, misconduct or subversive activities; 303 persons in all were dealt with

> under this regulation. In contrast with Ayub, the second military regime in its early stages kept the bureaucrats at arm's length from the decision-making process.

Corruption was an important matter, but the move was seen as a way to keep the Civil Service under control, I was told by a retired officer who had worked with Yahya. 'The message was clear. Mind your Ps and Qs.' The country's political and administrative system had remained untouched since the British had left. It was quaint – to say the least – but it worked and it depended upon high calibre civil servants.

Dr Humayun Khan, a Pashtun from Mardan and one of Pakistan's most distinguished public servants, explained the system of administration:

> The British left most of their colonies with a brilliant system of district administration which they had constructed on past practices in the country. The kingpin, under this system, was the Deputy Commissioner, who was responsible for revenue collection and law and order. He was also the coordinator of all government activity in his district, and the police came under him. All former British colonies continued with the system but introduced gradual changes which obliged the DC to be more responsible to public opinion and to the views of elected representatives from his area. This was particularly so in the matter of public sector development and not so much in administrative issues, where he was still expected to maintain a professional neutrality.

Life in the Federally Administered Tribal Areas, meanwhile, went on much as it had under the British. The FATA came loosely under the Governor of the North West Frontier Province, but the real power lay with the political agents, civil servants who represented the federal government and administered the Tribal Areas through the colonial-era Frontier Crimes Regulations and relied on the government-appointed *maliks* to control the tribes.

There was also the anomaly of the princely states, also dating from the days of the Raj. In the days of the Empire, princely states in India were administered by their own rulers, although the British controlled their external relations. The exact relationship between the states and the British varied from case to case. There were well over five hundred of these states, the most important of them – about one hundred and twenty

– given status by formal gun salutes to greet the ruler when he visited Delhi. The number of guns determined the importance of the state – the more the better – and it could change, depending on the British attitude to the ruler. Five states were entitled to twenty-one gun salutes in 1947: these were Hyderabad and Berar; Mysore; Jammu and Kashmir; Baroda; and Gwalior. At the time of partition and independence the rulers were to choose whether to accede to India or to Pakistan, or to remain independent. Twelve princely states opted for Pakistan. The most important were Kalat (later absorbed into Balochistan), Bahawalpur (Punjab), Khairpur (Sindh), Chitral, Hunza and Swat (Khyber Pakhtunkhwa). Most of the princely states were absorbed into West Pakistan in 1955, but some in the north of the country retained their independence as late as 1971. The process was to have, in the case of Swat, truly disastrous consequences for Pakistan.

Swat

Dr Humayun Khan was the political agent in the Malakand Division in 1969. This meant that – among his other responsibilities – he was the government's man in Swat – a valley in the upper part of the river Swat in the North West Frontier Province. He felt an affinity to the ruling Miangul family. His older brother Afzal had been at the Doon School in Dehradun (in India) with Miangul Aurangzeb, the Wali Ahad (heir apparent). Dr Humayun's family – lawyers and landowners mostly – were Yusufzai Pashtuns, as were many Swatis. Dr Humayun was later to become one of Pakistan's most distinguished public servants, serving as High Commissioner to Delhi and to London, and also as Foreign Secretary, the top Civil Service post in the department. Several times, over the years, he talked sadly about what had been done to Swat that had changed it from a lovely backwater into a hotbed of militant extremism.

When I asked him to recall the events leading up to Swat's incorporation into Pakistan his affection for the district was clear:

> [My] residence was atop a pine-covered hill, a thousand feet above the road linking the region with the rest of the country. It was here, on a balmy evening in March 1969, with a cool breeze from the mountains, that I was relaxing with my family on the lawn. A few days earlier, I had received Field Marshal Ayub Khan at the border of my jurisdiction and

> escorted him to Swat. He had just resigned as President of Pakistan and handed over power to the Commander-in-Chief of the Pakistan Army, General Agha Mohammed Yahya Khan. On this particular evening, the new President was to make his first major policy speech.

It turned out to be a very important address, in which he announced that the One Unit scheme, giving parity in the matter of representation between East and West Pakistan would be abandoned and the principle of one man, one vote would be adopted. This would give East Pakistan a permanent majority in Parliament and would, within two years, lead to the break-up of the country. He also announced the restoration of the four provinces of West Pakistan, which had been merged in 1955 to establish parity between the two wings.

Towards the end of this speech, Dr Humayun recalled,

> [Yahya] casually announced that the princely states of Dir, Swat and Chitral would be merged and would cease to enjoy internal autonomy. It was a somewhat misleading statement, in the sense that both Dir and Chitral had been taken over some years earlier and their rulers dethroned. Swat was the only remaining state with the ruler, or *Wali*, running his own administration. It had been recognised as a princely state by the British in 1926. During the 43 years of its existence, it had seen two rulers. Its founder, Miangul Gulshazada Sir Abdul Wadud, effectively tamed the tribes of Swat and established an effective administrative system which was a model of peace and orderliness. In advancing age, he abdicated in favour of his eldest son, Miangul Jehanzeb, who brought to his task an enlightened approach of improving health, education, communications and overall governance. Visitors to Swat could not help being impressed with the excellent roads, the well-equipped clinics and the numerous schools. In addition, there was a complete end to lawlessness and the system of justice was swift and easily comprehensible to the people. In this sense, Swat was a model state, unlike Dir and Chitral. Some years earlier, the ruler of Dir, who had little interest in the welfare of his people, had been removed when his loyalties to Pakistan became suspect. The young ruler of Chitral had been tragically killed in an air crash, so the government had taken over his administration. Swat was the only princely state remaining. Despite the manifest benevolence and effectiveness of the *Wali*'s rule, political

> elements in Pakistan who were opposed to Ayub Khan alleged that Swat was not being touched because two of Ayub's sons were married to the *Wali*'s daughters. That was the obvious reason why Yahya, determined to erase Ayub's legacy, made his sudden announcement without any previous planning or preparation. As the government's representative on the spot, I was not given any warning or instructions as to how the takeover was to be conducted. No thought seems to have been given to the legal or administrative requirements. We were all caught by surprise. Immediately after the President's broadcast, the *Wali* rang me up and asked, 'What are my orders?' I had always held him in great regard and he treated me with affection and respect. I could not dream of giving him any orders of my own, so I replied, 'Sir, I have received no instructions, so we maintain the status quo till I do.'

The following day, Dr Humayun had to go to Khar, the headquarters of the Bajaur tribal agency, which also lay in his jurisdiction. It was about eighty miles north-west over a barren and deserted road, which was only used during daylight hours.

> I accompanied the Inspector General of the Frontier Corps, Brigadier Mahmud Jan. At the Bajaur Scouts Mess, we were being entertained lavishly when, late at night, the teleprinter started rapidly ticking, with a message from the Martial Law Administrator in Peshawar. It said that black flags had been raised throughout Swat in protest against the merger and directed that some troops and artillery be moved to Landaki – the border post at the entry to the state. We were also ordered to return to the spot. We left Khar at 2 a.m. and were in Chakdarra, near the border at 5 a.m. The brigadier sat me down and took from me a detailed description of the *Wali*'s palace, the placement of the armed guards etc. He was preparing for a possible assault to remove the *Wali*. I asked him if he would first let me go alone and speak to the ruler. He was most understanding and showed confidence in me. He immediately ordered a convoy of Scouts' vehicles to escort me. I said this would defeat the whole purpose of my mission, because I had never gone to visit the *Wali* with an armed escort and people would think I was now making a show of force. Brigadier MJ, an experienced soldier, saw the point, so I left just with my driver, for Saidu Sharif, the capital of Swat, arriving at the *Wali*'s residence at 6 a.m. The staff knew me well, but they were still reluctant

to wake up *Wali Sahib*. They did so at my insistence, and we sat down over a cup of coffee and discussed the situation. We recalled that we had often talked of the inevitability of merger and how the *Wali* had been quite reconciled to it for a long time. I said I could not possibly handle the situation peacefully without his help. I requested him to summon all the elders and local leaders from all over and explain that he fully accepted the merger and did not want to show any signs of opposition. He graciously agreed and by 11 a.m. a representative *jirga* had assembled at his house and, in my presence, he addressed them. By the afternoon, all black flags had been taken down and I returned to Chakdarra to inform MJ that the crisis was over. He contacted Peshawar and, within the hour, the Martial Law Administrator and the Commissioner flew in by helicopter to assure themselves. I pleaded for the withdrawal of all forces and artillery from the border and they agreed. Next day, I was told to assume charge of the new post of Deputy Commissioner, Swat and to take over all administrative functions from the *Wali*. Without any laws, police or magistrates, I could only continue running things in the same way as the *Wali* had been doing, until alternative arrangements had been put in place. I refused to occupy the *Wali*'s office and worked out of a rest house in Mingora. I visited the *Wali* every evening to ask his advice on any problems that may have arisen during the day and he always helped me. This ad hoc arrangement continued for nearly a month and rumours began to spread that I had taken a bribe from the *Wali* to protect him. In fact, of course, through his wisdom, he had helped me overcome what would have been a grave crisis if the government of Pakistan had decided to use force. Very soon, a full-time Deputy Commissioner was appointed and new laws promulgated which were supposedly designed to bring Swat to a par with the rest of Pakistan. From the day this was done, the downhill slide started and today, forty-two years on, the idyllic valley of Swat, which attracted visitors from all over the world, is in violent turmoil, a hotbed of rebellion and under the tenuous hold of the Army. The people yearn for the days of the *Wali*.

The Birth of Bangladesh

In East Pakistan the separatists were gaining strength. In November 1970 a catastrophic cyclone there killed at least 400,000 people. The general's government was seen by many to have been callous and incompetent in its response. Elections the following month convulsed the country, with

Zulfiqar Ali Bhutto and the PPP taking a majority in West Pakistan, but Sheikh Mujibur Rahman's Awami League winning nearly all East Pakistan's seats, giving it an overall majority. The nightmare – long foreseen – was upon the country now. West Pakistan was still simply unable to countenance political domination by the despised Bengalis.

After futile attempts at compromise, Yahya suspended the Assembly, and the East went on strike. Yahya and his generals treated the Bengali problem as an insurgency, rather than a political problem, and clamped down brutally in March 1971. Accounts of Pakistani Army savagery reverberated around the world. Inevitably, civil war broke out, resulting in the slaughter of hundreds of thousands of people. In November, flooded by nine million refugees, India declared war on Pakistan and fighting erupted on the western border. Within six weeks, Pakistan suffered a catastrophic defeat with 90,000 of its men taken prisoner. The Army was traumatised and was forced to sign an instrument of surrender – the formal act of surrender in the East Wing. The Pakistan Army lost more than face. The independent state of Bangladesh was born. Pakistan was humiliated, losing 54 per cent of its population, valuable raw materials and much of its cultural diversity.

On 20 December 1971, four days after the ceasefire, General Yahya was persuaded (by the ISI, many believe) to hand over to Zulfiqar Ali Bhutto, who became President and Chief Martial Law Administrator, the same positions that Yahya had held. By allowing a popular civilian to come to power, the generals hoped to deflect criticism of their conduct in East Pakistan.

Mr Bhutto launched judicial, agrarian, health and educational reforms, intended to reduce social inequality. His programme of nationalisation, however, and the resulting outflow of capital heaped further damage on Pakistan, still recovering from the loss of the East Wing, and hit the business and professional classes hardest. He took on the establishment by destroying the Civil Service of Pakistan (replacing it with the emasculated District Management Group) and he established a nuclear weapons programme in order to match Indian military power and to limit the role of the men in uniform as the ultimate defenders of the state. (Ayub Khan had earlier refused to develop a military nuclear capability on the grounds that the country could not afford it.) Proclaiming his vision of Pakistan as an Islamic and a Socialist state, he meshed the forces of left-wing politics and conservative religion.

Bhutto's reform programme arguably destroyed more than it delivered, and unrest grew. In 1973 he had to call in the armed forces to quell a rebellion in Balochistan which resulted in 10,000 deaths. His recourse to military force enabled the Army to regain a foothold in public life after its shattering defeat in East Pakistan.

The Afghanistan Question

By 1973 a crisis was brewing in Afghanistan that was to change the region forever. Zulfiqar Ali Bhutto offered military help to the opponents of the government in power, a policy that was to continue for a long time to come. Pakistan's northern neighbours had always been a cause of concern. Afghanistan refused to recognise the border between the two countries, on the grounds that this border, the 'Durand Line', drawn by the British in 1893, annexed Pashtun territory against the will of the local people. Afghanistan was the only country in the world to vote against Pakistan's admission to the United Nations in 1947 and cross-border incursions from Afghanistan were a constant annoyance to the young state. In 1955 Pakistan's embassy in Kabul was sacked, and in May 1961 the Pakistan Army and Air Force repelled a significant incursion into the Bajaur agency. Mohammed Daoud, first cousin and brother-in-law of the Afghan King, and Prime Minister from 1953 to 1963, was obsessed with the idea of creating Pashtunistan, of taking territory from Pakistan in order to unite the Pashtun and to bring them all under the influence of Kabul. Nazi Germany had offered to support the Afghans over the Pashtun question – and more – if they would agree to attack the North West Frontier Province (NWFP) and distract British troops. The Afghans rejected the offer and remained neutral during World War II. The policy of neutrality later enabled Afghanistan to seek aid from the United States as well as the Soviet Union. But Daoud leaned decisively towards Moscow, accepting generous military assistance – aircraft, tanks and artillery and training – as well as massive loans. The Pakistan Army was convinced that Daoud was also supporting Pashtun and Baloch Marxists, as part of his effort to destabilise Pakistan.

The royal family was disturbed by the growing dependence on the Soviet Union, which was reinforced by Daoud's reckless hostility towards Pakistan. Unable to use traditional trade routes through the NWFP and Balochistan, Afghanistan had to rely more on supplies coming from the Soviet Union. Daoud was forced to resign in 1963, but in 1973 he overthrew his kinsman, the King, and declared Afghanistan a republic. His coup ushered in decades of violence and the virtual destruction of the country, as war inexorably followed war. The main opposition to the new Daoud regime came from Afghanistan's Islamist groups. Pakistan, under Mr Bhutto, began actively supporting 'mujahid' operations against the new regime.

Amir Sultan Amir, a tall Special Services Group officer – the SSG is Pakistan's special forces – who had recently returned from training in the US, was running the Parachute Training School in Peshawar at this time. I met 'Colonel Imam', as he was later to be widely known, with Major General Faisal Alavi, an old friend of his from the SSG.

> Major General Nasir Ullah Babar (later minister) was then Inspector General of the Frontier Corps – a locally recruited paramilitary force, with officers from the regular Army.
>
> In September 1974 I was asked to proceed to the Bala Hissar fort (HQ of the Frontier Corps in Peshawar) to meet Afghan students. That was where, for the first time, I met Babar. I really liked him and admired his brain. Later on I worked with him when he was a minister.
>
> He took me to the Auditorium, where I found a group of impressive young men, with bright, open faces and thinking eyes. They did not look Pakistani. Some had blue eyes and brown hair. All were fair. I was clean shaven then, and was wearing trousers and a bush shirt. Babar said 'This man is going to talk to you about non-conventional warfare' and then left. I said 'I've been told to teach you about "*cherimlyat*" guerrilla war' and began to talk. They were keen to learn and had a long list of questions. The naughtiest of my students, I later found out, was Gulbuddin Hekmatyar. Ahmad Shah Massud was also there. Most of the men I trained in those early days were killed later on. They would stay about seven days in Peshawar and then we would take them to the field, and show them how to use explosives. One of the things I taught them was making Molotov cocktails. This was a very dangerous activity. On one occasion I burnt myself and scorched my moustache without knowing. It was only later, when I looked in the mirror, that I realised what had happened. I looked very odd, with half a moustache.

The programme to train the mujahedin went on for two or three years. It was dropped, 'Colonel Imam' recalled, when Bhutto was deposed.

After mass demonstrations protesting against alleged electoral fraud in 1977, Bhutto declared martial law in Karachi, Hyderabad and Lahore and arrested opposition leaders. General Zia ul-Haq (the Chief of Army Staff), prodded by his restive Corps Commanders, overthrew Mr Bhutto on 5 July 1977. Two years later, following what was effectively a show trial, and on highly suspect charges of conspiring to assassinate a political enemy, Zulfiqar Ali Bhutto was hanged.

This was a catastrophic event for Pakistan. A retired general, who remembers the day his death was announced, commented that 'he was the most significant politician that we had seen since the death of Mr Jinnah. He was an orator of genius, he inspired people, he gave them hope. The brutality of his murder built terror into the life of the country.'

Having killed the former Prime Minister, General Zia tried to garner domestic support by introducing a programme of Islamisation. Under Zia, the public media was silenced and supposedly Islamic punishments such as floggings were introduced.

The Focus of World Attention

1979 was one of the most momentous years for Pakistan and its neighbours since Partition and Independence in 1947.

In January the Islamic Revolution overthrew the monarchy in Iran.

On the afternoon of 21 November the US embassy in Islamabad – hitherto considered a quiet posting for American diplomats – came under violent attack. The mob who stormed the compound had heard reports that the US was behind an invasion of the Grand Mosque in Mecca. In reality the situation in Mecca had come about when the leader of an Islamic study group, Juhayman al-Utaybi, convinced his followers in Saudi Arabia that his brother, Muhammed Abdullah al-Qahtani, was the Saviour. On this particular morning, Juhayman locked himself and his group in the Grand Mosque and attempted to have his brother-in-law ratified by the Imam as the Saviour. When the Imam refused, Juhayman opened fire.

The Saudis were slow to quash rumours that circulated about what was going on and before long the word had spread that the Americans and Israelis were behind the attack. This was compounded by the reported moves by President Carter to send US Navy ships to the Indian Ocean as a show of strength to Iran. Only weeks before the US embassy in Tehran had been taken over by Islamic students from a local university protesting over US support for the Shah of Iran. The timing was unfortunate, and buttressed the view that the US and Israel were combining forces to 'neutralise the Muslim world'.

The embassy was besieged, and diplomats, embassy staff and a visiting journalist huddled at the top of the building for five hours, before Pakistani troops arrived to rescue them. Two Americans died there that day. Americans were shocked and angry that the rescue mission had been so slow. The US relationship with Pakistan, already tense, deteriorated.

The Soviet Invasion of Afghanistan

At the end of December 1979 the Soviet Army moved into Afghanistan to prop up its failing government.

Pakistan became the focus of international attention as the Cold War-focused world watched avidly to see what would unfold in Afghanistan. Zia was determined to support Afghans who opposed the atheistic socialists. 'He was reminded that we had already trained teams,' 'Colonel Imam' told me. 'Experienced officers were gathered together but I was then in Siachen [the Siachen Glacier region in Kashmir] commanding 2 Pathan so I could not go at that time.' Brigadier Raza ran Pakistan's training programme.

International aid was slow to arrive. Zia described President Carter's help as 'peanuts'. As time passed, Pakistan was flooded with refugees whom it could ill afford to care for. When help from abroad eventually arrived it brought new problems. Pakistan was destabilised by the massive influx of foreign cash, with a $3.2 billion package promised by the Reagan administration in 1980, and millions more pouring in from Saudi Arabia, the Gulf states and elsewhere. General Zia evolved from pariah dictator to Hero of the Free World. Arms and equipment suddenly began to arrive for the Pakistan armed forces and for the fighters being trained to harass the Soviet troops.

'Colonel Imam' recounted what happened:

> At the end of 1981 Zia's training programme got going properly, with American help. I could not join it until 1983. Even at that stage the programme was still low level, with just a few men coming for training and then going back. But on the whole things were quiet. The

Americans were not really supporting us and were in fact discouraging us. Zia, however, was zealous. Some senior people were against helping the Afghans. They felt that the Russians might attack Pakistan. But Zia never faltered. We gave sanctuary to refugees and set up camps. But it was all very ad hoc at first. Then the United States realised that these people had the capacity to fight back and slowly they began to help.

The Russian Army was scared of the people we had trained.

I wanted to get close to the Soviet planners, and tell them you can't defeat the Afghans. In 1986 I contacted the Soviet Consul in Quetta. I wanted to tell him he wouldn't succeed. I had already tried to contact the Russians through the Afghans, but the thing leaked out.

DG ISI [Gen Attur Rahman] said: 'If you try that again I will hang you.'

But the Soviets came to know that I had a message to convey. A Russian diplomat saw me at the Ministry of Foreign Affairs and called me over. Without any introduction he said, 'Imam! Look, you have to understand that wherever a dog can go a Russian will go!'

'Yes,' I said, 'but an Afghan will go where a dog can't.'

'I don't believe you,' he said.

'You will!' I told him.

The Soviet Army was mechanised: they always travelled in vehicles. The Russian Spetsnaz troops put on Afghan clothes and grew beards; they looked a bit like Afghans but we managed to ambush them.

The mujahedin were flabbergasted. They had a lot of problems. They were careless, easily ambushed and often taken prisoner. For five or six months in late 1986 and early 1987 we ceased all activities. We went and taught the mujahedin to launch standby teams around Russian garrisons. We gave them walkie-talkies and taught them that anyone leaving the Soviet garrison in Afghan dress should be ambushed and captured. At that stage the hatred for the Russians was so great that the Afghans preferred to kill them than take them prisoner. I persuaded them that captives were valuable.

I interrogated a Soviet prisoner, an officer, for a couple of days, then had to leave. When I returned I was told that he had 'gone'. 'Gone where?' I asked.

'To hell,' they said.

The Soviets would bomb mujahedin positions intensively and then assault them on foot. So when the bombardment started the Afghans would move about 300 metres ahead of their positions and sit out the bombing behind the boulders.

Spetsnaz troops used to wear bulletproof jackets and helmets, so bullets were not effective against them. The mujahedin would therefore attack them with RPG 7s.

One soldier did it differently. He saw Spetsnaz troops slithering through grass towards him and leapt – like a leopard – onto a huge bear of a man. He suffocated him, and cut his throat. I asked him why on earth he had taken such a risk. He said, 'I wanted to kill him myself.'

There were many such stories. People really wanted to fight the Russians.

We constantly assessed the mujahedin, to make sure that the weapons and equipment were being used effectively.

Once, one of our good fighters came to me and said he wanted to wait four more days before returning to into Afghanistan. I said, 'You can have four weeks if you want. You're a good fighter. But why do you want to stay?' He said he wanted to stay because his sister was getting married.

So I took 50,000 rupees from an account and gave it to him, saying, 'This is for our Afghan sister.'

He went to the Bano Bazaar in Peshawar and bought her a wedding dress.

He told me the rest of the story three days later, after the marriage had taken place.

He came to me looking pale, and disgusted.

I said, 'What's wrong?'

'Colonel Imam, the money you gave me created problems. I bought her a wedding dress, bright red, and sent it to the ladies. But within minutes I heard a scream from their quarters. They were all weeping and screaming. We couldn't even go in, but my father went.

'When my sister was given the dress she threw it down, shouting, "How can I wear a dress the colour of the Russian flag? Burn it in front of me!"

'So I said goodbye to my sister in rags, in a darned dress. But she walked proudly!'

The Afghan women did a lot for their men. They were tough. They took control of families and sent young men to fight in Afghanistan. If one clan had more *Shaheed* [martyrs] than theirs they would encourage their young men to fight.

'Colonel Imam' was surprised by the fervour for martyrdom.

> I was in the Kunar Valley once, sitting in a group with some mujahedin, wondering why I saw the same few faces every time. 'Why is there no rotation?' I asked. 'I keep seeing you lot, but we have other volunteers.' They giggled a bit, then whispered among themselves and then – in typical Pashtun way – selected one of their number to answer the question. He said that his family, and the families of other seasoned fighters, would complain if new young men were killed before them.

'Colonel Imam' spoke at length of his adventures in Afghanistan, with a mixture of high purpose and boyish derring-do. In his telling of the war, his professional respect for the Soviet Army emerged clearly. 'The Russian soldiers were four times braver than any American,' he said.

He spent fifteen to twenty days a month in Afghanistan, usually entering the country from Quetta. I asked him whether he had ever met Osama bin Laden.

'Oh yes.'

'When did you first meet him?'

'In 1986, March maybe? I met him at Ali Khel. He'd been in Afghanistan for about six months. He'd brought money, and was building jeepable tracks and tunnels. He was not military at all. He was rather like a prince, very humble. He spoke Arabic and English, but lots of us spoke Arabic so language was not a problem.'

Political Musical Chairs

After the judicial murder of Mr Bhutto in 1979 his sons, Murtaza and Shahnawaz, fled to Afghanistan, from where they would plot against the new military government of their own country. In Afghanistan, then under Soviet-backed communist rule, the brothers joined forces with hundreds of other exiles from General Zia's persecution to form al-Zulfiqar, a left-wing militant group dedicated to avenging the death of their father. Over the next ten years al-Zulfiqar staged a campaign of bombings, robberies and assassinations in Pakistan – culminating most famously in 1981 with the hijacking of a Pakistan International Airlines flight from Peshawar to Kabul – an act condemned at the time by Benazir Bhutto. Al-Zulfiqar collapsed with the death of Shahnawaz Bhutto in 1985; his sister claimed he had been poisoned by agents of the ISI.

Murtaza returned to Pakistan only in 1993 with the second Premiership of his sister – although he then sought her deposition, forming his own PPP faction and accusing Benazir and her husband (future President Asif Ali Zardari) of corruption. Three years later, Murtaza was himself assassinated by police guards intercepting his convoy in Karachi.

In the months before Zulfiqar's execution, his daughter Benazir Bhutto was imprisoned. She would spend much of the next five years in solitary confinement at the pleasure of her father's killer. Though not overtly political in her youth, Benazir was young, glamorous and not afraid to capitalise on the credibility leant her by the popularity of her martyred father. She returned to Pakistan from London in the mid-1980s, and began drawing vast crowds to political rallies.

General Zia died in a plane crash in 1988. There has been speculation ever since about who might have engineered the accident. Conspiracy theories and suggestions of sabotage have rampaged and the crash remains a matter of mystery. There is, however, in my view no convincing evidence that this was anything more than a catastrophic machine failure.

After Zia's death General Aslam Beg (Vice Chief of Army Staff) consulted his colleagues and there was consensus among the Army leadership that elections should be held and a civilian government returned. Benazir Bhutto, became the first democratically elected woman premier in the Islamic world. The nation's hopes for better times, under the inspiring daughter of the slain leader were to be dashed. The following 'ten years of democracy' were marked by struggling regimes, corruption and incompetence. Benazir herself faced at least five charges of corruption, although she was never convicted. Leaving Pakistan in the late nineties, the rumours would continue to dog her in her life in exile.

Benazir Bhutto's relationship with the Pakistan Army was easier than that of her father or brothers. When she returned to Pakistan in 2007, following an amnesty granted by President Musharraf, she was cautiously greeted by the military as a potential ally in its struggle against militant Islamic forces within the country. This thaw in relations between Bhutto's party and the Pakistan Army was perceived by some as a betrayal of her natural democratic principles. Others, including the Western powers who had pushed for her to return, fight the general election and then – presumably – serve as Prime Minister under President Musharraf, saw it as a good omen for Pakistan.

Benazir's story ended in disaster. Like her father and at least one brother before her, she was assassinated. On 27 December 2007 while campaigning in Rawalpindi, a suicide bomber detonated beside her vehicle, the force thrusting her from her seat and crushing her skull against the roof of her car.

Afghanistan and the Taliban

The US lost interest in the region as the Soviet troops withdrew in 1989, souring the image of the West and leaving Pakistan to cope with more refugees as Afghanistan lurched through civil war and the Taliban takeover. 'It was brutal,' a senior officer who was serving at the time commented. 'They didn't need us, so they went. We had to try to clear up the mess.'

'Colonel Imam' was still serving in the Army when the Soviet forces left Afghanistan and he was then sent back to Herat to lead Pakistan's mission there. He told me about this:

> This was 1994. Pakistan wanted to open trade routes to central Asia. I was travelling with a big Pakistani trade convoy that was on its way to Ashgabat in Turkmenistan. We were meant to be there for the Turkmen national day. Benazir was there; the government really wanted this to work. But the convoy was stopped in Kandahar and I was taken hostage.

'Colonel Imam' laughed, but not in merriment.

> I was taken prisoner by my own students. They were my own boys! I was furious, and abused them. After a day they said, 'Ok, you can go.' 'But,' they said, 'Your government is supporting the Taliban.' These boys of mine were fighting against the Taliban, who were just gaining strength. Mullah Omar and Maulana Fazlullah had trained in our camps, but I did not know them then.
>
> Various fighters were emerging at that time, in different parts of the country. Kandahar was not controlled by anyone. It was the worst of places! The people there are very bad. There was lots of homosexuality and other vice, a lot of cases of rape. Mullah Omar had a reputation for honesty, but that was all.

Within days of this encounter Mullah Omar took Kandahar, four thousand volunteers fighting with him.

'Colonel Imam' was kidnapped again, in March 2010 when he was travelling in the Tribal Areas with another ISI veteran, Khalid Khawaja, a British journalist, Asad Qureshi, and Qureshi's driver, Rustam Khan. Khawaja was killed a month later. Asad Qureshi and Rustam Khan were released in September 2010. None of the captives knew what would would become of any of them, but when Asad Qureshi was being taken away, 'Colonel Imam' handed him his copy of the Koran. The old man presumably knew what was coming.

A video of the murder of Colonel Sultan Amir Tarar, 'Colonel Imam', was released in February 2011. He looks old and frail.

Hakimullah Mehsud, a Talib who had been thought to have been killed earlier, was seen clearly in the film.

'Colonel Imam' had long been reviled for his support of the Afghan Taliban. He was open about it. He did have a lot of time for the Afghan Taliban; he had trained most of them. But for the Pakistani Taliban he had contempt; he thought that they were using the cry of jihad for political reasons. He saw them, ultimately, as provincial nationalists.

After Benazir Bhutto's dismissal for corruption in 1990, elections brought Mian Nawaz Sharif to power. Anti-Western feeling grew as the US suspended economic and military aid over Pakistan's nuclear weapons programme (which had been continuing ever since it was started by Zulfiqar Ali Bhutto) and the first Gulf War slashed the huge remittances normally sent home by expatriate workers. Heavy monsoons in 1992 killed thousands and left more than a million homeless. Subsequent crop losses further battered the economy. Nawaz Sharif was blamed for his government's incompetent response to the floods.

In March 1993 President Ghulam Ishaq Khan dissolved the government amidst allegations of electoral fraud and corruption. After elections in October Benazir Bhutto returned to her former job as Prime Minister, only to be forced out again in November 1996, on similar grounds. Nawaz Sharif snatched victory after elections in February 1997, continuing the Pakistani political game of musical chairs. His attempts to crack down on religious fundamentalists and on drug trafficking failed as tribal and sectarian violence mounted.

After India conducted nuclear tests on 11 and 13 May 1998, Nawaz Sharif ordered public tests of Pakistan's nuclear weapons on 28 May. Although there had been an international outcry over Indian testing earlier in the month, Nawaz had little choice. He had been taunted by huge Islamist demonstrations and by opposition politicians. The public demanded a reaction to the Indian tests. The subsequent suspension of international economic assistance was overshadowed, domestically, by Sharif's freeze on $11.8 billion foreign currency in private bank accounts in Pakistan. *Time* magazine reported that 'Nawaz Sharif's cronies were tipped off early [about the move]... and were able to transfer their wealth out of the country. Meanwhile, middle-class Pakistanis scrimping to send their children abroad to college had their dollar savings wiped out.' The business community, Islamists and political opponents began to build pressure. The spectre of Pakistani default on external debt was eased, however, by support from the oil-rich Arab world.

Then, in August, US President Bill Clinton ordered missile strikes on training camps in Afghanistan, targeting Osama bin Laden in revenge for the bombing of American Embassies in Kenya and Tanzania. Public anger over the American attacks was so intense that some Westerners left Pakistan, fearing revenge by Osama's supporters. Bin Laden, the son of a billionaire Saudi businessman, had just created al Qaeda ('the Foundation') out of the international Muslim brigades who had driven the Soviet Union out of Afghanistan.

The country was becoming ever more unstable. Leading journalists were harassed, imprisoned, sometimes even tortured. Nawaz's friends seemed to be benefiting mightily as the country floundered. The sense of chaos was growing. Reuters described this as 'The worst financial crisis the country has faced, sanctions and allegations and counter-allegations by the government and opposition of massive, systematic corruption'. Army chief Jehangir Karamat commented publicly that Pakistan 'cannot afford ... vendettas and insecurity-driven policies', and that while there must be 'a neutral, competent and secure bureaucracy' there is a need for 'a security council at the apex'. Nawaz Sharif saw this as a personal attack. General Karamat resigned honourably on 7 October 1998, but the Army was angry. There were mutterings in the messes that he should have confronted Sharif.

Prime Minister Sharif then appointed General Pervez Musharraf (Commander of I Corps, Mangla) as Chief of Army Staff, calculating that this son of a *mohajir* (migrant) family would not wield great influence over the Punjabi-Pashtun-dominated high command.

Nawaz Sharif's relationship with his new Chief of Army Staff soon deteriorated, as he plunged into a controversial diplomatic initiative: 'Believing that every country, bureaucracy, or individual had a price, he thought he could do business with India and met with Indian prime minister Atal Behari Vajpayee in Lahore in February 1999', the long-time Pakistan watcher Stephen Cohen wrote of this episode. The Summit Communique made no reference to Kashmir, the issue over which three wars had been fought. At the insistence of the Army a brief allusion to Kashmir was inserted. It was too little in the eyes of the military, who – infuriated – declined to greet Mr Vajpayee when he arrived in Pakistan.

Later that spring, the Army crossed the line of control in the Kargil region of Kashmir, precipitating a strong Indian military response. The result of this episode, which he had not properly foreseen, unnerved Sharif, who pulled his Army back – upon advice from Bill Clinton during a trip to the US – in what was seen as an abject act of betrayal executed at American bidding.

Anticipating a coup, Sharif moved to sack General Musharraf, but he was outflanked by the military, who stood by their chief. It was Nawaz Sharif who was ousted, not General Musharraf. Once again the Army was in charge of the country.

After the 9/11 attacks on the US, Pakistan again found itself in the frontline of global conflict. President Musharraf, who had already signalled his intention to take on the extremists, immediately understood the opportunity that al Qaeda had handed him. He acceded to US demands for support, but made it clear that this could not be said publicly until he had met with his Corps Commanders. On 14 September the President told the Corps Commanders, intelligence chiefs and other senior Army officers of the stark choice that faced them: Pakistan could either join the American coalition or expect to be declared a terrorist state and be forced into a much tighter hole than they faced should they agree to cooperate. The consequences of being declared a 'rogue state' by the world's only remaining superpower were dire. If they agreed, the minimum would be required: hand over al Qaeda militants and clampdown on militancy. But if they were to shun the United States, Pakistan would be treated as a pariah military regime. It took six hours for the Corps Commanders to consent to General Musharraf's policy of support for the US. The Pakistan Army was now in the vanguard of the newly minted 'War on Terror' – and on the American side.

Fighting the War on Terror in the Tribal Regions

The Soviet war in Afghanistan led to radical social changes in the Tribal Areas. One of the most dramatic aspects of this was the improving status of the clerics:

> In the old days, mullahs were rather despised. They came into the hujra but no one thought much of them. They were tolerated only because they were religious men. The hujra – the room in a big house where the men of the family sat with their friends, neighbours and petitioners – was a crucial social institution, the meeting-place for the men of the area. But it is a dying institution; the mosque has taken over.

My grandfather used to call the shots', a retired Pashtun Brigadier said,' but now no one calls them.

> Madrassah students used to be called 'chanari'. Each mosque had a couple of them. Every afternoon or evening they would come to beg for food, boys of eight or ten years old. They were rather ridiculed, poor, insulted and humiliated. Now they are the power-brokers. These children had no idea of relationships. They were sent off to the mosque at the age of four or five. They had no family contacts, they never saw a woman. They were probably sodomised. We began to call them Talibs in the late 60s. The jihad against the Soviet Union changed everything. Suddenly these boys were given weapons and empowered.

A recently retired NCO talked to me about fighting in the tribal regions and his experience of the Inter-Services Intelligence Directorate (ISI). His knowledge of ISI activities would necessarily be limited; he would only officially be told what was necessary for him to know for his role in operations so his understanding of ISI intentions and capabilities might well be wrong. I was interested, however, by his interpretation of the role of the ISI in the Federally Administered Tribal Areas (FATA).

> Before the pacts with the militants there was a state of confusion and power struggles in the Tribal Areas. The political agents were trying to influence people to turn in foreigners and Taliban. The Army was doing the same. The Talibs were aggressive.
>
> Now there is only one power: the Taliban. The whole countryside is virtually under their control. In the Mehsud area there were two leaders; there was Baitullah [an old ISI beneficiary] and there was Abdullah – who had lost a leg in Afghanistan [in 1996].
>
> Abdullah had been taken prisoner in Afghanistan [in December 2001 in Kunduz] and handed over to the Americans by Dostum. But he was released from Guantanamo Bay and returned home. Abdullah was highly educated. He had, incidentally, a brother who was an army officer, a Piffer.
>
> Abdullah was becoming more popular. He masterminded the kidnapping of two Chinese engineers [in October 2004] and he was also a good speaker. People were impressed by his looks, by the fact that he had lost a leg but was still a leader and a fighter.
>
> The ISI are worried. They wanted one leader, one person they could handle. They are now retainers to both Abdullah and Baitullah, as well as to the head of the Wazir Talibs. The Taliban have offices all over Waziristan. They brainwash young men to fight the Americans.

I asked him about the Talib organisation. 'The basic level is the *halqa*, the local circle of Taliban, with members drawn from several villages, but all belonging to the same sub-tribe. Each has an *amir*, and a *naib amir*, the second-in-command. Baitullah controls seven main *halqas*.'

He told me that Baitullah had tried to set up a command structure with *tehsil* (sub-district) commanders, but that he found this too complicated and too expensive to run. So he believed that the *amirs* reported directly to Baitullah.

> The structures are now very simple and very straight. The local authority is the Taliban. The most dangerous aspect is the local office, which rules with martial law. The *maliks* are there, but they have no power. Pro-government *maliks* were all killed, or at least attacked. The others are now neutral. In many places, the political agent deals with a committee of Taliban rather than with the old *maliks*.

He reported that

> In Tank, for example, the Taliban office now manages government handouts. The political agent used to distribute funds to the *maliks*. Now, the funds for development go to the Taliban.
>
> The foreigners have been driven out of South Waziristan. So the Taliban there is only local. This strengthens them and it pleases them. People are very scared of the Taliban. They will kill anybody, and you'll never know who did it. But they have done one good thing. There is now no crime in South Waziristan. They enforce justice. Murderers are shot; they get the family of the victim to do it. If anyone is kidnapped the Taliban can find him within two days.
>
> But in the old days there was freedom. You could watch TV, fly kites, beat drums, play music. All that has gone. Only Islamic cassettes are allowed now.

The moment the NCO retired from the Army Abdullah Mehsud called on him, asking him to join up.

> He was very impressive. He was smart. Educated, handsome – tall, fair-complexioned with long hair, well built – and a good marksman. He speaks mildly and persuasively, although there is a tinge of immaturity. I had the impression that he was jealous of Baitullah, and others think the same. He accepted that I did not want to take up arms, but said we should keep in touch.
>
> Baitullah is more mature and serious, people say. But I have not met him.
>
> The Taliban drive around in Hilux Toyota pick-ups, without number plates. The cars are all smuggled so they don't have registration numbers. They are cocking a snook at the authorities, but nobody touches them.
>
> Everybody knows what they look like: short shalwar, above the ankle, and 'service shoes' [trainers] not *chappals* [sandals] like ordinary people. They wear camouflage jackets over their kameez, and sometimes a small turban, not the usual style, or a local black cap.
>
> They speak very respectfully to each other.
>
> They are becoming greedy, taxing the development money that they are given. People notice that they have become corrupt.

4

Fauji Life

The honour, safety and welfare of your country come first, always and every time.
The safety, welfare and comfort of the men you command come next.
Your own ease, safety and comfort come last, always and every time.

The notice in the Ingall Hall at the Pakistan Military Academy sums up the values that the Army instils in its cadets.

A coda adds:

It does not matter what happens to me, but it does matter how I behave while it happens to me.

When you pass through the high white gates of the Pakistan Military Academy (PMA), in the foothills of the Himalayas, you enter another world, leaving behind the muddle and grime and the signs of poverty that are all-pervasive outside. Within these walls, there is order. There is barely a speck of dust on the roads; everything is clean, newly painted. The grass is perfectly cut, the trees grow straight. Even the cement seems to shine. Everything has its place and everyone has his allotted role. This is the Army, after all.

A young man who succeeds – in the face of tremendous competition – in entering the Pakistan Military Academy as a gentleman cadet effectively renounces his freedom. For the next two years (and to a lesser extent for the rest of his working life too) his time will not be his own. His movements in and out of the academy will be controlled, and every aspect of his life and character will be considered to be the Army's business. Becoming an officer, he becomes government property.

The Pakistan Military Academy is the most vital institution in the collective psyche of the Pakistan Army. This is where all serving officers trained, and it is here in the drill square at Kakul that they became part of the Army. The shared experience of PMA is the first and strongest bond among officers of all generations. Training here is a formative experience; character development, physical excellence and discipline underline existence.

The slap of weapons on '*Salaam fang!*' ('Present arms!'), the crash of a hundred pairs of boots: this is the soundtrack to life at the academy. 'Fall in' is a simple exercise in accountability: from platoon up, officers must know and report how many souls are present and in parade state. More important, it is a constant reminder of submission: the individual yields to the greater whole.

Twice a year new recruits arrive at the double gates of the academy, each with a metal trunk with his name painted on it. Although most persuade their parents to leave them at the gates, some fathers (especially those who are themselves officers) insist on driving right up to the academy building. In every intake there will be a few cadets whose mothers embarrass them with over-emotional farewells, to the amusement of their peers. The independent and the poorer students have often travelled long distances alone and then taken the official transport from the station or bus stop.

Many of the new arrivals will never have seen anything like PMA, one of the most groomed spots on earth. To young men arriving from rural backgrounds it is truly awe-inspiring. For one of my visits to the Academy I hired a car and driver from an Islamabad hotel. The driver, who was not unsophisticated, had never visited PMA before and was staggered by the place. 'It is so beautiful,' he said. 'I could not have imagined anywhere so beautiful in Pakistan.' The academy is in no way palatial. It was the cleanliness and order that staggered the young driver.

Tradition, discipline and honour are elements of the Army appeal to prospective officers. Faisal Alavi, who was later to become head of Pakistan's Special Forces, explained: 'Joining the Pakistan Army as an officer had been a childhood ambition for me. The Army had always inspired me with its lofty traditions, messes filled with silver, insulated and neat way of life, uniforms and deeds of valour exhibited by many under the most difficult environments.'

Javed Alam, who was to retire as a lieutenant general, was the youngest of eight brothers, all of whom joined the armed forces. He had been advised what to say during the selection procedure, to talk about wanting to serve Pakistan and honour and so on. But when the interviewer asked him why he wanted to join the Army, Javed went for the truth: 'I need a job,' he said.

Before they arrive at the academy the cadets have been attached to one of the its three battalions, and as soon as the last lingering parents have been despatched, the young men are shunted onto coaches headed for the messes that are used as reception centres. Here they are formally assigned to a company and given a sheaf of papers to fill out in a very short time.

'Now,' according to a young officer who served as a platoon commander at PMA, 'the cadet sergeants and corporals descend on these poor souls and all hell breaks loose. Most of these boys (less those coming from shrewd Army background) are not exactly dressed as per the "code" PMA would like to see. Therefore the first thing they get is a crash course in dressing, which usually commences with a lot of cloth-tearing and dress-changing drills.'

The former platoon commander adds that the physical assessment of these boys in order to ascertain what kind of effort will be needed to turn them into proper officers begins at this moment.

The young men who arrive at the academy are the elite. Between 45,000 and 50,000 apply every year to train as officers in the Pakistan Army. PMA will accept about 1,000 of them.Twice a year – in May and October – the Academy admits 400 cadets for its two-year Long Course. There is also a one-year course (Technical Graduate Course) to train young men with relevant university degrees as officers for the Engineers, Signals and Electrical and Mechanical Engineers (EME) and the six-month Integrated Course, which turns out young officers for the Medical Corps, Education Corps, RVFC (Remount, Veterinary and Farms Corps), JAG (Judge Advocate General Branch) and Psychologists. The Army needs more officers, and there are plans to enlarge the academy by raising a fourth battalion. Shortage of funds has delayed implementation of this.

Students at PMA are always referred to as 'gentlemen cadets' (GCs) rather than simply cadets. This is a crucially important detail; the entire training programme is riven with character development. PMA aims to turn out rounded and polished officers.

The process of polishing up the GCs is tough. Faisal Alavi described his first day at the academy:

> We were being assigned the battalion/companies/platoons to report to, along with our room numbers and a number of handouts containing

> all kinds of instructions, mostly highly ominous. While we waited, in walked a tall middle-aged soldier in uniform who took a big look at all of us lazing in our seats and roared at the top of his voice, 'You look like a lazy lot. On your feet and out! Up! Up!' He was the battalion havildar major, we later learnt. We all tumbled out hastily, the thirty-five to forty of us waiting there. He was right behind us and shouted again, 'You lazy lot! I want you to have a quick run around this very building. Go!' We found ourselves running around the huge mess building. When we reported back to him, many of us huffing and puffing, 'One more round!' he shouted. And we found ourselves running again. This was followed by another two rounds of the mess complex! The awaited introduction to PMA had taken off.

After Alavi and his companions (including Zahid Hussain, who was to become Commandant of the academy, some decades later, and eventually retire as a lieutenant general) had unpacked their kit they met the senior gentleman cadet (SGC) from their platoon. The SGC

> was trying to put up a brave front, despite being thoroughly shaken from within, which we later learnt was because of the loud shouting and bullshit – as it was called – he had got on day one from the platoon commander, who was a major from the Armoured Corps and acted as if he had a vicious temper and utterly no compassion, with which he was able to instil a formidable amount of fear in the hearts of our entire platoon. We got a display of his temper the very next day on his first address to the platoon at 0600 hours where he again picked on the poor SGC and gave him a real dressing down as the platoon had failed to be in formation, five minutes before the given time. He shouted and roared at all of us, as we stood stupid and scared stiff, in front of him in formation. He talked of the high standards expected from us, especially in discipline, and how he'd kick the backsides of those who dared to falter or violate any orders. He blared that we were there in the Pakistan Military Academy only because of a selection procedure which had only identified 'potential', and now that we were in PMA, the 'potential' would be verified. 'Many amongst you will also fall out and will not get commissioned as officers!' he said sadistically. 'So you'll all have to work real hard here!' he threatened. We were all doubly scared.

GCs arrive from all over the country, and from every socio-economic background. So a major task for the academy is to bring them all up to the same cultural level. Many will arrive having worn shalwar kameez all their lives. The academy will provide them with their first pair of trousers. Some come from homes where English is spoken every day, others will have struggled with it at school. The time spent on etiquette and on mess procedure and behaviour at guest nights is indicative of the dramatic changes in Pakistani society over the last few decades, senior officers say. Cadets are no longer assumed to come from the upper middle class. In fact, PMA has been attracting boys from modest backgrounds for decades now. In 1971, Faisal Alavi recalled, 'there were some basic lessons for everybody, on the using and handling of the facilities. We were even instructed on how to use the toilet and sit on the seat: "Don't you dare sit on the commode with your big boots! You'll simply break it!", besides being told how to make use of the central heating.'

Mess etiquette was the next hurdle:

> We were all made to run in formation towards the mess complex. Layout and proper use of the fork and knife, napkins, starting meals, ending meals, how to sit, no crossing of legs! The instructions went on and on and on, till the memory storage portion of the brain went numb. Nobody to start a meal till the seniormost on the table starts his. Smoking after the meals would also require permission from the seniormost present on the table. 'We'll learn in any case,' thought all of us in the platoon identically, with their tired and switched-off minds.

These days, a large number of gentlemen cadets come from Military College Jhelum, which provides a good boarding school education for the sons of the other ranks, and from the Army's cadet colleges, boarding schools to which anyone may send their sons. A company commander at PMA, a polished and confident major who was himself an old boy of Military College Jhelum, made no bones about the fact that he preferred these young men to the others. 'They have a head start here. They know all the basics of Army life already, whereas the others have to be taught how to salute and march. I do favour them, certainly.' Suddenly he looked angry. 'These lads have been living in a barracks under military discipline all the years when the others have been lying in bed until midday with their parents waiting on them hand and foot.'

Other GCs are able boys who have come from local schools, with the occasional madrassah student making the grade for the academy. The country's great officer-producing schools are still represented, but fewer of their boys want to join the Army now.

Apart from schools with a direct connection to the Army, Lawrence College, at Ghora Galli near Murree, has probably produced more outstanding officers than any other school, Gallians, as they call themselves (motto: 'Never Give In'), seem cut out to lead: confident, fun loving, swashbuckling, they are better at command than staff jobs. Abbottabad Public School (motto: 'Character Is Destiny') has turned out a number of men who became outstanding general officers, including Major General Faisal Alavi (general officer commanding the SSG).

Another school based in Abbottabad is Burn Hall, which was started by the Catholic Mill Hill Missionaries, taken over by the Army in 1976 to be transformed into Army Burn Hall College. The Christian schools had an enormous influence in the first decades of Pakistan's history, providing some of the best education in the country. Most of Pakistan's elite went to a school run by priests or nuns, or they had close friends or cousins who did. Major General Mahmud Durrani remembered the priests at Burn Hall: 'It astonishes me, it really astonishes me now that I think of it, that these men had left their homes, left everything, to come and teach so far away. And they taught us well. And they were good men.' There was, of course, another side to it. 'I grew up knowing far more about Christianity than I did about my own religion. I regret that,' a retired four star told me rather sadly. 'But I was a choirboy, you know.'

St Patrick's in Karachi was started by the Jesuits. Although the Jesuits no longer run the school its Principal and Vice Principal are still Catholic priests. It lists three military men among its alumni. The first is Shaheed Rashid Minhas, *Nishan-i-Haider*, the Pakistan Air Force officer killed at the age of 20 (on 20 August 1971) when he forced his own aircraft to crash to prevent a Bengali instructor, who was trying to hijack it, from taking the aircraft to India. Then come two Chiefs of Army Staff, Jehangir Karamat and Pervez Musharraf.

Schools matter, evidently. But the Army believes that its own training can give a young man the advantages of a good education. When Ahmad Shuja Pasha, then a major general (now lieutenant general and Head of the

ISI) was Commandant of the Command and Staff College at Quetta he talked to me about the importance of inculcating standards:

> Why is the Army different from the rest of society? Why do boys from certain schools generally turn out to be reliable? How does this transformation happen? Training is part of the answer, but there is more. It comes, in the end, from a feeling of responsibility. Young men pick this up, in good schools or in the Army. A lieutenant will say that he wants to repay what he has been given, that he wants to serve. The Army is very different from the rest of the country.

After two years at Kakul, distinctions based on family background will be less evident. Every GC is considered to be a Pakistan Army officer in the making, and equivalent demands will be made of them all. The uniform is crucial here. However insecure a new GC may feel, the khaki gives him a sense of belonging and, simultaneously, of distinction.

PMA spares nothing in its quest for excellence. From dawn till dusk the gentlemen cadets are stretching their bodies and minds. They endure endless roll calls, parades, push-ups, sit-ups and running till they are ready to drop. A senior officer still remembered the exhaustion of his training. 'The calls for the "fall in" formations went on and on, unending. Normally a five-minute break followed a forty-minute period. And then again, "Fall In!" That had to be done fast and efficiently or we would be punished with frog jumps, front rolls or crawling up the PMA Road.' Day and night young men are tearing round the assault course or being punished for some infringement and having to perform non-stop forward rolls uphill. 'Roll like a ball, keep rolling till I tell you to stop.' Early in 2008 I was told that there were to be no punishments after 23.00, and none on the drill square. 'But you know,' a company commander told me confidently, 'these things keep changing. They decide that we are too tough, and should ease up on the GCs. They decide that we need to restore standards by toughening up. It's an endless cycle.'

In any case, the eased-up regime seemed formidably tough. Everything has to be done at the double at PMA, and endless inspections guarantee that everything has been done properly. 'The drill sergeant made us run in formation from one place to another, according to the rules. No walking, only running is what we were told. No first-termer could walk, he had to run and we had to be in a minimum pair of twos!' The GCs are driven without mercy; the Academy's instructing staff 'can't bear the sight of a stationary GC', a young officer recalled.

Then there are the exercises, many of which are designed to test the GC's willingness to obey what seem terrifying commands. The Acid Test, in the final term, is the most gruelling exercise of all and focuses on team work as well as individual endurance. The academy is in the Himalayan foothills north of Islamabad, but the weather is still brutal: 95°F by midday. First the cadets have to traverse a mountain carrying logs on their shoulders. Then they run nine miles with full gear to an obstacle course that forces them to swing over ditches, haul themselves over walls and slosh through an artificial swamp fed by a man hosing water from a truck. They are expected to complete the course within two hours thirty-five minutes in winter, two hours forty-five in summer. Some collapse along the way. Two or three cadets, out of about two hundred and fifty, will be unable to complete the Acid Test. They will be given a second chance, but only one. If they still can't do it, they will be unable to pass out.

The punishing schedule is necessary. PMA has four terms in which to turn the very varied young men who turn up at the gates into leaders of men, able to command instant obedience. They will have to take life-and-death decisions, they will have to be capable of doing everything they are going to ask of their soldiers and they will need the physical and psychological stamina to survive gruelling operations.

During their time at PMA the cadets will also ingest the Pakistan Army's most important teaching: look after the soldiers. An officer's first responsibility is to ensure the physical and emotional well-being of his men. Leadership depends upon gaining the men's trust. Soldiers will put up with whoever is in command, but the best officers are those they *want* to follow.

The regime is strict, but, in the end, the GCs discipline themselves. This is a fundamental lesson. In the chaos of the battlefield and in a frequently uncertain political environment, officers may find that they have only their own judgement to fall back on.

This is the meaning of the academy's honour code. It is intended to stress that the fear of punishment is not the foundation of discipline. The nation reposes its trust in the people who are commissioned into the armed forces and officers must justify this trust. At the academy, as future officers, GCs are choosing to live by the Army's values and to uphold its standards. In moments of crisis, whatever the cost, they have to act in accordance with these values.

The officers at PMA talk a great deal about standards, morality, trust, honour. The battalion and company commanders, in particular, spend the years they are posted here trying to influence the GCs. Character and professional skills are both crucial, company commanders at PMA believe. But character is the more important. Skills can be taught, but if they detect signs of a serious character flaw they will not hesitate to throw a cadet out of the Academy. A young man can be disciplined and guided, but moral turpitude – an expression that the Army's Adjutant General, Lt General Imtiaz Hussain, used, with deliberation, in two entirely separate conversations – cannot be tolerated. The directing staff at PMA constantly stress that the profession is unlike any other. The Army has to create an environment in which ethical behaviour comes as second nature.

The ruthless examination of character and striving for excellence that is instilled from the day a young man joins the Army gives military life its quasi-religious aspect. A Christian or a Parsi or a Sikh can serve in the Pakistan Army. Atheists do. But all are bound together by a willing submission to discipline and a battle for self-improvement that is itself doctrinal in character.

It sometimes sounds as though, in this puritan Army, there is no room for the boisterousness of healthy young animals. The stress on morality and character-building seems austere, and officers may sound as though they are imposing a joyless regime: drill, lectures, training, study. The legal prohibition of alcohol is taken seriously by the authorities at the Military Academy, so GCs at PMA do not relax in the way their Western counterparts would. Mobile phones are forbidden, I was told by a company commander. But how – you wonder – could anyone schooled in this regime have any fight left in him? The stories told by older officers of wild parties and famous pranks seem to come from another world. The answer is, inevitably, that the cadets are as high spirited as their predecessors.

With each passing term GCs are given greater freedom and gain greater confidence. Although there is not much time for relaxation, there is constant banter and teasing. The cadets give each other nicknames that may stick for life. There was a young man called 'Machar' (mosquito) when I was there, a very skinny boy who had – rather unusually – come to the academy from a madrassah, and 'Cobra', so called because he was very dark skinned. (PMA is not exempt from the general Pakistani obsession with fair skin.) I heard tell of a GC called Sajad who decided to smarten himself up a bit and began to sign himself 'Sadgit'. For as long as he serves in the Army the name will stick. The GCs slang reflects their obsessions. Steel helmets with webbing, horrible to wear, are called '*aqual choos*', brain absorbers, or '*kantop*', ear coverers.

The important appointments for GCs within the academy are usually referred to by their acronyms. So, the Battalion Sergeant Major is always the BSM ('Blood-Sucking Machine', as some GC wag called them.) These appointments are a crucial indicator of a GC's progress. The CSMs (Company Sergeant Majors), BSMs and the ASM (Academy Sergeant Major) and the even more important BSUOs (Battalion Senior Under Officers) and ASUO (Academy Senior Under Officer – the highest recognition for a GC) tend to become very grand and won't even look at a junior GC. The ASUO and the BSUOs are all in the running for the Sword of Honour at the passing-out parade, although a CSUO can grab it if he does very well.

These academy appointments and the awards – above all the Sword of Honour (given to the best all-round cadet of his course) – matter enormously to competitive young men. In every course there are 'one or two fools who can't stand not having an appointment but so want responsibilities that they hang around bullshitting the juniors, trying to take command. The other cadets hate it, and invented the position of ATM (Academy Thaekedar Major, or Major Taking Command) for them.'

Young men who go through the academy together become closely involved with each other, and will remain so throughout their lives. They talk endlessly: about the faculty, about home, about the next exercise, and – getting in training for a lifetime in an enclosed community – they also talk about each other. At PMA everybody is watching, all the time. The faculty are constantly watching the GCs, assessing them and evaluating their performance. The GCs are watching one another, to see what each is made of.

The academy's civilian contractors – including the barber, the tailor, the photographer and the cobbler – also watch the GCs keenly. These businessmen have, after all, been in Kakul longer than any of the men in uniform. The tailor's shop is called 'Haroon Jamil', and the owner is the direct descendant of 'Muhammad Ismail', who was making uniforms for the Indian Army and the princely states long before partition. The tailors here remember all the generals, but – significantly – their first boast is of having made a uniform for Shabbir Sharif, the Piffer major who was awarded the *Nishan-i-Haider* as well as the *Sitara-e-Jurat*, the second highest award for gallantry. Shabbir Sharif also made his mark, in the minds of the tailors here, by winning the Sword of Honour.

About 15 per cent of those who arrive at PMA, I was told by a company commander, fall by the wayside before the two years are up. Those who make it will be commissioned in an impressive passing-out parade. Parents and grandparents come, along with foreign diplomats and government officials. The Adjutant sits astride a white horse. The salute is taken by the Chief of Army Staff (or Vice Chief) or some other very senior general or politician. The GCs who are about to be commissioned march past and the Sword of Honour and other awards are presented.

Finally, to the strains of 'Auld Lang Syne', the new young officers march up the shallow steps and disappear from view into the academy building. Once they are inside a great roar is heard. At last the young men can relax.

The ten gentlemen cadets who pass out top of their course are allowed to choose their regiment. The next five may choose their arm of service. But the hard-earned privileges of the individual have to be balanced with the Army's needs, and a GC might be asked to reconsider if his preferred unit needs him less than another unit or arm of service. Even these star cadets are therefore asked to name three units, in order of preference. A GC whose father or grandfather was an Army officer is said to have a claim on his forebear's regiment (or battalion, in the infantry), and if he exercises this right the Army will generally honour his claim. A father or grandfather who served in the other ranks enables a GC to exercise a claim to the same branch of service – which will be granted – but he does not have an automatic right to serve in the same unit. Some in the Army believe that the position of a young officer whose father was in the ranks in the same unit is simply too complicated, and that is preferable to guide him elsewhere.

Other cadets can express a preference, but there is no guarantee that this will affect their destination.

GCs are much influenced by their platoon commanders, and many will therefore often express a preference for their commander's unit. Others will ask to follow in the footsteps of a charismatic Commandant. Some in each course seem temperamentally cut out for the Artillery, having mathematical ability and a methodical approach. All things being equal, though, the glamour of Armour tends to attract GCs.

The Military Secretary (MS) branch of the Army Staff (described as roughly equivalent to the human resources department in a corporation) works to ensure that talent is divided between arms and services. At the same time, there is an understandable feeling that the fighting arms (Armour, Infantry, Artillery) deserve the ablest young men. This apparent tension in fact resolves itself because the fighting arms simply need more young officers.

About ten days after the passing-out parade the newly commissioned lieutenants arrive in their units. New officers turn up in every cantonment, eager to lead men. This, after all, is what the Military Academy has been teaching them to do.

But now the unit will take over and show them how things should be done. After the rarefied atmosphere of PMA, this induction may come as a rude awakening. An ebullient young officer recounted his first interview with his commanding officer: '"You've spent the last two years doing stick drill and reading improving literature," the CO barked at me. "Now forget it, forget everything you learnt. All you need to know is that very shortly we will be going to the Tribal Areas, where you'd better assume that every man you see, and plenty you don't, will want to kill you. OK?" As it turned out, it was good advice.'

In the first few months it is really the NCOs and JCOs, and even the soldiers, who mould their officers. Yet again, young lieutenants find themselves being looked over. The new lieutenants are watched carefully, examined with an eye that is both critical and protective. These young men arriving in the unit will be part of the family forever. Whether they bring disgrace or glory on the unit, rise to the stars or fade out early on, they will be part of the unit's story. There are about twenty-five officers serving in a unit at any one time (out of a total of about eight hundred in an infantry unit, and around four hundred and sixty in an armoured regiment). Old men, who have long since left the regiment, wait anxiously to hear news of the newcomer. The most important verdict is that of the soldiers themselves.

Officers come and go, and the men recognise their types. But, although they are ruthless in their assessments, the soldiers want the young lieutenants to do well. Their own self-respect depends upon the calibre of the officers in the unit. They help, cajole and encourage their lieutenants, longing for them to prove themselves. The soldiers will forgive a great deal in a junior officer. They are prepared to overlook some professional inadequacies, well aware that basic special-to-arms training – for the Infantry or Artillery or whatever – usually sorts these out. They know that lieutenants may struggle with administrative work, and will cover for them. But they do expect their officers to be physically fit and to be able to match their stamina; they will have no respect for a lieutenant who is not able to run alongside them. Still more serious than unfitness, for the men, is selfishness. This is the unforgiveable sin. If it becomes clear that a young officer is more worried about his career than about the welfare of his men they will write him off. The *jawans* watch young officers ingratiating themselves with the bosses. It is nothing new. They register the offence; they continue to obey the young sycophant and to show him the respect due to his rank, but he will never command their ultimate loyalty. The judgements of the other ranks are ruthless. To an outsider they will not speak ill of an officer: they will say nothing. The non-comment is more shocking than anything that they could say. The affection of the men is not a necessary qualification for advancement. There are general officers whose units do not like them. But 'he is not popular with his unit' is a damning indictment, a taint on any reputation, no matter how illustrious the career in every other respect.

When a lieutenant arrives in his unit he will spend most of his time with the soldiers. 'Our culture does not allow us to get away from the men. In units, we are meant to be with them... The more time you spend with the soldiers, on duty and off, the more cohesive the unit will be,' Brigadier Haroon – Commander of 8 Independent Armoured Brigade – said in Kharian in 2008.

Officers often play practical jokes on the callow lieutenants during their first day or two in the unit. The Armoured Corps specialises in this. A captain in civilian clothes may approach the new boy, asking whether he wants his clothes ironed, and at what time he would like to be woken in the morning. The younger man's squirming, when he meets the captain in uniform the next morning, gives great pleasure all round. New lieutenants have sometimes been asked to sign for some absurd piece of equipment. It is almost unheard of for them to admit that they have never heard of this particular piece of kit. The pranks are innocent, and a young officer's reaction will be remembered decades later.

Army life has its own rhythm. Every January annual training objectives – collective and individual – are set, and the training cycle begins in earnest the following month. At the end of the year one month is devoted to bringing those who are weak in a specific area up to scratch. Twice a year the troops are taken to the field for collective exercises, the culmination of the cycle.

'GHQ develops the programme for the collective training, and decides the level. They tell us whether it will be at unit, brigade, divisional, corps or even Army level. Directives come down to us, but within the framework of the objectives commanding officers are given the liberty to organise the training as they see fit,' Brigadier Haroon told me.

Another annual rhythm, that of the religious calendar, governs the lives of military people and their families. The hard element of this is *Ramazan*, the holiest month of the year, when all adult Muslims are enjoined to fast. This is one of the pillars of the religion, taken seriously by anyone of a religious disposition. Soldiers and officers want to complete the full month's *rozas*, fasts, even when *Ramazan* falls in summer and the days are blisteringly hot and painfully long. Whenever possible, the Army slows down during this month, although not to the same extent as the rest of the country. If a unit is on operations there may be no way to make the days less arduous. In the autumn of 2005 I travelled to Kashmir and nearby areas that had been devastated by an earthquake on the morning of 8 October. This was during *Ramazan*. Helicopter and fixed-wing pilots are forbidden to fast when they are flying. It is laid down that they must not. Islam is not inflexible; there is plenty of scope to make up the missed *rozas* later on. But I realised, that month, that fixed-wing and helicopter pilots who were working flat out rescuing survivors and delivering supplies to areas that had been cut off, flying far longer hours than normal, were in fact fasting scrupulously.

Older officers regret the passing of mess life as they knew it. A retired major general from the Armoured Corps, a quiet man who does not drink alcohol himself, says that Zulfiqar Ali Bhutto's ban on the sale of alcohol in the 1970s changed the Army for the worse.

> The club used to be the focal point of unit life. There would always be somebody there. But the messes went dry at about the time that everybody was getting television, then video. Our Army never subsidised food in the mess (unlike the British Army) so why would officers go? No drink, bad food. So people withdrew to their own rooms, they stayed in and watched television. Without the community life those officers did not gain the breadth of vision and imagination that mixing with everybody would have given them.

Technically, lieutenants are platoon commanders when they are first sent to their units, but where possible newly commissioned officers are placed under senior subalterns who show them the ropes. The Army believes that young officers have to understand the jobs that they will be asking their *jawans* to carry out. Arif Hassan, who rose to be a lieutenant general and served as Commander of X Corps, reports that, as a young officer, he stared out as a tank driver, then became the gunner then, during manoeuvres, acted as loader. Some young officers are even expected to live in the barracks with their soldiers, in order to understand life in the ranks. An Infantry officer will spend between about a year in his unit, 'getting the hang of things', before being sent for basic special-to-arms training. Lieutenants in Artillery and Armour regiments leave for their specialised training after six months.

For Infantry officers, this training will take place in Quetta (at the School of Infantry and Tactics) and for armoured corps and artillery officers at Nowshera (at the School of Armour or at the School of Artillery). The courses last fifteen to twenty weeks, and during this time the young lieutenants remain firmly part of their units.

'My men called me often when I went to Nowshera,' a cavalry troop commander commented. 'They were worried. The soldiers in my troop needed me to do well.'

After he has completed his basic course, an officer will begin to think about his mid-career course, which he will usually do four years later, probably as a senior lieutenant. This is the first turning point in an officer's career. If he does well in it he will be in the fast track for rapid promotion. The course includes a junior staff course element, intended to equip young officers for staff duties in their units and to begin to prepare them for Staff College.

An officer who has finished his mid-career course will usually be in his sixth year of service, and will be ready to become a staff officer. He will be given a Grade 3 (G3) appointment, in operations, intelligence or logistics. The Military Secretary Branch (which handles postings and promotions) tends to move high fliers towards the operational side at this stage.

Pakistani officers comment wryly that those who join the Army in the hope of a life of action rather than study will be disappointed. An officer's life is punctuated with courses and periods of study: promotions from lieutenant to captain and captain to major are by examination. During his first ten years of service, they reckon in GHQ, an officer masters his field and – even more importantly – is groomed for command.

Entrance to the Command and Staff College at Quetta (which prepares officers for higher command) is the second turning point in a military career, and men are allowed up to four cracks at the entrance examination. To enter the college an officer needs a bare minimum of eight years of service behind him (most will have been commissioned for about ten years).

After Staff College an officer will either return to a posting in a unit or he will be given a Grade 2 staff job. Very promising men may find themselves at GHQ at this stage. Some will have been spotted as high flyers, and, once the MS Branch is satisfied that the Staff College assessment was correct, they will be part of the pool of officers identified for 'special handling'. Promotion is not accelerated for these fast-stream officers, but they will be given more, and better, opportunities.

The Army is competitive. Lieutenant General Waseem Ashraf, then Adjutant General, commented in 2005 that it was like a tall pyramid. Between 50 and 60 per cent of those who pass out from PMA will make it to the rank of lieutenant colonel; 20 per cent will become brigadiers; only 2 per cent will earn the crossed sword and baton insignia of a general officer. Crude ambition is thought ugly, but young men aspire to do well.

Officers of every rank are rapidly superseded in the Pakistan Army. There is a fixed period for service in every rank. When this has expired a man must leave the Army if he is not promoted. Very occasional exceptions are made, but overall the Army squanders a lot of good manpower by sending men home who are performing well, and could continue to do so for some years. The present system stresses excellence, but the Army loses a lot of experience.

Most officers hope for a posting abroad with a UN mission; a stint with the Blue Berets is prestigious, it brings valuable operational contact with foreign military personnel and it is well paid. Pakistan is the largest single troop-contributing nation for United Nations missions and its troops generally acquit themselves well. Pakistani soldiers notably rescued trapped American troops in Mogadishu in Somalia in 1993, in the grim episode that the film *Black Hawk Down* is based upon. When American troops were trapped in the Madina Bazaar area of Mogadishu, soldiers from 15 Frontier Force extricated them. To the annoyance of the Pakistan Army, the blockbusting film leaves its troops out of the story.

High flyers may well be sent on courses abroad, particularly to the US, UK or China. These courses – whether officer cadet training, staff courses or specialised training – are valuable, and enhance an officer's standing (although they may also generate jealousy and suspicion that the officer has been beguiled by the Western way of life). But they too tie up valuable manpower in an Army that is overstretched and short of officers.

By his seventeenth year of service an officer will have been given fairly broad experience, and will be ready to be promoted to lieutenant colonel, if he passes the Promotion Board. The Army is trying, at every level, to encourage younger commanders and has therefore reduced from nineteen to fifteen years the necessary length of service for a lieutenant colonel.

A special category of officers exists at this level. FCO stands for Fit for Colonel Only, and such a man will – by definition – not rise further.

Every officer wants to command a unit, preferably his own, but not all will be able to. The Command Selection Board sifts out those who are 'not fit for command'. Damning as this sounds, the Military Secretary's Branch insists that it is simply a recognition that some good officers are better at staff jobs than command. A man on whom this verdict has been passed can still rise to be a brigadier. Those who are considered fit and are lucky enough to be given a unit will command it for at least two years, and possibly up to four. A lieutenant colonel may well also do a term with a UN contingent and a staff job before his allotted seven years are up. Another Promotion Board decides who should be made up to full colonel. The Army's highest fliers bypass the rank of colonel altogether, gliding from lieutenant colonel to brigadier. Others serve for a year as colonel, and are then automatically promoted to brigadier. Otherwise, a colonel serves two years before adding the third pip of a brigadier.

The next crucial career trial faces colonels: selection for the War

Course at the National Defence University in Islamabad. 'If you do outstandingly here, you've got it made,' a serving general commented. 'And unless you really goof you will make it to major general.'

Although the Pakistan Army is so closely modelled on its British antecedent it has its particularities. In every rank an officer is meant to complete a command, a staff and an instructional posting. It is surprising, to an outsider, that such talent is tied up in the Army's training institutions. The advantage of this is that, at every stage of their education, officers are presented with the most inspiring role models available. This certainly contributes to the overall development of the officer corps, but it is also a surprising use of talent in an Army which suffers from an endemic shortage of officers. As I have said, a great many officers are, at any one time, out of their units for training courses of one sort or another. Some – the ablest of their generation – will be doing courses abroad. Others will be occupied on United Nations missions around the world. Still more will have been superseded while there was still good work to be had out of them. The shortage has been exacerbated by the losses of the last few years during operations. Young officers have been killed, and many more wounded, on operations in the Tribal Areas.

One of the Pakistan Army's favourite occupations is speculating about postings and promotions. Everyone does it, at every level. In the summer of 2006 General Ashfaq Kayani, who was then running the ISI, admitted that he himself indulged in the fun of private 'local boards', trying to work out who would, or should, move where in the endlessly fascinating merry-go-round of Army jobs.

Postings are hard to predict, but promotions far less so. It is usually more or less clear who will be moving up in the next round, although there are always a few surprises, a few careers that could go either way. Nothing can be taken for granted until it has been confirmed. A man who had been on tenterhooks for some time told me that the Chief informed him at a wedding that he was to be promoted to lieutenant general.

Another two-star, similarly anxious for news, was informed in a telephone call. It went, he recalled later, like this:

'Is this Maj General?'

'Speaking.'

'I am calling from the Army House; the Chief will like to speak to you.'

'Hello Sir.'

'Hello, how are you? I have decided to promote you to lieutenant general.'

'Oh! Thank you sir.'

A few more words were exchanged, regarding the added responsibilities in becoming part of the highest policy- and decision-making group of the Pakistan Army, then: 'The Military Secretary will call and inform you of your next assignment. Good luck and goodbye.'

Lieutenant General Munir Hafiez, a Piffer from 7 FF (Frontier Force), wrote that on hearing the news he

> slumped into [a] chair and was overwhelmed with a strange feeling of extreme satisfaction & achievement. Where was I going, command or staff? Command, I hope, because that is what one looks forward to in every rank. The day of joining PMA came back vivid & lucid, standing to attention with my platoon of thirty-odd, hair cropped, eyes fixed and hearing the full throated expletives of the platoon sergeant.

Recalling his passing-out parade, and the years since as he had risen from second lieutenant to major general, Munir told me that he thanked God for his luck. He was still more thankful when the Military Secretary called two days later with the news that he was to command a corps and report in ten days' time.

> In line with infantry tradition, the ceremony to pin the badges was held at the battalion I was commissioned in and later commanded. There were some sitting there who had been sepoys when I had joined and were now senior JCOs. My first CO (who had difficulty walking) and many others who had seen me as a young officer were all there.

7 FF, Coke's Paltan, is a distinguished unit, raised by Captain John Coke in 1849. It had, like most old battalions, been given various different designations as the British Indian, and later Pakistan, Army kept being reorganised. But the unit's identity was clear. It remained loyal to the British during the 1857 mutiny, and was involved in retaking rebel-

held Delhi. It was involved in the Umbeyla Campaign (1863–4) – an expedition to suppress rebellion on the frontier during which two of its officers were awarded the Victoria Cross – and the Second Afghan War. It performed well against hostile tribes in Waziristan in the 1890s and was again deployed on the frontier during the First World War. In 1915 Jemindar Mir Dast was awarded the Victoria Cross while on attachment with another unit, and serving in Belgium. During the Second World War Coke's fought in Malaya. In 1948 it distinguished itself in the Kashmir War, and it 1965 it fought with great gallantry at the Battle of Chawinda (an account of the Battle of Chawinda is attached as Appendix One). But despite its glorious record, the promotion of an officer to lieutenant general was a great event for the unit.

> A matter of extreme pride engulfed me as I watched the faces of the officers, JCOs & ORs exuding their share of pride over one of theirs achieving this rank. I [had] thought two stars was it, but as I drove out after wearing the rank and flying my Corp's flag, it was a totally different feeling of authority and responsibility and the mind was thinking beyond the mundane.

The new lieutenant general packed his bags and headed to Bahawalpur, to XXXI Corps HQ, and was briefed on the corps order of battle.

> [This was] another dose of mental absorption. Here I was, being informed of the array of military assets at my disposal and those assured to me for training and combat. It was a complete fighting machine comprising, intrinsically, arms and services for a complete operational cycle of the defensive & offensive battle. What hit me most was that I was charged with the lives of close to 60 thousand of all ranks, a phenomenal amount of military equipment and above all the defence of part of my motherland. I had to ensure, through a high degree of leadership and professionalism, that I measure up to the responsibility – a daunting task.
>
> The Commander of a corps has the Army policy and direction as a guide but acts fairly independently. The coordination with GHQ is continual but more by the staff with GHQ. The personality and conduct of corps commander travels all the way and reflects down to the lowest level. The canvas of operational responsibility and liberty is fairly large

and allows for a wide application of the intellectual and professional capabilities. I made full use of this liberty during my command.

Army officers are beset by enemies, usually of the pernicious local sort who will seize any opportunity to accuse the military of nepotism or corruption or any other vice. The higher an officer rises the tougher it gets. Munir was alert to the threat:

> At this highest pedestal within the Army hierarchy I was acutely conscious that I was literally in a glass house. No movement of the corps commander goes unnoticed by all those under his command, which then travels horizontally in the Army as well. Every word I spoke and action I took, howsoever innocuous, could be interpreted according to the level of understanding of the recipient. I therefore had to be extremely fair in my dealings, both professional and private. My conduct was being micro-watched so my family and the life I led could not be a make-believe. Leadership was viewed through a microscope. The answer was simple, be simple and be natural. Those under command accepted a natural behavior faster than a put-up show.

The commander has to ensure that morale is maintained so that the corps will be ready 'when extreme sacrifice is required'. This can only be done through rigorous training and through attention to the welfare of all ranks. Munir was surprised to discover how much latitude a corps commander has to undertake projects to provide better facilities for all ranks. 'That I could provide for my officers and troops without recourse to bureaucratic frills and hurdles gave me immense satisfaction.'

But, for all the power he wields, the corps commander has no direct command over his forces.

> 'Till the time I was a division commander, I had direct involvement and considerable contact with my troops. The corps commander provides policy/operational direction and cannot be at all times involved with his troops. That domain ends at the division commander. I tried my best to break this barrier but for obvious reasons could not. War comes the way

of lucky corps commanders who lead their troops into battle. I, unfortunately, fell in the unlucky category.

The Soldiers' Lives

Young officers have to look out for trouble between the different local groups among the soldiers. Punjabis, for example, are loyal to their *graain*, men from the same village. In any company, and in any battalion, there is a tendency for one group to dominate. Each unit has a specified ratio of 'classes', or provincial nationalities among the troops. The toughest mix to handle, I was told by officers, was 50 per cent Punjabi, 50 per cent Pathan. There is plenty of racial banter among the troops, but is generally good-natured.

Urdu-speakers, from families who migrated from India, are derogatorily referred to as baiya, the Urdu word for brother.

The Pashtun sometimes call Punjabis *daal khor*, 'lentil-eaters', implying that they are simple rural folk. Punjabis describe the wild Pashtun as *kharru*, 'uncouth'. Urdu speakers call Punjabis – whom they see as unsophisticated – *daggas*, 'bulls' or 'oxen'.

The Punjabis don't eat beef. After all, a Pashtun told me, most of them were Hindus a few generations back. 'The Punjabis also think mutton a bit smelly. But they can't get enough goat. Whereas we [Pashtun] love mutton and beef.'

The Pakistan Army takes pride in looking after its soldiers and the care that is given to them is extraordinary, by any standards. Like the British Raj, with its paternalistic *maa-baap*, mother-father government, the Army looks after the welfare of its enlisted men while they are serving, and for the rest of their lives. It continues to care for them when they leave the Army.

Soldiers' accommodation is free, and medical treatment is provided free for soldiers' parents and children. If the local combined military hospital cannot treat the disease of a soldier or one of his family, the patient will be referred to another hospital in Pakistan. Lt Colonel Mansoor, then commanding officer of 25 Cavalry, told me that he knew of several cases where the Army had paid to send patients to the UK for medical treatment. Men or dependants who need to go to hospital are helped with transport, either on the routine buses or by ambulance. Every unit has three or four ambulances available. 25 Cavalry had sixteen *shaheeds*, martyrs who had given their lives for Pakistan, the colonel said.

The regiment had helped their families and still keeps in touch with their children and grandchildren.

Soldiers are well fed. Rations for soldiers I visited in Kharian included mutton twice a week, beef twice a week and chicken twice a week. But the Army is frugal and keeps track of everything. Worn-out items of kit and clothing are inspected, within the unit, and claims for replacement sent to the Ordnance Board.

The troops are tough. Soldiers (and their officers) posted to Siachen, for example, live in posts at altitudes of between 20,000 and 22,000 feet for up to six months (the highest Pakistani post is at 23,400 feet). They live in cramped fibreglass igloos with about six other men, fifteen days journey away from any sort of civilisation.

During an extended trip to the Northern areas I talked at length to officers and men of the Siachen Brigade. A Captain described the relentless battle to survive the cold:

> The shortage of oxygen is exhausting and leaves you breathless all the time. Constant headaches, and guarantee frostbite on any part of the body that is exposed. You never feel normal. With very low atmospheric pressure you feel as though you might explode. In these conditions everything freezes within seconds.

I asked him how cold it was in the winter. 'At 60 below, the thermometer broke. It wasn't just the temperature. There can be blizzards of up to 120 kilometres per hour that may last up to a month.'

To keep the igloo warm the men burn kerosene. Soldiers say that they often cough up soot from the kerosene for weeks after leaving the posts. The troops are provided with the world's best clothing and equipment for these conditions, and with just about every sort of food that can be tinned. For water, they melt snow.

In a post on the glacier there will an officer, a lieutenant or a captain, aged between twenty and twenty-seven. There will be two or three sepoys, one or two naiks (corporals) and perhaps a havildar (sergeant) who may well be in his late thirties.

I spoke later to another officer who had served in Siachen. He told me that the weather was not the worst thing about life up there:

> All we did was think. We almost went mad. But monotony is the worst enemy. No one sleeps for more than a couple of hours. We would play cards for hours on end. Officers and men all take a turn at sentry duty outside the igloo. In these conditions you have to earn the respect of the other ranks. You have to reach to the soldier's level.
>
> Motivation is sometimes psychological, sometimes spiritual, often material. Sometimes officers give sweets that have been sent to them to the soldiers. You LONG for the chocolate yourself, but you know that it is better to save it for the troops.

Phone calls home from Siachen are a strange procedure. The men at the posts can speak only to an operator, who relays messages to and from wives, parents and children. Life has become easier. With the improving security situation troops can move by day; earlier, in order to avoid Indian fire, movement was only by night.

It remains hard, though. Everyone who has served in Siachen has dramatic stories to tell:

> One night, a lance-naik was taken ill. The team's Medic believed that he was suffering from HACE (High Altitude Cerebral Oedema). Descending from the post at night is suicidally difficult, but the igloo's lieutenant strapped the lance-naik to his back and a very fit naik offered to go with him. The pair managed to descend, carrying their comrade, to a point where personnel from the sector could meet them, and transport him to a point from where he could be evacuated by helicopter. But the lieutenant and the naik still had to face the sheer climb back up to their post, barely visible as a speck on the mountain.
>
> The wife of one of my jawans gave birth to a son. He was given permission to go to visit them, and fell 4000' to his death that same evening.
>
> A packet of chocolate sent by my father reached me after forty days. I wept when it arrived.

Experienced NCOs are a godsend in Siachen and wherever else the Army is deployed. Several commanding officers have told me that they have been surprised to see what these men are capable of in the heat of battle.

'We often treat our NCOs as though they are children, in a way, almost like the soldiers. Listen, and you'll hear it. We worry about their welfare, we do everything for them. We think they need looking after. I've seen them in battle, and some of them put the officers to shame, they are so brave and so capable', an officer told me in Waziristan.

The Pakistan Army has a category of personnel above the NCOs – the Junior Commissioned Officers (JCOs) – that has no equivalent in Western armies. Under the British, the Viceroy's commissioned officers were Indians, bridging the gap between the generally British officers and the native soldiery. The Pakistan Army has preserved the category, and the JCOs are a valued link in the Army chain. 'All soldiers dream of becoming JCOs', I was told by a JCO in Peshawar, 'and', he grinned, rather bashfully, 'all JCOs dream of sending their sons to Military College, Jhelum' so that they will be able to get into the Pakistan Military Academy and be commissioned. The JCOs are selected from among the non-commissioned officers, on the basis of merit and long service. The highest Junior Commissioned Officer rank is subedar major, or risaldar major in the Cavalry. It is possible for a JCO to be given the rank of lieutenant or captain, if he performs well.

Officers defer to the subedar/risaldar major's knowledge in anything concerning the welfare, security and administration of the enlisted men. 'Every morning, the first person I see is the risaldar major,' Lieutenant Colonel Mansoor told me.

> He's the spokesman for the troops. He has nothing to do with training or life in the field, but he is an open channel to the troops. He will report very serious matters concerning the welfare of soldiers, or pass on complaints that a meal was not properly cooked. Remember that food is an important issue for soldiers. They work hard and they have a right to be decently fed.

The length of time that the JCOs serve in the unit makes them an invaluable source of knowledge. Lt Colonel Mansoor pointed out that 'a sepoy [a private] may serve for eighteen years, a non-commissioned officer for twenty-three years, a junior commissioned officer for twenty-six years, a risaldar for twenty-eight years and a risaldar major for thirty-four years. There is nothing that a good risaldar major does not know about his regiment.' Another, younger, officer in Kharian told me that the risaldar major is seen, bizarrely, as 'the mother of the unit'. All the officers go with the unit when it moves out on exercises, but the risaldar major stays behind. He holds the fort until the officers return, while the CO's wife takes responsibility for looking after all the families.

There have never been enough married quarters for everyone in the Army. When General Kayani became Chief of Army Staff in November 2007 he made it a priority to provide more housing for the JCOs, NCOs and soldiers. Most units that I visited had family accommodation for about 10 per cent of the other ranks, who were often allowed to bring their families to live with them for one year only. Many soldiers said they preferred not to uproot their wives and children, who lived in villages and would find cantonment life strange and difficult, for one year. The shortage of housing is hard on families, admittedly, but the men are able to spend quite a lot of time at home. The Army is generous in granting leave: two months a year – in one stretch if they are lucky – for soldiers, NCOs and JCOs.

Unit Welfare Responsibilities

The Regimental Welfare Fund is responsible for distributing funds to help personnel who are in need. Sometimes people will be given money, but more often the help will be a loan, with easy repayment terms (and no interest of course, in this Islamic Army). There is also a Shaheed Fund, to help the dependants of the unit's martyrs. Here, the help is more likely to be an outright gift, rather than a loan. Some of the old regiments have a great deal of money, and are therefore able to be more generous. In extraordinary circumstances Army units will make a great effort to help. After the 2005 earthquake all the officers of 6 Lancers, serving and retired, were expected to donate 500 rupees, a young major from that regiment told me. This was on top of the statutory one day's pay that was deducted from all public servants, civil and military, to help with earthquake relief.

Loans are available to enable enlisted men to build houses when they retire (after a reasonable period of service they will be given a plot of residential or agricultural land on retirement). Army people are also helped to perform their religious duty and go on the Haj, the pilgrimage to Mecca. Attention is paid to the welfare of the men at every level, from GHQ down to the unit.

When a man dies in service his family will be able to keep their accommodation for five years, and the children will be educated free. During a visit to Kharian I spent a lot of time with the officers and men of 25 Cavalry and 26 Cavalry. The regiments have much in common. Both were raised in the 1960s, and both performed well in 1965. Each has produced generals and won gallantry awards, each has *shaheeds* to remember. The commanding officers of these two tank regiments must have seen a great deal of each other during the time that they were both in Kharian. Lieutenant Colonel Mansoor, 25 Cavalry, was everyone's idea of a proper cavalry officer, smart, with a clipped moustache and a slightly languid air. I met him in the evening, wearing a very smart blue blazer with shiny buttons. His neighbour, Lieutenant Colonel Ishfaq Khan, was a quiet man, who chose to wear a pale shalwar kameez with a jacket on top, and a *pakol*, the soft, circular woollen Pashtun hat. It was evident that he was a pious man, although he did not talk about religion. He spoke about the need for a commanding officer to be accessible to his men, and yet to maintain discipline. These two colonels could hardly have been more different, you might think. But within the Army individual differences do not matter much. The welfare of the troops concerned both men.

The JCOs and NCOs of 26 Cavalry are a very impressive group. It occurred to me, as I sat with them in their mess, that in a crisis I would as soon rely on these men as any on earth. They believe that their regiment is unusual; the officers encourage them to make suggestions about whatever is going on. 'We can affect what happens, we really can change things. Even if it's a small matter, it makes a difference. For example, today we had to arrange a *darbar* (meeting) for the outgoing brigadier. It was going to be held outdoors, but the weather was bad, so then it was going to be held in the gymnasium. We suggested the idea that we could have the *darbar* in an auditorium not far away that belongs to another unit. They [the officers] listened to us, and that's what happened.'

Pakistan Army officers have to be prepared to be teased by the men, just occasionally. The JCOs often organise what they call a pantomime at the end of a big exercise. This is often really like a revue, and 'the main aim is to bring out the weaknesses of the personnel, especially senior people. The soldiers are brilliant mimics, and they always pick up things during exercises that they can use. Everybody comes to watch – we'd probably do it at brigade level – and they usually laugh at themselves.'

The best source of information in the Army is the 'Langar Gup', the cookhouse gossip. The Langar is always right, the men say, 'but the timescale is often wrong'. For example 'we knew that the officers were going to lose their batmen eleven years ago, eight years before it actually happened'.

Major General Tahir Siddiqui, the general officer commanding 6 Division, talked of the relationship between men and tanks. 'The time comes', he said, 'when your heartbeat synchronises with the engine.' The Armoured Corps is different from the rest of the Army. Following the British tradition, an armour battalion is called a regiment. These units have been able to preserve their separate identities. There are even small variations in mess kit uniform. In 19 Lancers, I was told, even second lieutenants carry bamboo canes.

Regiments still have a defined 'class' composition, 'class' meaning provincial identity. 26 Cavalry is 65 per cent Punjabi, 25 per cent Sindhi and 10 per cent Baloch. The regiment used to be 75 per cent Punjabi, but as the Army strives to become more inclusive, the mix is changing. The regiment's JCOs told me that it is meant to be moving towards being 50 per cent Punjabi, 25 per cent Sindhi and 25 per cent Baloch.

The soldiers pass their time, whenever they are waiting for something to happen, playing draughts, or ludo, or caran board, a sort of billiards board game. The new recruits are better educated than before, and easier to train. 'A soldier will pick up in an hour something that it would have taken two days to teach ten years ago,' I was told. But you still have to bawl at them. The NCOs have their own trade secrets. Liquorice (*malethi*) is very good for the throat, after a hard day shouting orders at soldiers.

One of the gravest issues facing the Army at the moment is the threat of the Taliban penetrating the institution. There have been numerous attempts to lure soldiers and officers into the ranks of the extremists, but susceptible individuals are – the Army believes – generally spotted.

There have even been several attempts to subvert SSG personnel. Before Major General Faisal Alavi took over as GOC (general officer commanding) a group called Hezb-i-Islaam (HQ in London) which preaches the Caliphate managed to penetrate the SSG. A young Asian with a Kenyan background turned up in Pakistan (under cover of a teaching job), befriended an SSG officer and through him met a young (also SSG) Captain whom he managed to subvert. This happened while Alavi was in China. By the time the affair was uncovered three SSG Captains had been fully recruited, and another three were halfway there. It was only when a seventh – a Shia – was approached and reported this that the affair came to light. The SSG officers were arrested and finally broke down under interrogation. A trap was set for the conspirators, and it then emerged that other officers had also been dragged into the affair. The SSG and 111 Brigade had been targeted, units whose personnel might be in a position to assassinate President Musharraf and Corps Commanders. One of the SSG officers involved, Captain Farouk, was at the time in the President's security detail, guarding Mrs Musharraf. He had worked out that the President was most vulnerable on the golf course. The other diehards were Captain Saad-ullah and Captain Yawar.

As Alavi arrived to take over as GOC SSG he was told to read all the material concerning this case in the DG Personnel's office in the AG Branch.

The young Shia officer who sounded the alarm over this affair went first to the SSG Commander, Brigadier (later General) Haroon Aslam who reported it directly to the DGMI, Tariq Majid.

A retired Infantry major general used to take me for drives in the mountains around Islamabad. We often went to the Margalla Hills, sometimes right up the rocky and twisty road to the Peer Sohawa and looked over to Murree. At other times we got no further than Daman-e-Koh, in the lap of the mountains, where there is a garden and a rather good restaurant. He was a confident driver, manoeuvring his cool, clean car up the steep roads. He had a good war record and came from a solid background. He had never known shortage of money or connections. I found talking to him very useful. He still took a keen interest in the Army and its doings, as well as in wider strategic issues. My friend had been expected to go far in the Army, and felt some hurt that his career, distinguished though it was, had stalled and that he had not made three-star. It was misty, and beginning to drizzle as he spoke of the anguish he felt when this became clear. He was desolate, and felt that his life, and all his work, had come to nothing. He told me that, in the depths of his despair, he prayed for peace. He had never asked anything of God before, but in those months his pleas were passionate. The prayers were answered, he said. A position came along that took him far enough away from the fray for his wounds to heal, and yet kept him connected to the Army he loved. He knew that his story was embarrassing, but he told it in a soldierly way, religious experience recounted in a staff report.

The major general felt that recurrent confrontation and collusion with politicians had blackened the Army's reputation and had, arguably, hampered its military effectiveness. The Army had been dragged into sorting out differences among politicians, frequently at the behest of the politicians themselves, and it had worked to bring people together to form parties or coalitions. Time and again the men who had been elected to govern had brought the country to the brink of catastrophe. The generals had had little choice but to intervene, but these episodes had distracted the Army from its real job and had damaged its image domestically. Civilian resentment at the scale of resources apparently devoured by the military was disturbing to younger officers and to soldiers, he said, and this resentment was fostered by the opacity of government defence spending. But, in the end, we came back to the refrain that the Army was the most effective organ of the state.

5

Inside the ISI

The killing of Osama bin Laden of 2 May 2011 thrust the Inter-Services Intelligence Directorate (ISI) under a most unwelcome spotlight.

It seemed incredible, to many commentators at home and abroad, that bin Laden should have been living in Abbottabad, near to the Pakistan Military Academy, for some time without the ISI, or for that matter Military Intelligence, having any idea that he was there.

Surely, it was said, the ISI must have known that he was there and probably been supporting him.

But, within the Army, the only feasible explanation for the bizarre and humiliating situation was that the ISI had indeed been unaware that bin Laden was living with several wives and children almost in their midst. There were are only two remotely possible alternatives:

a. The ISI knew where he was and was protecting him,

b. The ISI knew where bin Laden was and agreed with the US that the killing should be presented as an American operation, to protect the government of Pakistan from hostile public opinion.

The first of these was not credible. Since 9/11 the ISI had had four Heads: Lieutenant General Ehsan ul-Haq (2001–4), Lieutenant General Ashfaq Parvez Kayani (2004–7), Lieutenant General Nadeem Taj (2007–8) and Lieutenant General Ahmad Shuja Pasha (Oct 2008–).

The first three were appointed by, and beholden to, Pervez Musharraf. Ehsan ul-Haq and Ashfaq Kayani were both ambitious men, intensely aware that their next appointment might be to the post of Vice Chief of Army Staff – virtually the top job since the President was the Chief – answering their wildest dreams. Otherwise, there would be a consolation prize job or comfortable retirement. Neither General Ehsan ul-Haq nor General Kayani would risk destroying a lifetime's work and hopes in order to shelter bin Laden. Further, although General Ehsan ul-Haq was beholden to Musharraf when he was DG ISI, he has been on the conference circuit since retirement. Would he have been able to resist sharing such gossip on his travels? Lieutenant General Nadeem

Taj was one of the most loyal men in the Pakistan Army. He had worked closely with General Musharraf as his Military Secretary and then as Director General Military Intelligence (DG MI), and was related to him by marriage. No one who knows him could imagine that he would ever countenance any activity in the ISI that ran counter to Musharraf's policy. Whatever the ISI did from 2001 to 2008 concerning the location of Osama bin Laden would have been what the President ordered.

It is not likely that Musharraf would ever have wanted to shelter him. If, however, for the sake of argument we imagine that for some strange reason of state, Pervez Musharraf had sanctioned the ISI sheltering bin Laden for a while he would surely have done something about him by 2007. He was, by then, coming under intense criticism about the ISI's relationships with Pakistan-based militant groups that were attacking NATO forces in Afghanistan. Pakistan – handling a very serious terrorist threat – had understandable reasons to maintain contact with groups based on its soil who did not threaten the state but operated roughly in the same area as those who did. But it was hard to persuade western officials, faced with an increasingly difficult campaign in Afghanistan, to be understanding about Pakistan's needs. They were demanding action, ever more angrily.

In 2007 Musharraf could have regained US confidence by producing either Osama bin Laden's head on a plate or his address.

Since Musharraf's retirement General Kayani – as Army Chief – has wielded enormous power. If Osama bin Laden was being sheltered in Pakistan, it would have been up to Kayani to decide what to do with him. Kayani has also come under great pressure from the US about Pakistan's role in the war against terror. He has every reason to be aware of American capabilities, military and political, and would not want to risk their wrath.

Any incoming Army or ISI Chief who discovered, upon taking up his job, that Osama bin Laden was being protected might well decide that he was a hot potato: dangerous in Pakistan's custody, lethal if discovered in the country. He could have been removed quietly. It is hard to believe that any or all of these four men would have thought it a good idea to harbour the most wanted man or earth, responsible – directly or indirectly – for the deaths of tens of thousands of Pakistanis and others.

The second option, that the ISI agreed with the US that the killing of bin Laden should be presented as an American operation, is only slightly more credible. The timing does not make sense. In the wake of the Raymond Davis (the American who shot dead two men in Lahore) affair the Army Chief would not want another violent demonstration of US power undermining the dignity of Pakistan and its Army.

Admittedly, the Army and the government might be concerned about the impact on public opinion if the Pakistan Army killed the great jihadi. But it would have been clear to anyone thinking ahead that reaction was likely to be far worse if the US was known to have done it alone. Furthermore, the US government would presumably have muted the hostility towards Pakistan if there had been real cooperation.

So, the theory that the ISI was unaware of Osama bin Laden's whereabouts is the least improbable possibility.

The house where bin Laden was living was described in the media as 'next door to the Pakistan Military Academy'. A retired ISI officer who took an interest in the case after the killing (and stresses that he no longer has access to any restricted information) told me that the house was half a mile away from the Academy, as the crow flies. There were other buildings in between PMA and bin Laden's compound, he said, as well as Nilour Spur, an area of high ground that is known to all GCs from map-reading exercises. 'The Academy and Osama bin Laden's house are not intervisible,' he says categorically. There was no reason for the authorities to know who is living in every room in Abbottabad. The compound was only a little bit odder than a lot of buildings in Khyber Pakhtunkhwa. Pakistan runs on gossip: Osama bin Laden was more likely to survive with only a handful of trusted friends helping him than with the knowledge of the authorities.

If the ISI had known where he was they would either have protected him properly, or otherwise dealt with him. Leaving aside the successive chiefs, a string of handlers would therefore have had to be in the loop if the ISI had been helping him. The ISI would have had to ensure that neither the police nor the Army interfered with him or his hosts. They would have had to try to make sure that no one found him by mistake.

This would have meant that someone in the police force would have had to know that the house should not be touched. Similarly, someone in the Military Police would probably have had to be aware that something very sensitive indeed was going on in that house.

It is credible that no one locally knew who was there. Although the country is gossipy, there are also a lot of people with reason to keep themselves to themselves. Tariq and Arshad, as the brothers who built the house were called locally, appeared to be tribesmen who had been involved in some sort of family feud that had possibly involved drug-dealing. The brothers were civil to their neighbours but kept themselves to themselves. Their wives lived in purdah. The story was well designed to keep people at bay, without exciting too much interest.

The bin Laden episode is arguably the most disastrous in the ISI's history. The directorate is, however, used to controversy.

For many years it has seemed that all roads in the minds of conspiracy theorists lead to the ISI. The ISI's senior leadership is aware of its menacing reputation and of the damage that this has done to the country's image.

A former Director General of the ISI discussed the directorate's reputation. Critics of the organisation tended to shift their ground, he said, first accusing the directorate itself of supporting the Taliban, al Qaeda and other terrorists, then blaming 'elements within' the ISI, and then retired officers. They talked also of its role as 'kingmaker' in Pakistani politics, creating political players and then bringing them down. The danger of these 'vicious' allegations, the general said, was that they could sow doubt. Talk of a 'government within the government' might unnerve Presidents or Prime Ministers and while any DG ISI had to address these issues, there was the risk that he might be led to be unreasonably suspicious of his own subordinates and undermine the directorate. The worst possible outcome would be for sensitivities over the reputation of the ISI to lead to its destruction. The directorate existed to acquire intelligence, as tasked by the government of the day. It would be a disaster to dismantle it.

It was useful to think about how your enemies saw you, the former DG said. There was no doubt that the ISI's adversaries rated it very highly. But the directorate had been a victim of its own success in many ways.

The former DG said that he had been thinking about these issues lately, and wondering about the motives of those who assaulted the ISI. Foreign intelligence agencies might possibly have an agenda, but why should domestic critics be so remorseless in their attacks?

The ISI in Afghanistan

The ISI orchestrated the opposition to the Soviet Union's invasion of Afghanistan. The CIA, Saudi Arabians and others helped, 'but the whole show was run by the ISI', the former DG said. Some in Pakistan's Foreign Office say that the country's policy towards Afghanistan at that time was decided by the ISI. They are correct. We are meant to supply intelligence, not to act on it. It is the same within the Army. The MI is there to provide the intelligence upon which the Army acts.'

But during the years of the Soviet–Afghan war, there was an intimate connection between policy-making and intelligence-gathering, with officers of all ranks actively involved. Some ISI officers were able to pass as Afghans and others developed very close relationships with the Afghan resistance. Strong relationships were, not surprisingly, forged between people who worked together during those tough times. The ISI *was* very closely involved with the mujahedin.

'This was the first time that intelligence-gathering had become mixed up with running operations, but the system worked well. It was an odd situation. Afghanistan's politicians were all in exile in Pakistan, while the fighters pitched themselves against the Soviet troops.'

The aftermath of the war was more complicated, and the general said that the ISI did not detach itself in time, and, in fact, became more deeply involved. 'We should have detached ourselves when the Soviet Army withdrew. Or, with hindsight, we should have used our knowledge of the country to guide the Afghan political leaders.' All the warlords who struggled for power were well known to the ISI.

As it was, the ISI general said, Pakistan retained its presence in Afghanistan but did not influence the course of events as the country collapsed into brutal civil war.

'Then, in due course, came the Taliban. The success of the Taliban in the mid-1990s came as a surprise to us'. The Taliban began to be noticed as a force in 1994. By 1996 they had taken control of the capital, Kabul. 'The Afghans were fed up with war, and the Taliban filled the vacuum.' The ISI did not create the Taliban or plan its takeover of Afghanistan. 'But we certainly interacted with it, once it had emerged.'

Mullah Omar was difficult to handle, with the arrogance of ignorance. Even by 9/11, though, when Pakistan had to send someone to Kabul to talk to him, General Mahmood Ahmed (then DG ISI) went.

This sort of relationship could not be switched on and off, the general insisted. While the Taliban was in power in neighbouring Afghanistan, a relationship emerged between the ISI and the Taliban, to the extent that the directorate did not want anyone else to handle the interaction. Whenever anyone had to deal with the Taliban, even on fundamental foreign policy issues, the ISI was consulted and so its ownership of the relationship was strengthened.

US reaction to 9/11 swept away the Taliban. But none of the key players in the new Afghanistan was a stranger to the ISI. The directorate knew Hamid Karzai and the others 'inside out'. Karzai was appointed Afghanistan's interim leader in December 2001, though between the warlords and the Taliban, he controlled little beyond Kabul. Having been director of information in the anti-Soviet Afghan National Liberation Front, Karzai initially supported the Taliban before he decided that it was unduly controlled by Pakistan's ISI, and went into exile... in Pakistan. He returned to Afghanistan during the US-led invasion and – well educated and Westernised – was promptly groomed by the US for leadership.

The ISI was so deeply involved in Afghanistan that it had become difficult to make a graceful exit. 'We became too possessive', and the Afghan issues, as a whole, came to be seen as an ISI responsibility. Nothing could happen without ISI clearance, and this habit became so ingrained that even the ISI itself came to believe it. ISI's own senior retired officers believed that the directorate ran the show on Afghanistan.

Even in 2007, the general said, the police tended to telephone the ISI if they arrested any Afghan. Because of this long-standing relationship, even Pakistani politicians tended to think that they needed ISI help on Afghan-related issues. A senior military officer who served in the ISI more recently told me that this is still pretty much the case.

The former DG told of a conversation with Akram Durrani, then Chief Minister (CM) of the NWFP, about the movement of people between Afghanistan and Pakistan. The CM knew that the border was porous, but felt himself powerless to act. 'He told me that, although there were twenty or thirty posts, nobody was checking these people as they moved about. These posts were manned variously by the political agents, the Frontier Corps and the Army. So I asked him why he was telling me about this. He smiled. "Nothing happens in the Tribal Areas unless the ISI wants it." I told him that this is not how things work. Neither the Governor, nor the FC, nor the Army take orders from me.

But one of our problems is that the impression of ISI ownership is very strong.'

The former DG elaborated on the ISI's image in Pakistan. There was a tendency, he said, to think that the ISI's remit covered almost everything, and that all law enforcement involved the directorate. But the ISI, the general insisted, was an intelligence agency, not an enforcement agency. It was the ISI's own mistake to have allowed this impression of omnipotence to arise. Some of the ISI's younger officers, gratified by the directorate's image, have tried to reinforce it. Pakistan's other intelligence agencies sometimes presented themselves as ISI operatives when engaged in covert operations, to impress those with whom they were interacting. The problem was compounded when any mention in the newspapers of 'agencies' was inevitably interpreted by most readers as a reference to the ISI.

The ISI was, in fact, burdened by its own history.

Lieutenant General Kayani was appointed DG ISI in 2004, with no background in intelligence beyond the familiarity of a corps commander and former DGMO with the work of the intelligence agencies. Having satisfied himself that the directorate was running properly, he set about revolutionising its image. This entailed altering perceptions of its remit within the government and the security apparatus as well as within the directorate itself. President Musharraf and Lieutenant General Kayani agreed on a campaign to persuade the law enforcement agencies to shoulder their proper responsibilities and to make this process clear to all. A message was to go out to the four provinces, to local government, Army and police alike, that the buck could no longer be passed to the ISI.

In an attempt to address this issue, Lieutenant General Kayani asked for a meeting of all provincial Chief Secretaries and Interior Secretaries, representatives of the police, the paramilitary forces (Frontier Corps NWFP and Balochistan, the Sind Rangers and Punjab Rangers) and the ISI sector commanders to be convened in the Ministry of the Interior offices. The DG ISI does not, by convention, attend meetings in other ministries, so the fact that this meeting was run by the Interior Secretary was intended to send a signal. Lieutenant General Kayani addressed the meeting and stressed that the ISI did not have, or want, ownership of law enforcement issues. 'Law and order in the provinces is your responsibility,' he told those present. If they needed additional assets they should ask the Ministry of the Interior to provide them. If anyone had broken the law he should be arrested at once: there was no need for ISI clearance. Lieutenant General Kayani wanted the Ministry of the Interior and the paramilitary forces to become more accountable, he wanted the system to become more transparent and he wanted the message to reach the Afghans and the Taliban. Anyone on the published UN list of individuals and groups associated with Al Qaeda or the Taliban (which imposed a freezing of their assets and a travel ban) or on Pakistan's additional list (with about forty more names) should be arrested and deported. There was no need for those involved in law enforcement to refer everything back to the ISI or to seek its approval.

Lieutenant General Kayani asked those present to implement this policy at once, rather than going down the usual bureaucratic route of submitting plans. He wanted change immediately, he said.

The meeting was anything but routine. It was a very carefully considered attempt to bring Pakistan's law enforcement agencies to maturity and force them to take on their statutory responsibilities.

ISI consent could no longer be used to provide all the agencies responsible for law enforcement in the troubled areas with total cover for their actions. They had to begin to take responsibility themselves. The ISI view – where it had one – should not always prevail, since security was not the only consideration in many circumstances.

Terrorist suspects apprehended since that meeting have been handed directly into the custody of the provincial authorities, I have been told by very senior ISI officers.

The ISI and Kashmir

The ISI has been criticised over the years for training and supporting Kashmiri militants.

President Musharraf invested enormous effort into reaching an agreement with India over the future of Kashmir and tasked the ISI to demonstrate that it was not training fighters and sending them across the Line of Control.

Some outsiders continued to insist that, whatever was being said in Islamabad, the mujahedin themselves believed that they were being assisted. The former DG ISI pointed out to his foreign interlocutors that he could call all the militant leaders together, and tell them to go to hell. But, he said, he could not guarantee that they would not pass the message on their followers. The ISI did not want the existing organisations to splinter into ever more extreme factions of whose existence it would not even be aware. It wanted to retain its ability to deal with the leaders of the militant groups. Hafiz Saeed (a well-known jihadi, founder of the the militant *Lashkar-e-Taiba*, 'Army of the Righteous') and others would not be persuaded, after twenty years, that they were wrong. A tough military approach was possible, but it would be ineffective. Handling the existing groups and weaning them away from militancy was a better approach. So the ISI set up rehabilitation camps and publicised their existence. British and American officials asked to visit the camps, but the ISI stressed that this would ruin the effort. The British compared the situation to Northern Ireland, but Lieutenant General Kayani told them, 'You are assuming that that all these people are prepared to be rehabilitated. But they are not.'

But the government was persisting, providing training and assistance and encouraging these people to marry and settle down, while at the same time trying to ensure that they did not cross the border into Kashmir. It was important to stress, the former DG said, that the ISI was not solely responsible for this effort. He had tried to make this clear to all concerned. Checkpoints in Azad Kashmir were run by the police and Army as well as the ISI. There were some Army personnel at every checkpost. This was made easier when troops were sent to Mansehra for earthquake relief work. No one, the former DG stressed, could guarantee that there would not be any incidents in Kashmir. Although almost one third of the Pakistani Army was facing that direction, and there was a very heavy Indian presence on the other side, nothing could be guaranteed.

For the time being, he said, he was telling the militants that they were benefiting from government policy and should give the political process a chance. But the militants were restive, and were asking what was the likelihood of agreement being reached on the status of Kashmir. He had to persuade them to keep faith with the government. But, the former DG went on, the militants saw no light at the end of the tunnel. 'We have run out of arguments, and the present situation is not sustainable. No government can stretch its policy beyond the limits that public opinion will tolerate.'

Successive heads of the ISI have made a point of meeting regularly with Kashmiri militant leaders, either individually or in small groups. They have done this personally to ensure that the message was consistent and clear, and laid great stress on ensuring that it was passed down the chain of command, and that the police and Army were constantly acting in accordance with government policy. 'It must be clear that the ISI is not playing games. They need to see manifestations of what I tell them. They need to understand that we will prevent them entering the launching areas.' The militants had to be worried, the former DG said, or they would not take the new policy seriously.

Several sections of the ISI (including Internal, Technical, Counter-Terrorism and Special Operations) were involved in work on Kashmir, the former DG said. But he stressed that only he was in possession of all the facts on every aspect of ISI policy on Kashmir.

The former DG commented, ruefully, that his conclusion on Kashmir was that 'even if we stand on our heads the Indians will not agree to give up *anything*'. Escalation was not in Indian interests, but the general felt that it was difficult to make any progress towards a permanent solution. The ceasefire had allowed the Indians to lay better defences, including sensors, although this was rarely mentioned. Earlier they had been unable to leave their bunkers.

The Pakistan Army was over-stretched. 10 Corps (much the biggest in the Army – 12 Div. alone was the size of some corps) was occupied with the perennial problem of Kashmir. There was a serious problem of rotation, and this level of commitment could not be sustained indefinitely.

So Pakistan wanted a peace deal with India. But the ball was in India's court.

The Structure of the ISI

The ISI has about 25,000 professional personnel. This includes officers from all three armed forces, posted to the ISI for a period of up to four years. Some officers serve for longer. The senior leadership of the ISI comes from the armed forces. There is also a cadre of civilian professional ISI officers, understandably convinced that they run the show. The military come and go, but they remain. If the constant allegations of collusion between the ISI and the mujahedin have any substance whatsoever, it can only be these old ISI hands who are responsible. Even here, though, it is hard to believe that they would have survived so long; there is no evidence for it. The people I came across were thoroughly professional, conducting themselves like responsible, serious civil servants.

There are also civilians serving in the ISI on contract. These are usually academics or journalists. In my experience these men and women do much to bring the directorate into disrepute. For several years a lot of the ISI's media handling was carried out by these contract officers. All of them seemed overwhelmed with self-importance, hugely enjoying the sinister glamour of being part of the ISI. A former junior academic used to boast to me that he could have me thrown out of the country.

The ISI is run by the Director General, a serving lieutenant general. His deputies – major generals – are, confusingly, also referred to as DGs. The structure of the ISI is altered from time to time, but it remains basically as follows, I have been told.

DG Security is the key job in the ISI, an insider told me. 'Everything of any real consequence comes under the DGS. He handles all CT [counter-terrorism], intelligence-gathering, counter-intelligence and local snooping'. The ISI's Political Wing – which maintained contact with politicians – used to come under DG Security. It was reported in November 2008 that President Zardari had closed the Political Wing, which had been established by his father-in-law, Zulfiqar Ali Bhutto, in the 1970s.

DG Analysis is a highly prestigious post; a number of previous occupants – including Javed Alam, Safdar Hussain and Sikander Afzal – have gone on to become corps commanders. Until the end of 2001, contact with foreign officials in Pakistan was handled by DGA.

DG Internal's responsibilities include counter-terrorism. After 9/11 a new Anti-Terrorism Cell was set up, with US help. The intention was that the CIA and the ISI would be able to collect and collate information together. Mutual suspicion has dogged cooperation ever since. ISI insiders blame former DG Ehsan ul-Haq for opening up too many lines of communication to the Americans within the directorate. When all liaison with foreign governments and agencies went through DG Analysis the relationship was easier and neater; they say now that wires are getting crossed. Nevertheless, the US funding greatly increased the ISI's CT capability. 'Officers serving here were suddenly to be seen running around in brand new cars and jeeps. They have safe houses all over Islamabad.... Money has been poured into this cell, which now has capabilities for intercepting and tracing email communications, extracting material from computers and so on.' Pakistan's CT capability remained limited, given the terrorist threat it faced. Some years ago I was told that the Anti-Terrorism Cell could monitor one hundred and fifty mobile phones at any one time, although Pakistan was still unable to monitor satellite calls. The ISI's capabilities are said to have increased significantly since then.

DG External is responsible for ISI activities abroad, with ISI officers working under diplomatic cover at embassies and undercover.

DG Technical is responsible for communications and IT, and usually comes from the Corps of Signals, or from the Electrical and Mechanical Engineers.

London bombings

Counter-terrorism cooperation with the UK is carried on separately.

The ISI provided useful information that contributed to the arrest of the 21 July London bomb plotters. A senior ISI officer said that he had been involved in the decision to intercept the plans, although he personally would have allowed the intelligence operation to run longer.

But the ISI was aggrieved that, when the news first broke, insufficient credit was given to Pakistan's role. The DG is said to have contacted London and said, 'Hey!' The British replied that they did not generally speak publicly about the role of partners in intelligence operations, except the Americans. But the DG had, he said, asked the UK to acknowledge Pakistan's contribution.

The Kashmir Cell

The Kashmir Cell was set up some time after the Afghan Cell and also relied upon SSG and ex-SSG personnel to train fighters and launch operations. ISI officers refer to this cell by different names, Section 24 is the most common (the Afghan cell was Section 21). It is now inactive in terms of launching operations, but it still exists, maintaining contacts with Azad Kashmir and with those who were involved in the struggle there. It seems that a lot of the Kashmir fighters are now moving to the Tribal Areas.

Some SSG personnel joined the fighters in Kashmir after retiring from the Army. The men who did this were usually those who had been training the fighters. For a long time it was considered respectable and even laudable to do this.

Some years ago, before Musharraf became Chief of Army Staff, a serving SSG havildar deserted to join the fighters in Kashmir. He carried out several operations and was taken prisoner by the Indians. He escaped and returned home a hero. He was pardoned for his desertion by the Chief of the General Staff (General Aziz). He returned to Kashmir continually until he was killed by Indian Special Forces.

Large numbers of SSG and ex-SSG personnel became very effective, while working as ISI trainers; they went off on government duty for a couple of years and stayed for life as volunteers.

The ISI's great strength is human intelligence. Its forte, not surprisingly, is said to be gathering intelligence on India. In this regard, an ISI professional told me, it has often operated successfully through Nepal.

6

General Musharraf

General Pervez Musharraf ran the Army – and the country – during some of the toughest years it had known. He handed over command of the Army on 29 November 2007, after nine years at the helm, and resigned as President of Pakistan on 18 August the following year. He had steered the country through the aftermath of the 9/11 attacks on New York, supporting the coalition war in Afghanistan while dealing with the fallout from that war in Pakistan. He tackled the growing militant threat within Pakistan at the same time as dealing with the worst natural disaster the country had ever faced, the earthquake of 2005. During his period in office the economy did well; its GDP doubled. The media was released from rigid government control and scores of new television and radio channels, newspapers and magazines were started, all benefiting from unprecedented freedom. By the time he resigned, however, he was deeply unpopular.

General Musharraf was appointed Chief of Army Staff on the night of 7 October 1998. He was summoned from his home in Mangla, where he was then commander of 1 Corps, to Islamabad. He was ordered to go immediately to Prime Minister Nawaz Sharif's house, without informing the serving Chief of Army Staff, General Jehangir Karamat. General Musharraf was uneasy about this, as he recalled later, in his autobiography: 'It is not normal for a prime minister to call a Lt General like that, and at night, when the Army chief is available next door to sort anything out.' But the Prime Minister's Military Secretary summoned him, so he set off on the ninety-minute drive. Before he had reached the capital news reached him that the Chief had resigned, and that he was to replace him.

General Pervez Musharraf was a gunner by profession, commissioned into 16 Self-Propelled Artillery Regiment in 1964. A couple of years later he tried out for the SSG, and served eight years with the Special Forces. He was the son of migrants from Delhi, educated people with a tradition of government service. It is frequently said that Prime Minister Nawaz

Sharif selected Pervez Musharraf as Army Chief because he was without powerful social-professional links. He was an Urdu-speaking mohajir, he did not come from one of the powerful cavalry or old infantry regiments and anyone from the SSG was vulnerable to the jealousy of those who had tried out for the Special Forces and been rejected. Musharraf's assets, according to officers who have known him for a long time, were his ability, his energy, the loyalty he attracted and his ability to hold his team together.

The Army was at this time seething with anger towards the Prime Minister. After months of unrest General Jehangir Karamat, the Chief of Army Staff, had just resigned.

'JK had an outstanding mind, but he should not have allowed the political government to push him around. He only had three months to go until retirement and he should have said, loud and clear, "Don't mess with me."'

Pakistan was in a precarious position, virtually bankrupt, with mounting sectarian violence. Shia mosques were being attacked, their clergy kidnapped and the mosques occupied. Dispassionate observers, civilian and military alike, were also concerned about the rise of fundamentalist Islam. In the North West Frontier Province tribesmen were said to be inspired by the Taliban regime in Afghanistan and destroying televisions and music cassettes.

Ahmed Rashid, the Pakistani journalist and scholar, wrote gloomily in *The Nation* (11 April 1998) about the second Nawaz Sharif regime:

> As Nawaz Sharif's government slipped into inertia six months after being voted into power in February 1997, most major Islamic parties publicly declared that they had lost faith in parliamentary politics and aimed to mobilise a mass movement for an Islamic revolution by the end of the year.

Rashid foresaw madrassah students who had fought in Afghanistan, armed, trained and motivated, joining such a movement.

He went on: 'With Pakistan's civil state machinery eaten away by corruption and ineffectiveness and growing public disillusionment with the political system, the law and order agencies would be unable to cope with an Islamic movement which would be violent and self-sacrificing. Almost immediately, such a movement would come up against the Army.'

The writer believed that middle and lower-ranking Army officers would be unwilling to fight the militants. 'The threat of an Islamic revolution in Pakistan', he concluded, 'has never been greater.'

The Army was deeply disturbed by everything it saw and laid contingency plans, in case of a breakdown of law and order.

In 1999 Brigadier Faisal Alavi, the commander of the SSG, was summoned by the then CGS (Lieutenant General Mohammad Aziz Khan).

> [General Aziz] said that security measures had to be taken in case of any attempt to overrun the President's House or the Prime Minister's House. The following day the Commander moved an SSG company to the Air Force base at Dhamial, under cover of training with aviation.
>
> Apart from this SSG company the only troops in Rawalpindi were the two battalions of 111 Brigade. At that time one was guarding the PM's House, one the President's.
>
> A meeting was held at Willoughby Road in Pindi, the SSG Rest House and Commander's Residence. The DG Military Operations (Shahid Aziz), Cmdr 111 Brigade (Salauddin Satti), the Director of Military Operations (Brigadier Haroon Aslam), the commander of the battalion guarding the Prime Minister's House (Lt Col Shahid) and the officer in command of the SSG ZARRAR company (Major Haroon ul-Islam, who was to be killed during the Lal Masjid siege in 2007) were there. And so was I, as Commander SSG.
>
> This meeting followed an earlier session at the GS. I moved first from the GS to my house, with the O/C Zarrar Company, and the other participants arrived at fifteen minute intervals.

'Did Nawaz Sharif suspect that the Army was going to mount a coup?' I asked a general who had retired in 1998.

'Probably. He generally thought people were out to get him.'

Was the Army in fact laying plans to topple Nawaz?

'No, but we were very worried about the way things were going. Nawaz might do anything.'

The major cities felt as though they were on the brink of catastrophe, a brigadier who was serving then told me. 'People seem to have forgotten what those last Nawaz years were like. The mood was, in my opinion, worse than anything we have seen since.'

On 12 October 1999 Nawaz Sharif made a bungled attempt to rid himself of General Musharraf as Chief of Army Staff by effectively hijacking the commercial flight on which he was returning from a trip to Sri Lanka, forbidding it to land in Pakistan. The Army moved swiftly and competently and Pervez Musharraf replaced Nawaz Sharif as head of the government that same day.

Foreign governments voiced disapproval of the military takeover and Pakistan was suspended from membership of the Commonwealth.

At home, an overwhelming majority welcomed General Musharraf's takeover. An Islamabad intellectual told me that she had written to congratulate the general; she had never – before or since – written to a public figure who was not a friend or relation. Her letter reflected a widespread feeling that Pakistan had been sliding towards catastrophe, and had been rescued by the takeover. Professor Ian Talbot wrote later that 'some people came onto the streets to welcome the Army – thus providing a fitting epitaph for an era in which Parliament was at worst a bear-pit, at best the fountainhead of patronage politics'.

Pervez Musharraf adopted the title of Chief Executive – rather than 'Martial Law Administrator', as Zia had been – stressing that his was to be a modern, reforming government. There was to be no martial law, Musharraf decided. On 17 October 1999 he addressed the nation:

> Quite clearly, what Pakistan has experienced in the recent years has been hardly a label of democracy not the essence of it. Our people were never emancipated from the yoke of despotism. I shall not allow the people to be taken back to the era of sham democracy.

He announced a seven-point agenda:

Rebuild national confidence and morale.
Strengthen the federation, remove inter-provincial disharmony and restore national cohesion.
Revive the economy and restore investor confidence.
Ensure law and order and dispense speedy justice.
Depoliticise state institutions.
Devolve of power to the grass roots level.
Ensure swift and across the board accountability.

Good governance, he told the nation, was the pre-requisite for achieving these objectives.

Musharraf's first years were successful. In 2000 he became President, partly in order to be able to represent Pakistan at the important Agra Summit with India. The summit achieved nothing. For President Musharraf, Kashmir was key. He insisted that progress had to be made on that front, before any other.

The new President was concerned to introduce reforms that would give real power to local elected bodies. The existing local government system had evolved from the British colonial system.

However, the devolution plan – the cornerstone of the democratic reforms – was not, in the end, a success. It cost the President the support of many in the Civil Service, the 'bureaucracy' as it is always called in Pakistan.

The existing system was anachronistic in some ways, based on a nineteenth-century colonial model. But it worked. Dr Humayun Khan, who had begun his professional life in the Civil Service of Pakistan, explained his reservations about the reforms. Pakistan, he said, was throwing the baby out with the bathwater:

> A system which had evolved over two hundred years was abolished overnight. The main reason cited for this was an imperial legacy and that DCs [district commissioners] were no longer responsive to people's needs, they were corrupt, high-handed and incompetent. But this was due to a deterioration of personnel more than faults in the system. Z. A. Bhutto had set off this decline by removing all constitutional safeguards for the civil services and decreeing that loyalty to the regime, rather than integrity and efficiency, would be the criterion for advancement in a civil servant's career. Army Generals too, had developed a certain antagonism towards 'bloody civilians' over the years.
>
> Conceptually, there was nothing wrong with the idea of decentralisation of power and pushing it down as close to the people as possible. The devil lay in the motivation behind the reforms and the controversies it would generate because it impinged adversely on a fundamental tenet of the Constitution, which was provincial autonomy.
>
> When the reforms were introduced in August 2001, there were no provincial assemblies so an identical ordinance was passed by the governors appointed by Musharraf in all the four provinces. The motive was suspected to be the creation of grassroots organisations, apparently representative, but directly dependent on the Centre which would provide a civilian constituency for the President.

District councils, tehsil councils and union councils, each headed by a Nazim, would be expected to deliver the vote to the Government Party in elections. The provincial governments would be by-passed.

The second flaw was that the whole reform exercise was handed over to a bookish General [Lieutenant General Tanvir Naqvi] who had no experience of administration and no knowledge of realities at the grassroots level.

The unrealistic assumption was that an elected District Nazim, who was to replace the DC, would not be a partisan figure, but would be elected on a non-Party basis. He would be totally impartial and be directly accountable to the people of his district. This was a pipe dream. Once the political parties realised that the office carried considerable power, they entered the fray and all concepts of fairness and justice went out of the window. As a safeguard, each Nazim was assisted by a District Coordination Officer, an experienced bureaucrat who could guide him in technical matters, but since the DCO's career was in the hands of the Nazim, most of them complied with politically motivated decisions. Where he showed any independence, the administration was paralysed.

Finally, of course, the old adage applied that the proof of the pudding lies in the eating. The new set-up proved to be an administrative disaster. Local political rivalries made fairness and impartiality impossible. The law and order situation went completely out of hand, the police went out of control, there was no accountability at all and the poor had no avenues of redress.

There is evidence to show that the various Nazims and Councils were active in the 2002 elections, where Musharraf's 'King's Party' won. By the time of the 2008 elections, the traditional political parties had entered the devolution structures, and the PPP and PML-N came into their own. Evidence of administrative decisions being taken on the basis of party, clan or sect was also there, reflected in the fact that, over a period of five years or so, in the NWFP alone, more than fifty Nazims, at various levels, were murdered because of personal feuds. Throughout this period, serious breaches of law and order were a regular occurrence, but there was not a single case of a Nazim, who was responsible for security, being taken to task. Immediately after the formation of elected provincial governments in 2008, Punjab took the lead in dismantling the system, followed by the NWFP and Baluchistan. Only Sind wanted to keep it on because the MQM won the Council elections and its Party Nazims controlled the key areas of Karachi and Hyderabad.

> Small wonder that, as soon as Musharraf went, all four provinces threw out his reforms and started moving back to the well-tested system of the past. But the damage has been done and the effects of this seven year aberration will first have to be overcome before the country sees any semblance of good governance. In my view, the greatest disservice Musharraf did to Pakistan was to destroy its administrative structure.

Pervez Musharraf's instincts were liberal and his vision for Pakistan was that it should be a moderate, modern, Islamic state. He was convinced that the vast majority of the population shared this ideal and that given time he would be able to turn the country round.

The events of 9/11 soon overshadowed everything else, though. The attention of the government and of the President himself now had to be focused on handling the fallout.

After 9/11, with Pakistan's support so vital, the Western attitude to President Musharraf changed almost overnight. No longer reviled as a military dictator, he was now lauded as a vital partner in the war on terror. The US and UK liked what they saw of Pervez Musharraf, but the 'uniform issue', as it came to be described, niggled.

Western governments advised the General that he should give up his role as Chief of Army Staff, in the belief that it would be easier for him to remain Head of State as a civilian. Despite personal regard for him, there was a feeling that governments should not be run by military men. Within Pakistan, things looked different. There, it was clear that power lay with the Army.

Musharraf's supporters were worried that, the minute he gave up the Army job, he would be weakened. So senior officers were concerned to reassure him that the Army was behind him and wanted him to remain its Chief.

Major General Nadeem Taj, the DGMI, approached Faisal Alavi just before a Formation Commanders Conference. He whispered that he wanted Alavi to speak about the uniform issue.

The DG suggested that Alavi should speak as soon as Musharraf arrived, before he opened the conference. When the usual reading from the Koran was over, General Musharraf asked whether any of those present had anything to say, before he began the proceedings. Instantly, even before Alavi could open his mouth, Major General Mehdi, the Director General of the Punjab Rangers, spoke. He was reading from a piece of paper, so had clearly been given some notice that he should speak. He talked at length of the economic situation, of law and order and of the raft of problems facing the country.

'Mehdi!' Musharraf interrupted impatiently. 'What do you want to say?'

'Sir, what I really want to say is that you should not take off your uniform.'

Alavi leant forward.

'Yes, Faisal? You have something to say?'

'Sir, in all my life I have never agreed with anything that Mehdi has said. But today, for the first time, I agree in totality.'

Everyone laughed.

Then Shahid Aziz spoke and Ahsan Saleem Hyat followed in the same vein.

So Musharraf thanked everyone for their support and said that he would bear in mind their views.

President Musharraf once said that his greatest blessing was a happy disposition. Certainly he seemed to have a great capacity for cheerfulness. He impressed the bureaucracy with his ability to master a brief: 'he developed a much better grasp of all the important issues than any politician I had ever worked with', a civil servant told me.

I met him often when he was President. As Chief of Army Staff it was he, ultimately, who was responsible for giving me access to the Army. What most me struck me was this: General Musharraf talked about the problems facing Pakistan in a way that was far saner than most of the civilians I knew. He talked about poverty, disease, lack of education, lack of opportunity, despair. These were the issues that he brought up when he was discussing what had to be done for Pakistan.

Something else surprised me, too. When he talked about people, civilian or military – and he was interested in people, I noticed – he always began by highlighting their individual characteristics. He did not use the taxonomy (Punjabi, Gujar tribe, Baloch Regiment or Pashtun from East Punjab, Burki tribe, 19 Lancers) that others relied on. One year I spent Christmas with the President and Mrs Musharraf in Karachi and met Javed Alam, an old friend of the General's, in the Corps Guest House, where I was staying. The President was pleased to hear that Javed was in town. 'Javed Alam's here? Good! Do you know what is unusual about that man? He has phenomenal upper body strength!'

President Musharraf's loyalties were strong, I observed. He tended to see the good in people, and to continue to believe in his friends and allies until he had very good reason not to.

In 2011, in his London flat, I asked General Musharraf about the war on terror, as it had been fought in Pakistan.

'In the very early years, 2001 and 2002, we were simply reacting to events. Then, once we had defined the Taliban threat, we focused more on Pakistan. At that time there were no Taliban in Pakistan, apart from Afghans who were running with al Qaeda. At first, our issue was hunting down al Qaeda in the cities and the mountains.

'We did not – then – have sophisticated means of surveillance. The ISI relied on human intelligence. Later on the Anti-Terrorist Wing of the ISI developed these capabilities. The attacks on me [two assassination attempts in December 2003] boosted our efforts. These attacks showed just how far the terrorists could reach. Kayani, then X Corps Commander, took some officers from the MO Directorate to work on developing technological capabilities. He selected bright young men, and they did well. I was impressed by the way Kayani handled all this, and therefore posted him to the ISI.

'From 2002 onwards we worked on a three-pronged approach – military, political and socio-economic – to the problem of the militants . On the military side, the key decision was to move two Divisions – 7 and 9 – to South Waziristan. Politically, we tried to wean the Pashtun away from the Taliban. I coined the phrase: "All Taliban are Pashtun, but not all Pashtun are Taliban."'

The issue of public support for the Taliban greatly concerned the government. President Musharraf wanted to do more to develop the economy in the Federally Administered Tribal Areas (FATA) and he was disappointed that the US and UK did not deliver help that they had promised.

> The US promised billions of dollars that never arrived. The Americans did not deliver.
>
> I liked the idea of weaning the Pashtun away from the Taliban, and tasked the corps commander to hold *jirgas*. We started the *jirgas* in 2003, at the same time that we initiated development works: road construction, opening dispensaries, schools and so on. We did not work out the parameters of the *jirgas*, though. Perhaps we should have done.

> But what upset me was the blunder on the other side of the border. Nothing was done to wean the Pashtun in Afghanistan away from the Taliban. There was a vacuum in Afghanistan. By 2003–4 the Taliban resurgence was underway.
>
> At about this time the Pakistan Taliban were beginning to really gain strength.
>
> But in military terms, we thought that the battle had been won in Afghanistan. The Pashtun should have been given a dominant role in Kabul, and then they would have moved away from the Taliban.
>
> We wasted two years, because of this.

The General felt strongly that the US had blamed Pakistan unfairly for failing to combat the Taliban. The vital mistake, he insisted, was made by the American-led Coalition in Afghanistan. Pakistan, as usual, paid the price for other people's folly.

The Army's deal with Baitullah was a mistake, the general conceded.

> It was done in a hurry, through weakness. Safdar should certainly NOT have gone to meet the militants. Safdar is energetic and outgoing, but he had not mastered the finer points of handling the situation.
>
> Baitullah violated every agreement he entered into.
>
> Owais [Governor of NWFP after General Orakzai] later refined the system of *jirgas*.

It was in 2007 that things began to go disastrously wrong for the Musharraf Presidency.

The Taliban were gaining strength in the Tribal Areas, even though the Army had by this time been deployed in operations against them for six years. There were almost constant attacks on military and civilian targets in Pakistan's cities and small towns. In Islamabad the drama of the Lal Masjid, the radical mosque in the city centre, dragged on for the first half of the year. President Musharraf's government tried for months to persuade the armed militants who had barricaded themselves inside the mosque to surrender, without success. Eventually, in July, the Army stormed the buildings. The President had been criticised for allowing the standoff to continue for so long, but now – perversely – critics blamed him for having sent in the troops.

A second crisis unfolded at the same time. In March President Musharraf sacked the Chief Justice of the Supreme Court, Iftikhar Muhammad Chaudry, on charges of 'misconduct and misuse of authority'. Throughout my years in Pakistan I have heard dozens of people, civilians and Army alike, complain that that its ineffective legal system was one of the country's main problems. Suddenly, however, Iftikhar Chaudry was treated as a hero and Pakistan's lawyers emerged as a force to be reckoned with, backing the Chief Justice in his refusal to accept his dismissal. Liberals came out onto the streets in the cities, joining the lawyers in their demonstrations.

The United States and Britain were piling pressure on Pakistan over allegations that the ISI was supporting Pakistan-based Taliban groups who were launching attacks on coalition troops in Afghanistan. Their conviction that the Pakistan Army – and presumably its Chief – had been deceiving them for years soured their relationship with President Musharraf. These suspicions were not new; they had been voiced for years. The Western allies believed, though, that recently accumulated evidence proved ISI–Taliban collusion.

The United States and Britain were at this time also insisting, ever more ever strongly, that Benazir Bhutto and Nawaz Sharif, the country's two exiled political party leaders, should be allowed to return home to take part in the general election in January 2008. The President was open to the idea that Benazir should be allowed to return, although he strongly resisted the suggestion that Nawaz Sharif should also come back. It seemed likely that the PPP would win the largest number of seats in the election, but that it would not gain an absolute majority. Western governments liked the idea of Benazir Bhutto as Prime Minister, with Pervez Musharraf remaining as President. Before the January elections, though, the President had to be re-elected by the National Assembly, the Senate and the four Provincial Assemblies.

Before his dismissal Chief Justice Iftikhar had been attempting to end the President's ability to allow terrorists to be handed over to the US, a move that would have further worsened the general's already difficult relationship with his allies. He was also likely to block the re-election of the President.

All these issues became increasingly entwined in a crisis from which Pervez Musharraf's Presidency did not recover. He was re-elected in October, but by November he felt it necessary to declare a State of Emergency to avert constitutional chaos: the Supreme Court seemed to be about to declare his recent election invalid. The move was a grave mistake, as he was later to admit, but it was born of desperation.

By 2007 General Musharraf had decided to take off his uniform. He agonised for a long time over whom to appoint as his successor.

As Vice Chief (a post that only exists in Pakistan when the Chief has a day job running the country) General Musharraf had appointed Ahsan Saleem Hyat, a good man and a person of integrity. The Vice Chief carried much of the day-to-day burden of running the Army. He stood notably apart from the fray, trusted – it appeared – by everybody but not expected to take sides. The Vice Chief was, however due to retire.

The real contenders were these:

General Tariq Majid, Commander X Corps. As Chief of the General Staff from 2003 to 2006, he had occupied a pivotal position. He was in overall charge of operations, and controlled the Army's key directorates, including Military Operations, Military Intelligence and the Inter-Services Public Relations. Tariq Majid (an infantryman; 28 Baloch) was a brooding man, described by colleagues as 'difficult', 'rigid' and 'lugubrious'. He had a reputation for scrupulous financial integrity, for having fiercely avoided situations that might leave him beholden – even if only in the imaginations of other men – to businessmen. This contributed to the somewhat puritanical image. Tariq Majid seemed to be an isolated figure in the Army. Colleagues spoke of him with respect, but not warmth. However, General Musharraf had worked with Tariq Majid earlier and thought him intelligent, competent and dependable.

General Ashfaq Parvez Kayani, DG ISI, was a more immediately likeable person. He was reserved, but friendly and rather funny. He was never far away from his cigarettes, which he smoked with a holder. It was well known that he was the son of an NCO, and he was respected for having risen so far. Old acquaintances said that he had always been charming but completely focused on his profession. When other young officers talked about girlfriends or motor bikes he would be discussing the next course in his sights, the next examination. Everyone liked him, but he was not thought to have many close friends. One of his strengths was that he had even fewer enemies. He was given his A for the War Course at the National Defence University, I was told, not only because he was able, but because none of the instructors argued against giving it to him.

There were rumours of bad blood between General Kayani and some other officers two decades ago. Back in 1988, General Kayani was doing a course at Fort Leavenworth. Some at the Pakistan embassy in Washington were outraged at the family's bills for antenatal treatment and delivery. Feelings ran high on both sides. But this was virtually the only story I heard that put him in any sort of questionable light.

There was something endearing about General Kayani, I thought. I interviewed him one evening in the rest house in the garden of his official residence. Just as I was beginning to think that I should leave, the telephone rang. The General indicated that I should relax and take some more green tea. He talked for a long time, happily slipping between English and Urdu. The conversation did not sound entirely businesslike. There seemed to be plenty of laughter, and gossip as far as I could gather. Eventually, the call ended.

The General smiled. 'That was the President,' he said, rather sweetly.

All summer, the Army – and the country – speculated endlessly. Who would Musharraf choose? I saw the rivals, Generals Kayani and Tariq Majid, at several events during those months. They eyed each other ravenously. Proprieties were observed, this was the Army after all, but the hunger was palpable.

If the Army had had a vote, Lieutenant General Kayani, the DG ISI, would have romped home. Many people saw Tariq Majid as the front-runner, however, and believed that he had been groomed by General Musharraf for the post.

Any lieutenant general might be appointed as Vice Chief of Army Staff, in principle. However, had the President selected anyone other than the two favourites, by tradition everyone of the seniority of the new Vice Chief or younger would retire. So the younger the man the greater the shake-up.

Finally, on 2 October the announcement came. Lieutenant General Kayani was to be appointed Vice Chief of Army Staff.

On 28 November General Musharraf resigned from the Army. Henceforth, the Army's loyalty belonged to General Kayani. But there was no massive switch of allegiance. The institution was what mattered, not individuals. Initially, in any case, many assumed that Pervez Musharraf would remain as Head of State.

So long as he could pull through the next few months – the argument went at the time – the President would be in office for longer than Kayani would be Chief, and for longer than the Prime Minister (whoever that might be) would be around.

There was much speculation in the Army, therefore, about the identity of the next Chief. Nadeem Taj was thought to be the front-runner, being groomed by Musharraf to take over from Kayani in due course.

General Kayani held open house at the Signals Mess in Rawalpindi to celebrate his appointment as Chief. But the electricity failed, so it was held in the dark. 'Ominous, that,' a lieutenant general who was there commented. No one that I spoke to afterwards had seen Tariq Majid that evening. Almost everybody else who counted in the Army was there.

The Army wanted the new government to succeed. Officers and men cared about the fate of the country, and the country needed stability. Even those who were most loyal to Pervez Musharraf, and who most disliked the individuals connected with the PPP government, wished Prime Minister Gilani and his team well. A great many officers supported the PPP's traditional left-leaning views and would have voted for the party if they had voted at all (few in the armed forces seem to be registered to vote).

After the assassination of Benazir Bhutto an English television correspondent asked President Musharraf whether he had blood on his hands. Tony Blair had been asked the same question a few years before, referring to the death of the scientist David Kelly, so the impact of the question was muted to British ears. But to President Musharraf the question was impossibly insulting. He was furious. He talked about his family background, a reaction that sounded odd to British ears. But it was a relevant response: he was stressing that he did not come from a murderous feudal family where killing was commonplace. His Urdu-speaking family was decent and hardworking. It was true.

7

Tackling the Militants

The ISI and the CIA had retained their links even after US interest in Afghanistan dwindled with the withdrawal of the Soviet Army in 1989. But in the days, weeks and months following the 9/11 attacks the relationship intensified. The ISI was keen to cooperate with the US. It was not in Pakistan's interest that fighters from Afghanistan should be flocking into the Tribal Areas nor that the region should be destabilised by the fallout from the war. Pakistani officials were also aware that US hostility might be more potent than its goodwill.

The CIA Islamabad Station Chief, Bob Grenier, asked to visit Pakistan's border region shortly after 9/11. The ISI's DG Analysis, a lieutenant general, escorted him into the Federally Administered Tribal Areas (FATA). It was fortunate that this man held that position at the time. Confident, relaxed and convivial, he was good company. He was not a career intelligence officer; like almost all ISI officers he had spent most of his life working in ordinary Army units. But he knew the US, he had a taste for the work, and he understood the ways of the Americans well. He and Grenier went without fuss in a couple of civilian cars from Miramshah. They crossed the unmarked border into Afghanistan and spent some time walking around the area, on both sides of the border. The general recalls seeing a B-52 bomber overhead as they prowled the scrubby hillsides.

Over the next couple of months the General took a series of other foreigners on the same trip, and he took Bob Grenier to the border again. 'I kept saying, to all of them, that we needed ground and air mobility, thermal night vision equipment and secure communications. "Give us these and we'll seal the border so tightly that nothing can get across,"I told all our visitors.' The Pakistan Army has complained ever since that the Americans wanted them to prevent border crossings but would not share proper equipment with them.

Operation Enduring Freedom was launched on 7 October 2001 at about 17.00, local time, with air strikes against Taliban forces and al Qaeda targets. Aerial bombing and cruise missile attacks were to pound Afghanistan for weeks to come. On 8 October people came out onto the streets of all the major cities of Pakistan to protest against the war. Most Pakistanis were disturbed by the latest foreign assault on their neighbour, appalled by the ferocity of the air attacks.

Although President Musharraf had agreed to support the war, he had grave concern about the way it was to be pursued. Coalition ground forces would have to enter Afghanistan either through Pakistan or from central Asia to the north. It would not have been politically possible for the Pakistan government to allow the invasion to be launched from Pakistani soil. It was clear, however, that the Northern Alliance – the umbrella group that involved most of the non-Pashtun groups who had opposed the Taliban – would benefit if the coalition entered the country from the north. Most of the warlords who had brought Afghanistan to its knees during the civil war that raged after the Soviet Army's withdrawal were now connected to this group. Although the Northern Alliance included some Pashtun fighters, most belonged to Afghanistan's other nationalities, Tajiks and Hazaras, Uzbeks and Turkmen. The Northern Alliance was hostile to the generally Pashtun Taliban, and was seen as being, by extension, anti-Pashtun. If the Afghan Pashtun were to feel disenfranchised at home, they would inevitably look to Pakistan for support.

Pakistan did not want another influx of refugees, nor did it want to have to support the Afghan Taliban. So President Musharraf was keen that the Northern Alliance should not be portrayed as liberators. He argued that the coalition war should be swift, that there should be minimal collateral damage and that the Northern Alliance should not be allowed to effectively replace the Taliban. President Bush gave him an undertaking that if and when the Taliban were driven out of Kabul, it should be declared an 'open city' until an interim regime could be established. But as the Northern Alliance troops rolled across the country it became clear that they did not feel bound by any such deal. When the Northern Alliance fighters entered the important Taliban stronghold of Mazar-i-Sharif on 9 November 2001, the American Secretary of State, Colin Powell, urged the Northern Alliance troops to stay out of Kabul. They entered the city three days later. President Musharraf was angered by the apparent muddle of the war. The ISI, which had invested so much in Afghanistan, was deeply concerned. 'We could only hope that a better balance between the Northern Alliance and the Pashtuns would emerge in time. We assumed, however, that it would be a couple of years, at the very least, before this could happen,' a very senior ISI officer commented later.

Although President Musharraf's help had been crucial to the coalition's successful invasion of Afghanistan, the Army was irritated that the US failed to coordinate with Pakistan on crucial issues.

'We suggested to the US that they should not drive fighters towards our borders,' General Ashfaq Parvez Kayani (Director General Military Operations, the Army's key operational job, at the time he was talking about) said some years later. 'We hoped that the coalition would encircle the al Qaeda forces.' But the planners at Centcom (US Central Command, headquartered at MacDill Air Force Base in Tampa, Florida) seemed to take no account of Pakistani concerns. There were differences at that time between the CIA and Centcom, Kayani reported. 'The CIA was very possessive of Afghanistan, and there were problems between the Director of the CIA and the DoD [Department of Defense].'

General Kayani commented wryly: 'We first learnt about Tora Bora [December 2001] from the television.' There was, he said, no coordination with the US. 'We watched the American forces driving towards us,' pushing enemy fighters into Pakistan. 'But no one was manning our borders.' The Pakistan Army was doing what it could, but a crucial opportunity to prevent any incursions had been lost.

Between October and December 2001 Pakistan's response to the Afghan war had been to 'beef up' its posts on the western (Afghan) border and occupy new posts. Guarding the borders to prevent the incursion of militants was the responsibility of the Frontier Corps. Even this was well-nigh impossible in the wild and mountainous terrain of South Waziristan. Shortage of modern equipment exacerbated the Army's difficulties.

In December 2001 President Musharraf took the second crucial decision in Pakistan's war against terror. Having supported the coalition's invasion of Afghanistan, he now launched Operation al-Mizan (Justice). Pakistan Army troops (as well as the locally-based Frontier Corps, who were already there) moved into the Tribal Areas. The aim was to kill or capture militants who threatened the state, and its initial focus was South Waziristan. There were several clashes, in the autumn/ winter of 2001–2 between the Frontier Corps and militants entering Pakistan, but it was not until 2002 that the Army really began to take on the militants.

From the middle of December al-Mizan's aims were broadened, including efforts to engage the tribes in an attempt to pacify the area. This was, General Kayani stressed, entirely a Pakistan initiative. The tribes were alarmed by what they had heard of American power and the Pakistan government seized the opportunity to persuade the Pashtuns, while they were briefly unnerved, to allow Pakistan Army troops into the Tribal Areas. 'We identified the window of opportunity and used the possibility of American pursuit of fighters from Afghans to say "You have a choice. Either we guard our borders and check foreign fighters or you accept the risk of a spillover from Afghanistan."' The tribes agreed to allow the Army and the Frontier Corps into all seven areas. This was, almost literally, uncharted territory. It was only a year since the Army had been allowed into the Tribal Areas for the first time, in order to build roads and initiate development projects.

However, it was at least partly successful. About 250 fighters fleeing Afghanistan – all Arabs and other foreigners – were captured after they had crossed into Pakistan in December 2001 or the beginning of 2002.

'After the Tora Bora bombings [in December 2001] we had them on the run,' a key general commented later. 'We said that no foreigners would be allowed to cross the borders. The Army and FC had road blocks all over Waziristan. All traffic was checked. The rebels did not have free access to roam wherever they wanted. We were putting them under pressure and this affected their ability to operate in Afghanistan.'

In the early stages of the war CIA officers were obsessed with finding Osama bin Laden. Officers who were in the ISI at the time report that they were quite often woken up in the early hours of the morning with some bizarre request. One night, the story was that a Predator was tracking four people who had hopped out of pick-up trucks about five kilometres from the border and were now heading for Pakistan. 'We need them stopped as soon as they reach your territory,' the American voice told the Pakistan general. The ISI passed the request on to the Frontier Corps, who immediately deployed and picked up the four men. 'But none of them was more than 5ft 8in or 5ft 9in in height and among them was a teenaged boy who was brought to Pakistan for kidney treatment. We had ambushed the group, and imprisoned them on the basis of flawed information. But we had to work hard to persuade the Americans that we should release them. The relationship with the US was lopsided and it endangered government credibility in the Tribal Areas and in the rest of Pakistan.'

During early operations in the Tribal Areas, Army officers suspected that operational information was being leaked to the militants. Time and again the Army would arrive at a suspected terrorist base to find it recently abandoned. The stove would still be warm and the house seemed to have been abandoned in a hurry. Many in the Army became convinced at this time that the leaks could only be coming from within the ISI.

The Americans were bringing a lot of pressure to bear on Pakistan, insisting that militants had to be dealt with. Although US intelligence in Pakistan has frequently been criticised for being late and wrong, some of the Pakistan Army's senior commanders in recent operations insist that US satellite intelligence was the most useful information available to them. The ISI relied on human intelligence, which was frequently contaminated.

During the winter of 2001–2 renewed tension with India distracted Pakistan from its efforts to tackle the militants in the Tribal Areas. Terrorist attacks on Indian-controlled Kashmir's Legislative Assembly on 1 October 2001 and on the Indian Parliament on 13 December provoked diplomatic hostilities that appeared to bring the two countries to the brink of nuclear war. Seven people were killed in the attack on the Indian Parliament before the five terrorists were themselves killed. The Indian government blamed two militant pro-Kashmir groups, Lashkar-e-Taiba and Jaish-e-Mohammad, both ISI backed. Pakistan counter-claimed that the attack was a drama staged by Indian intelligence agencies. Despite UN and US calls for restraint, India launched Operation Parakram, its greatest mobilisation since the 1971 war, and the two sides faced each other along Kashmir's Line of Control, poised for war.

At the height of the drama more than a million troops were lined up, facing each other on the border.

Hurried international diplomacy – with Colin Powell's deputy, Richard Armitage, and others scuttling around south Asia – and some vestige of restraint led the neighbours to de-escalate. Tension seemed to ease further after Powell's January 2002 visit, but military minds in Pakistan remained very much focused on its eastern neighbours.

A Lieutenant General who was occupying a key position at the time uses these events to explain the ISI's initial response to the war in Afghanistan:

> Up to 2001 FATA was very peaceful and [it was] the route to supply the Taliban [in Afghanistan] who were supported by us. Post 9/11 and especially after Tora Bora the ISI was very slow to reorient itself to face the new challenge. This was considerably augmented by the 'Escalation' in 2001–2002 as the primary focus had to be India rather than what was previously our back garden. Given the limited resources that the ISI had, all our effort was directed towards India while FATA was left to fester. XI Corps was dislocated from NWFP and was concentrated in Strategic Assembly Areas to strike India if war was imposed on us and therefore not available for any support in the concerned area. The move back from this situation had to be managed as we learnt of Indian formations moving back, especially those from Eastern Command, and therefore took nearly six months. On returning from a field deployment the natural emphasis is administration, including leave, rest and recreation etc. Historically our intelligence effort had been directed eastward and while a supply infrastructure was in place since the early 1980s, no effort was made to install [an] intelligence-gathering network [in FATA] as no threat was perceived. Such networks take time to establish and mature. So I feel that there was a definite distraction by the Indian deployment.

Throughout the winter of 2001–2 the militants were gaining strength in the Tribal Areas. On 1 April two people were killed and twelve injured in a bomb attack on a bus at Spin Qaira in South Waziristan. Later that month a government college in Miramshah was damaged by a missile. Pakistan media reports claimed that US troops had been stationed at a nearby vocational training centre until the last week of April. In June three missiles were fired at a Frontier Corps camp in North Waziristan, where the Provincial Governor, Syed Iftikhar Hussain Shah, was staying. A week later a building that was being used by US forces was targeted in a rocket attack. The building was not hit but the incident further alarmed both GHQ and the Americans. It was becoming clear that the militants had useful intelligence.

Within a week the Pakistan Army launched its first significant operation against the extremists in the Tribal Areas.

The View From the FATA A Pashtun soldier explained the tribes' viewpoint to me. He came from a modest tribal background, but was Army trained. Both influences were evident as he talked. He had the quiet dignity of a Pashtun man, with the alert edginess of a soldier who has seen a lot of fighting.

> The Frontier Crimes Regulations gave [the authorities] immense powers. A man could be imprisoned for life. The system of collective punishment meant that if a man did wrong, the whole sub-tribe would be punished: shops would be sealed and the tribe forbidden to enter the settled areas. They would be unable to trade at all. As well as the Frontier Scouts, the political agent has a police force – the Hasildars – who are used before the Scouts are called in.
>
> The Waziristan tribes, the Mehsuds and the Wazirs, were the fiercest under the British and they still are the fiercest now. These people are different from the others. They even speak a Pashtu very different from the rest of the Frontier.
>
> The Mehsuds and the Wazirs have not been properly supported by the Pakistan government. Pakistan has paid them peanuts compared to what the British had been doing for them.

The British ruled the Tribal Areas through a political agent (a civil servant) and *maliks*, government-appointed tribal leaders.

> The power of the *maliks* came largely through cash. They used funds given to them by the British to pay off the tribesmen. Some, like the Fakir of Ipi, fought them and fought the government of Pakistan after 1947. But most people did not rock the boat.

Before 1947, 'the people were quite happy, not being pressurised either by the Brits or by the *maliks*'. For decades after the British left, their system rumbled along.

> In 1998 there was a movement against the *maliks*. The Shaman Khela [sub-tribe] *maliks* were misappropriating government handouts that were intended for schools, tube wells and so on, and selling to other tribes the equipment that they had been given.
>
> So a movement was started by the tribesmen, under their own tribal

> *Sardar* [chieftan]. During this movement they blew up the *maliks'* houses and formed a *lashkar* [a tribal militia] and went around beating drums. They told the families to get out and then blew up the *maliks'* houses. So the *maliks* lost all credibility. The *maliks* lost respect because they were too selfish, too greedy.

Then came the time of the Talibs. *Talib* means 'student', but it became a loose expression for local (Afghan/Pakistani) tribesmen loyal to Mullah Omar. During the Soviet War a lot of tribesmen joined the jihad. The ISI trained Afghan refugees but a lot of tribesmen joined too.

The Russians were seen as infidels, communist and atheist, cruel invaders of a Muslim country subjugating the people and committing atrocities towards the women. When the Soviet Union pulled out they left anarchy behind in Afghanistan, leaving the way open for the Taliban..

The soldier takes up the story:

> A lot of the Arabs who had fought [the Soviet Union] in Afghanistan had never left [the Tribal Areas]. Once the Taliban came to power the area became a safe haven. These foreigners were respected and welcomed by the tribes. After the US invasion of Afghanistan, the foreign fighters were given shelter by the tribes, and shown great hospitality. But this time around it was different. The foreigners went to the richer tribals and paid them pretty well. They paid in US dollars, dirhans and other currencies. A lot of them were Arabians who opposed the Saudi regime.
>
> The Talib training schools were so good that they were almost military academies. It was only after a while that we realised how powerful the Talibs were. We began to realise that every second or third house was Taliban.
>
> So the power of the *maliks* was reducing and that of the Talibs was growing. When the Taliban and foreigners arrived, there was strong pressure from the US on President Musharraf and on the Army and from them onto the Governors and political agents to get rid of the foreigners. This was a dilemma. The foreigners were respected, old allies.

Operation Kazha Punga

In June 2002 the CIA passed on intelligence that about thirty al Qaeda fighters were staying on a militant base in South Waziristan near Kazha

Punga, a village near Azam Warsak. Based on the US intelligence, an assault was planned. This was the operation in which the Pakistan Army first drew blood, and it illustrated the Army's weaknesses at that time.

Three Americans (believed to have been CIA operatives) accompanied the Pakistan Army during this operation, according to information provided to me by men who were on the operation.

On the night of 25 June 2002, a mixed force, comprising of 23 Baloch Company (only about thirty-five men) and a similar number of Frontier Corps Tochi Scouts (under a captain),was deployed to search out the militants. According to Army sources the orders for this operation were passed to 9 Division by the then Corps Chief of Staff, Brigadier Shahid Iqbal, at about 16.00. 'He insisted that the operation should be carried out at once. The Brigadier maintained that the Corps Commander was asleep and that the first thing he would do when he woke up would be to enquire about the progress of the operation. The mixed force under CO 23 Baloch and the Company Commander was therefore despatched to Kazha Punga in haste, nudged by the division and by [116] Brigade,' a senior officer reported later. 'The Tochi Scouts promised to send eighty-five Scouts, but only thirty-five were actually sent. 23 Baloch turned up without their recoilless rifles and mortars, despite the fact that they came in vehicles ... The inherent slackness and the non-seriousness of proper analysis of the operating environment was disastrous.'

The plan was that the militants' compound should be surrounded by 23 Baloch with the Scouts forming an outer cordon. These troops arrived in vehicles before first light. The American CIA personnel arrived last, with the ten SSG men who were there to protect them. The commanding officer of the SSG's 3 Commando, Lieutenant Colonel Raza, and Major Imtiaz (one of his company commanders) were also there. Initially, the troops deployed around the wrong house. The correct building was then encircled by 23 Baloch, but 'in a rather casual and unprofessional manner. The FC scouts stood aside in a group, apparently uninterested in the operation,' according to a soldier who was there.

The political agent, a major from 23 Baloch and the Frontier Corps captain approached the building and hammered on the door. Since the man who opened the door seemed not to understand any Pakistani language they assumed that he was a foreign fighter and bundled him into a jeep but only after he had shouted some warning to those inside.

The government forces seemed to have no plan at all and were thrown into confusion when the next man to appear at the door told them there was a woman in labour inside the compound. Nevertheless, he said, the troops could enter and search the premises. He asked only that they should wait ten minutes, so that the woman could go into purdah. After a while he opened the door again, and held it for the soldiers. They walked straight into the trap. Within minutes the major from 23 Baloch and the FC captain had been killed, along with six other regular soldiers. Two militants emerged from the building, one firing to the left, the other to the right. The few SSG personnel present reacted quickly, an officer returning fire from one side and an SSG sniper from the other. Both the foreign militants were shot dead.

But there was now a stalemate. The Americans ran off, followed by six of the SSG men who were supposed to be protecting them. The rest of the SSG personnel stayed with their CO, who was trying to help 23 Baloch assume control. A lance naik who took part in the operation later described the scene: 'The CO of 23 Baloch seemed to be in a state of shock. He kept lamenting on whether his men who had not emerged out of the compound were dead or alive and wounded and seemed to have lost his mind in reasoning out anything.' Lt Colonel Raza was on the scene and took over, deploying the 23 Baloch men more effectively. However, the Scouts 'appeared to be rudderless without their captain and again cluttered into a corner'. Raza was now trying to calm 23 Baloch CO's nerves, conferring with him in a nearby tube well building. Outside, where it was now dark, confusion reigned. The foreign militants (mostly Uzbek) suddenly broke through the door 'in a most daring and professional manner. The first two emerged with speed and fired with RPG 7s at the machine guns that were guarding the exit. As the soldiers ducked for cover over thirty foreign fighters sprinted out, firing randomly in all directions. They made straight for the orchard less than a hundred yards away, killing two more soldiers of 23 Baloch who lay in their direction before melting away into the darkness.' The infantrymen were so disoriented that, they said later on, they had thought the fleeing foreigners were SSG soldiers in local dress.

This dismal operation lead to much soul-searching in the Pakistan Army. At the end of the day the Pakistan Army had lost two officers and ten soldiers from 23 Baloch and the FC. Admittedly, two Uzbeks had been killed and one captured alive. But Operation Kazha Punga forced the military to confront the unpleasant fact that it was not competent at counter-insurgency operations. After this, GHQ relied ever more on the SSG to tackle these trained and motivated foreign fighters and their local allies. At about this time SSG teams began to train infantry battalions that were being sent to Waziristan.

The operation, which had been planned by 9 Division (Kohat) led to the sacking of Brigadier Ijaz, who commanded 116 Brigade. 'He was a brilliant and brave officer,' a lieutenant general said some years later. 'But in the Army you take responsibility.' The commanding officer of 23 Baloch unit was also replaced. Shortly afterwards Major General Saeed, Commander of 9 Div, was moved out. Lt Col Raza of 3 Commando was blamed in the enquiry that followed for not taking over the situation and missed out on promotion as a result. The SSG thought that Lt Colonel Raza, who had only had ten soldiers with him, had in fact performed well. But these protests went unheard. Some felt that the infantry was determined not to shoulder all the responsibility for the botched operation.

At GHQ in Rawalpindi a very senior officer later expressed the view that the fallout from the failed operation at Kazha Punga was not well handled. 'There was great bitterness, rancour and buck-passing in XI Corps.'

General Kayani commented later that this operation illustrated the vulnerabilities of the Army at that time. The troops were overconfident, assuming that the men in the compound were telling the truth. In their concern not to inflict collateral damage they overlooked the danger of the situation. The Army had to learn to be more cautious, without going too far. Operating in these areas is perilous. Every family has weapons and every house has a picket.

Throughout the spring and early summer of 2003 there were sporadic attacks in the Tribal Areas. In April a hundred and twenty-five Russian-made rockets were found in a truck of animal feed in South Waziristan, and in June a telephone exchange in North Waziristan was attacked. July saw nine people, some of them military, injured in a bomb attack on the bazaar in Miramshah and at least three people killed in Saadgai.

The Commander of XI Corps, General Orakzai, told me that, in mid-2003, the US passed on intelligence that al Qaeda fighters were gathering in an inaccessible, mountainous part of the Mohmand Agency. 'The operation was planned for 4 June 2003, but was then postponed for two weeks at their request. So we launched the operation on 20 June, but even after the delay the US troops were not in place. We had asked them to deploy troops on the Afghan side, on the known routes through the mountains but they did not bother to do so.' General Orakzai took the Army into several regions, such as Khyber and the Shawwal area of North Waziristan, that had been no-go areas. The first development work in the FATA was started by him, and this achievement is always acknowledged. But he is often criticised by other Pakistan Army officers for his unwillingness to take on the tribesmen at this vital time. 'His understanding with the locals was that the Army was only there to prevent incursions over the border. He kept the lid on things, insisting that there was no real problem.'

General Orakzai stressed that, as a Pashtun himself, he spoke with authority. The Pakistani writer Ahmed Rashid later said of him: 'A tribesman from FATA who boasted of his inside knowledge of the tribal mind, in fact Orakzai appeared totally insensitive to tribal needs' (*Descent into Chaos* (2008), p. 277). This was exactly the view of a number of senior officers involved in these operations. 'General Orakzai never lived in the Aurakzai Agency. His relations live in Hangu. He is not a tribal *malik* or anything. He has no place in the local hierarchy,' a younger officer who served in XI Corps told me bitterly.

Hamid Khan, then a major general, was appointed Inspector General of the Frontier Corps (IGFC) in February 2003. General Hamid had been commissioned into XI Cavalry, Prince Albert Victor's Own (PAVO), one of the old cavalry regiments. PAVO, as distinguished as any regiment in the Pakistan Army, wears its grandeur lightly, without pomposity. Its officers tend to share a humorous and ironic view of the world. General Hamid had been commanding an armoured division in Kharian before coming to Peshawar. But he was a local man. He was a Pashtun, a Mohammadzai from Charsadda whose father, Mohammad Hashim Khan, had been Vice Chancellor of Peshawar University. The family was known and respected.

'Within a month of me taking over the President called a conference. Should we, or should we not, move into Mohmand Agency? If so, who should do it? I said that it should be the FC. We know the local culture and any difficulties will be containable.' General Hamid was convinced that the Frontier Corps could handle things in a much lower-key way than the Army. He describes the Frontier Corps' first encounter with the militants during his tenure, when he took them into the Mohmand Agency in June 2003:

> Most of the area was cleared without resistance. In fact, when I landed to see the progress the local elders garlanded me. Shortly afterwards, though, trouble broke out.
>
> After the FC had moved into the Mohmand Agency Lt Gen. Orakzai began to shift troops on to the border. I said, 'Don't. I have cleared the dominating areas. Let's hold them.' I told General Ehsan [DG ISI] the same.

As General Hamid had predicted, clashes erupted when the Army closed up to the border area.

> We had occupied all the dominating features along the Durand Line, but we were still moving into the area. I was on the frontline and General Orakzai came to visit me. It was his habit to collect local people together to talk to them. The militants could see us from their higher positions and as soon as he arrived the militants opened fire. After forty minutes or so I had to evacuate him in my jeep.

In General Hamid's view, the decision to move troops up to the Durand Line, the disputed border with Afghanistan, antagonised the Afghans. The regular border clashes that erupted afterwards were a result of this decision, he maintained.

Upgrading the Special Services Group

There had been no large-scale Army operations against the militants since Kazha Punga. That operation had highlighted the need to improve the SSG's capabilities. With this in mind President Musharraf ordered the creation of an SSG Special Operations Task Force (SOTF) specifically to take on operations against the militants in the mountainous terrain of the Tribal Areas. Pakistan's Special Forces were to be better trained and better equipped, and raised from brigade to division strength. The post of Head of the Special Services Group was upgraded to a two-star slot. On 14 August 2003 Major General Amir Faisal Alavi, who had earlier commanded the SSG from 1999 to 2001, was appointed as the first general officer commanding the SSG.

The operating environment, always difficult, was becoming ever more perilous, Alavi explained:

> As operations progressed, the Taliban went witch-hunting for US and ISI/MI spies amongst the local population and bodies of such suspected spies began to be found all over Waziristan with their throats slit and a note in Pushto attached to their bodies explaining that the person had been caught, tried, proved to be a spy and anybody spying on the Taliban/al Qaeda would meet a similar fate. Resultantly, the ISI and MI watched helplessly as they saw their sources drying up. Under these circumstances, more reliance now lay on the technical information provided by the Americans, duly vetted from Tampa, Florida, where all this information was collected, collated, interpreted and then passed to the CIA fellows in Pakistan to share with their Pakistani partners. That would result in quickly called conferences in the Military Operations Directorate where the DGMO (Director General Military Operations) would give out the recently received target information along with real-time aerial photographs and all other information passed.
>
> This would be presented to the Vice Chief /Chief of General Staff in the presence of those whose troops would be participating in the forthcoming operations. Hence, the Corps Commander XI Corps, the GOC SSG and the DG Aviation or the local aviation base commander were mostly there. The DG MI and DG ISI (S) also attended in order to give their intelligence inputs. But the ISI was there to provide intelligence. Planning was the job of the MO Directorate.
>
> During the planning conferences, tea and sandwiches were served whenever the Vice Chief or the Chief of General Staff [CGS] attended. Smoking was obviously allowed as both the Vice Chief and the CGS smoked. So the others also lit up. Tea and snacks had their place in a corner to which everyone had access. After the initial briefings and the rattling out of the intelligence inputs, the MO Directorate would spell out their tentative plan for tackling that particular target/targets. A general discussion ensued, thereafter, in which every commander who was participating gave his own views regarding the plan, often seeking amendments for his troops' own role, the final decision of which lay with the seniormost officer present. The amended plan would then

be presented in the next sitting, a few hours later, which once approved would see the conference coming to an end and all commanders taking off towards their own commands to disseminate orders for implementation. The operation would then take off at the planned timings with the MO Directorate monitoring it and giving the required briefings on the progress of the operations to the Vice Chief /CGS.

Normally, the operation went in right after the conference. At times troops were briefed during movement as time was short.

Operation Angoor Adda

'Operation Tight Noose' was conducted very close to the Angoor Adda border checkpost on 2 October 2003. This was to be the first outing for the newly formed Special Operations Task Force. Many in the Pakistan Army felt that this was the first operation that did anything to boost American confidence in the country's anti-terrorism policy. Richard Armitage (US Deputy Secretary of State) was in Kabul at the time but had cancelled his onward visit to Pakistan. Hearing of the success of this operation he rescheduled his visit.

During this operation the notorious al-Khadr (an Egyptian known as *Cannadi*, 'the Canadian', because of his North American passport) was killed in an exchange of fire with the GOC SSG (Major General Faisal Alavi) and his command group as they bumped into him during the final clearing of the brush where he lay in hiding. The Americans had a ten million dollar bounty on the head of al-Khadr, which was duly paid to the Pakistan Army (and used to set up a welfare fund for killed and injured Army personnel and their dependants). Hassan Maksoom, the Uighur leader of the military wing of the East Turkestan Movement, was also killed in this operation to the great relief of the Chinese.

(The East Turkestan Islamic Movement (ETIM) is fighting to turn China's Xinjiang province into the independent state of East Turkestan. It is believed to have links to Al Qaeda.)

The Americans had been monitoring a complex of five adjoining houses, about two kilometres away from the Angoor Adda checkpost, for many months and were by now sure that it was a militant hideout. They were convinced that most of the attacks on the US base at Shikin, a couple of kilometres due west of Angoor Adda were being launched from this spot. Detailed satellite imagery of the target was passed by the CIA to GHQ. The Special Operations Task Force (SOTF), along with

Zarar Company (the Anti-Terrorist Company) were tasked to perform the operation. Initially it was planned to be an air assault operation at first light with the SSG being dropped all around the target area and then forming a quick inner cordon before clearing the area. However, the operation was advanced by one day when the Americans reported that a group of about thirty-five jihadis had just crossed the border after attacking the US Base at Shikin carrying with them one of their dead who had been killed in a fire-fight there. Major General Faisal Alavi wrote later, in an email to me:

> GHQ planned that we should bag the group immediately before they returned. So the plan was revised. Now the SSG was to take off immediately for Angoor Adda, in vehicles, and undertake this arduous thirteen hour journey to close up to the complex on foot after disembarking near Angoor Adda. This was intended to achieve complete surprise and that it did!
>
> The SOTF under Brigadier Nazareth Bashir had the cordon in place just before first light. This was commendable keeping in view the distance they had travelled on vehicles and the final couple of kilometres walk up to the target to achieve surprise. But they only just managed to do it.

Major General Alavi, who was monitoring the operation from the Military Operations Directorate Operations Room, received a call on his Thuraya phone from a young SSG captain who was sitting next to the CIA operatives whom he was there to protect. The CIA personnel were monitoring the operation on their laptops through the Predator drone that was circling the target area. The captain informed his general 'that – apparently – the occupants of the complex suspected that something was happening as they had seen four or five men peering out of the same window in one of the buildings'. A message was immediately relayed to the SOTF commander that the Army's movements had been detected.

> He reacted accordingly, announcing in Pashto that the troops were elements of the Pakistan Army and that they wanted everybody to come out of the five compounds with their hands up. Gunfire from the buildings was the only reply. Knowing that there were women and children

> in these houses, the SOTF commander requested the Jihadis at least to send out the women and children. The firing then stopped as the women and children piled out and were guided to a safe place. Then the fire-fight resumed with the SOTF severely pounding the buildings. Cobra attack helicopters joined in with their machine guns blazing. The fire-fight continued for hours. Reports of the dead and captured Jihadis started pouring in at GHQ. Approximately six of the Jihadis had been killed and fifteen captured by the time Zarar Company moved in, clearing the compounds and capturing a great deal of explosive material, an armoury of weapons, mines and ammunition.

GHQ, reassured by the reports that were coming in, decided that it would be safe to send journalists to the site. The DG ISPR (Inter-Services Public Relations), Major General Shaukat Sultan, was informed, and a helicopter was put on standby. All available foreign journalists were bundled into a Mi 17 helicopter which took off for Angoor Adda by late noon. Major General Alavi, who said later that he went to see his troops to 'give them a pat on the back', travelled with the journalists.

When the press party landed it emerged that the battle was still going on. The BBC's Zaffar Abbas reported: 'A fire-fight was still taking place nearby, Cobra helicopters flew overhead and local tribesmen looked on with a mixture of anger and amazement from their homes.'

Leaving the journalists at Angoor Adda, General Alavi

> dashed to the site to see the situation on ground. Reaching the location of Karrar Company (the reserve company in this operation) [he] spoke by Thuraya with the SOTF commander who said that at least four of the diehard Jihadis had disappeared into the thick brush and the folds of the ground between the compounds. Trying to follow them, the SSG had been greeted with fire and grenades. Two soldiers had been injured and one soldier forming the cordon had also been killed by a direct hit to the head.

The Chief of the General Staff (Lieutenant General Shahid Aziz) and the Vice Chief of Army Staff (General Yusuf Khan) began calling General Alavi, frantically instructing him 'to ensure an early winding up of the operation as the Pakistan Army had never operated in the Tribal Areas here earlier and was at a loss to predict the response by night of the Jihadi elements in the area'. Alavi was by this time showing the captured weapons cache and the prisoners to the journalists. The journalists 'went scurrying back to Angoor Adda, to their waiting helicopter, the moment a machine gun burst from an undisclosed location landed nearby,' General Alavi chuckled later.

Alavi took charge. It was now 4.30 p.m. and it was fast getting dark.

The operation had to be ended before last light and the entire force safely quartered for the night at Angoor Adda. General Alavi called Major Raja Sanaullah (Karrar Company commander) and told him to bring his men up through a *nullah* running parallel to the target area.

> I guided the company up to the highest contour of the target area from where the ground rolled down in the shape of terraces. Lining the company all along the target area and placing myself in the centre, I ordered the company to roll down the slopes to search and clear the last of the Jihadis hiding in the contours of the ground. The search force was now in a position of advantage as they were looking down at the enemy, who would find it extremely difficult to hide. Finding two dead Jihadis still holding onto their weapons, the company moved downhill, conducting speculative fire into the brush. Fire then erupted and Sepoy Ishtiaq, who was standing to my left, fell down dead. A bullet had entered straight into his heart from an oblique left side where the bulletproof jacket had only its straps. My command group and I fell to the ground and returned fire, the fire-fight lasting a good ten minutes till the low cries of a man in pain, coming from the terrace below, made me order the stopping of all fire. The troops peered down to see the legs of a man sticking out of a bush.
>
> The big bearded dead Jihadi who was pulled out from the scrub later turned out to be Al Khadr himself. But at this time we did not realise who we had bagged. Neither did our Intelligence. These identities were subsequently revealed to us by the Americans, once they examined the bodies. Meanwhile, the cordon party reported having seized one more Jihadi as he tried to slip away. He turned out to be an educated Punjabi youth from Sheikhupura who was there to undergo Jihad by fighting the Americans and had a passion for attaining martyrdom.

After the firefight the area was quickly searched and sterilised. By last light a company of 23 Baloch had arrived from Angoor Adda to cover the withdrawal of the SOTF and Zarar Company. An hour later the operation was over and the bodies of the jihadis and the seized materiel were moved to Angoor Adda. Amongst the captured was the teenage son of al-Khadr, who had been shot in the spine and was paralysed from the waist down (his two brothers had been captured by the Americans in Afghanistan and quarantined at Guantanamo Bay).

General Alavi discovered more about the fate of this boy later on.

> He was released a few years later and flew to Canada with his mother. He was arrested upon arrival, handed over to the Americans and flown to the same place where his other brothers were imprisoned. This is the story of just one motivated jihadi family. One can surely guess that there are many others like them who believe in their cause.

Shin Warsak

In January 2004 the ISI reported the presence of up to two hundred Uzbek fighters at Shin Warsak, a couple of miles from Wana in South Waziristan. They were thought to be working with the most important local militant, a glamorous young Ahmadzai Wazir from the Shakai Valley called Nek Mohammad.

The ISI had an agent there, who was in touch with them by satellite phone. He claimed to be with the Uzbeks. An operation targeting the base was planned. Major General Tahir's 9 Division was in the lead, with the SSG intending to raid the buildings where the militants were staying. There was some dispute, when the operation was being planned, over the roles of the SSG and XI Corps. General Yusuf, the Vice Chief, supported Alavi's argument that the infantry should provide both the outer and inner cordons around the objective, with the inner cordon set in place first. Alavi recalled, years later, the unblinking gaze of the recently appointed Chief of the General Staff, Lieutenant General Tariq Majid, as General Yusuf endorsed his argument.

Early on 8 January the SSG landed in helicopters near the group of buildings that the ISI had identified as the militants' base. General Alavi was at GHQ in Rawalpindi, dependent upon Brigadier Nazareth (of the SOTF) for information. He was dispirited by the first news that reached him of the operation. The cordon that should have been thrown round the target at a distance of 500 yards – just out of range of small arms fire – was in fact one kilometre away on all sides. A number of villagers' houses were inside the cordon, so the militants might have slipped away into these buildings.

> The infantry fired a couple of rockets at the buildings, and a woman came out carrying an AK47. Everybody was appalled, but she surrendered and was taken into custody. Then no one else came out of the building. So the SSG was given the order to move in.
>
> The ISI people in GHQ reported that they were still in contact with their source inside, who insisted that the militants were all still there. But General Tahir was telling us that the situation was 'very odd. The villagers are all standing on the roofs of their houses, calmly watching us'. The local political agent was with the SSG (as was usual at that time) and he went into the buildings and talked to the men he found there, telling them that the Army wanted to search the premises. They did not object and the soldiers moved swiftly through the buildings. They found nothing but small arms and a little ammunition. But the 'lady searchers' [nurses, family health workers or policewomen recruited by the political agent] ran into trouble when the women refused to allow them into some areas. The searchers insisted and came across a stash of Uzbek, Kazakh and other passports and piles of training documents in foreign scripts.
>
> The SSG took the thirty or so people from the compound in for questioning but they were profoundly disappointed. The ISI had insisted that this was a major base for foreign militants. Either the intelligence was wrong, the SSG concluded, or the militants had been forewarned of the operation and so the bulk of them had fled.
>
> Before trudging rather despondently back to Wana the SSG troops took action against Nek Mohammad's property, flattening buildings that belonged to him.

The tribe's retribution was swift.

Alavi went on: 'The unfortunate 23 Baloch which had formed the inner cordon was ambushed by the militants as they were returning on vehicles to the safety of Wana Garrison.' Six men were killed in this ambush.

Later that night, the militants vented their anger on Wana Garrison, firing RPGs, rockets and machine guns from close range at the protection posts of the garrison. Within minutes three soldiers of a Piffer regiment that was guarding the perimeter had been killed and several others wounded.

Alavi concluded: 'This operation had fared badly. No Uzbek or any other militant had been caught or killed or even seen but the infantry had suffered eight dead and some wounded.'

An officer who was then a three-star general assessed the operation afterwards:

> We made a mess of the whole thing. Our source was flawed and none of the troops acquitted themselves particularly well, including the SSG. Then our people made the attack on Wana even worse than it was. The Pakistan Army was trigger-happy. They opened up out of fright. But good trigger control is the sign of a professional army. The militants performed better. They waited until it was dark to attack 23 Baloch and then they taught us a lesson by attacking the cantonment.

Two years into its counter-insurgency efforts the Army seemed to be getting nowhere. Not only were the militants becoming more brazen in the Tribal Areas, but President Musharraf was grimly aware that two narrowly unsuccessful attempts to assassinate him in December 2003 had been hatched by networks based in the FATA. American demands that Pakistan should do more were also growing. The political authorities and the Army began to step up pressure on the tribes to cooperate in eradicating militancy and over foreign fighters. Army officers' complaints that Lieutenant General Orakzai was too soft on the tribes were growing. 'He soft-pedalled all the way through,' an artillery officer lamented later. 'All the time he was Corps Commander the militants were getting more and more dug in, both in Waziristan and elsewhere.' Nevertheless, by the end of 2003 the government's message was beginning to get across: the tribesmen were to hand over foreign militants, or face the consequences.' In March 2004 Lt General Orakzai retired from the Army and was replaced as Corps Commander Peshawar by Lt General Muhammad Safdar Hussain. General Safdar had served as the ISI's DG Analysis, an important and influential post. He was a wiry, energetic infantryman (commissioned into 2 Baloch) with a good record. He had held command in difficult places before, as brigade commander in Skardu and then as general officer commanding Force Command Northern Areas, and was said to have acquitted himself well. Safdar had his own style: a photograph of Mr Jinnah with a cigar and a glass of something that looked like whisky hung on the wall of his office at the Corps HQ in Peshawar. It was a beguiling image of the *Quaid*, but not one that many three-star generals would choose to display. Safdar seemed to be a man who would do things his own way, and who was not worried what others thought of him.

Within days – almost within hours – of General Safdar's arrival in Peshawar he was plunged into one of the Army's most difficult situations since the counter-insurgency operations began.

Operation Kalosha

On Monday 15 March 2004 President Musharraf addressed a Grand Tribal *Jirga* on the lawns of the Governor's House in Peshawar. *Dawn* newspaper (16 March 2004) reported:

> Repercussions will be very serious for the country if the operation fails in Wana,' he said, stressing that the tribesmen would have to cooperate with the government in this regard.
>
> 'We have confirmed that 500 to 600 foreign suspects have been sheltered in the South Waziristan region. But we don't want them to get weapons and training from here and create disturbance across the western border,' he said.
>
> He urged tribal elders to expel foreign suspects and their local sympathisers from the region. He reiterated an earlier offer that foreign militants who surrendered would not be handed over to any foreign country.

General Hamid Khan, then IGFC, described Operation Kalosha:

> On 15 March we received intelligence – from the Political Administration and from our Frontier Corps sources – that there were some important militants based near Kalosha, a few miles away from Wana in South Waziristan. There has been lots of talk that we do nothing about terrorists but often, as on this occasion, we have reacted very quickly. We planned the operation to involve the South Waziristan Scouts and the Dir Scouts.
>
> 'President Musharraf was in Peshawar that day and I informed him then the operation was being launched at dawn the following morn-

> ing. This was just a few days after Lt General Safdar had taken over as Corps Commander. I stayed at the Bala Hissar Fort because President Musharraf was visiting.
>
> As the attack was launched, in the heavily built up small town of Kalosha, Uzbeks and others came out from all directions.'

The troops had walked into a trap.

Pervez Musharraf described this moment in his autobiography: 'Our forces were in a low-lying area while the terrorists had occupied the surrounding hills and mountains. There was a hail of fire from the mountains, and our troops suffered heavy casualties in men and materiel. A pitched battle ensued, with the terrorists dominating the area.'

General Hamid Khan took up the story:

> By midday I realised that we needed Cobra gunships and contacted DGMO, Major General Yusuf, at GHQ. But the helicopters were in Multan and arrived too late. By evening my troops were falling back and I thought they needed support. An infantry battalion was tasked to help but they could not reach my troops. The Frontier Corps had deployed in blocking positions. The Commandant was at the front, in the heat of the battle and as the soldiers withdrew the command and control was not good.
>
> With the enemy closing in on them, twelve men had already run out of ammunition. A soldier who had one round left managed to shoot a militant, but the group was taken prisoner. The soldiers were Massuds and the Massud tribe later threatened the Wazirs in order to get the men released.
>
> The South Waziristan Scouts were simply not prepared for this type of operation. The Commandant was superseded after this.

Within a few days seven thousand regular Army and Frontier Corps troops, as well as Cobra helicopters and fighter aircraft, were involved in what had started out as a simple cordon-and-search effort. The operation lasted, according to President Musharraf, from 16 to 28 March.

They aimed to take an important base. Tahir Yuldashev, the co-founder and leader of the Islamic Movement of Uzbekistan (IMU) was there. Founded in 1991, the IMU's aim was to overthrow the Uzbek government and establish an Islamic state. Unsuccessful in Uzbekistan, it moved to Afghanistan, suffered heavy losses during the US-led invasion, and moved again – to Pakistan. It has close ties with al Qaeda and the Taliban.

It was later claimed – wrongly, in the assessment of responsible senior Army officers – that Ayman al-Zawahiri, the al Qaeda ideologue, was also there.

'Yuldashev was injured but escaped,' General Hamid told me. 'We intercepted their communications for a few days afterwards but with the help of local people they were both able to slip away… Over the next few days the Pakistan Army lost fifty men. Everybody seemed to be attacking us. We were coming under fire from every building.

'This operation showed us that we were up against a much larger force than we had realised…'

Major General Faisal Alavi also talked about Operation Kalosha:

> The operation was to rescue the surrounded FC personnel who had gone for an operation by themselves at Shin Warsak against Nek Mohammad and others. On surrounding Nek's house, fire opened up at them from all directions, including the areas behind them. The FC realised that they had been surrounded. XI Corps launched its infantry to pull the FC out of its precarious situation. The infantry, most of whom this time came from 7 Division, fared badly. 22 Punjab lost twenty-two dead and many more injured on being ambushed just after their landing there by helicopters. Militants with automatics sitting on ridge tops opened up at the clumsy infantry, which until now had not realised the environment that they were operating in and on landing got into a formation to check out their states. The militants could not have got a better target.

One hundred and sixty-three militants were reported – by Inter-Services Public Relations – to have been arrested during Operation Kalosha. Fifty, the Army spokesman announced on 29 March, were released after interrogation. General Alavi commented later that most of the prisoners had been brought to the SSG's facility at the Attock Fort.

> They were handcuffed to the walls of the barracks. We had some spare accommodation, but some soldiers had to double up as a result of the influx. All the prisoners were interrogated by the MI and ISI, and one by one they were let go. This was a persistent problem during my time as

> GOC SSG. The MI had no facilities to detain large numbers of people. Sometimes the SSG was told to hold them over in Bannu, sometimes in Pindi. There was no systematic way of handling these prisoners. After an operation, [seized] weaponry and prisoners were handed over, but there was no time to document them properly. Time was always short. Helicopters usually left [the site of the operation] loaded with weapons and ammunition, but they were only documented when, after landing, they were taken to the MI storehouse. Later on, they would be sent to the Ordnance Branch of the Army for disposal.
>
> After Kazha Punga, Shin Warsak and [Operation Kalosha, the] first, infantry only, operation of XI Corps, the weaknesses and vulnerabilities of the infantry of the Pakistan Army came to light very phenomenally. They were ill trained and ill equipped to effectively battle the well-trained and highly motivated insurgents. Their knowledge of Frontier Warfare operations and Anti-Insurgency operations was vague. Troops being inducted to fight in the Tribal Areas needed to undergo special training. Many SSG training teams were despatched to brigades and units in XI Corps under a crash programme. Lt General Safdar himself relied more on his SSG bodyguards then his own infantry. Each time the SSG tried to get its bodyguards back from all senior commanders to bolster its strength, Lt General Safdar would ensure an extension of his bodyguards through his unit mate, the CGS, Lt General Tariq Majeed. The SSG as always preferred to operate independently under GHQ. This subsequently led to friction between the SSG and XI Corps.

Operation Kalosha, in which the Frontier Corps and the Pakistan Army had been humiliated, ended in a deal with the militants, and Nek Mohammad, 27, the militant leader, emerging as hero. He was said to have driven Yuldashev to safety in his Toyota.

On 27 March 2004 Lt General Safdar concluded the Shakai Valley agreement with Nek Mohammad.

'Safdar did not handle the tribes well,' a Lieutenant General (from an infantry regiment) said later. 'He went public on everything, and was loudmouthed. The ISI did not like his style, and this caused a constant undercurrent of friction.'

It seemed to make sense to deal with the Ahmadzai Wazirs. They were a small group in South Waziristan, far outnumbered by their rivals, the Masuds, who sat astride the crucially important road link between

Wana and the outside world. The Ahmadzai Wazirs, angered by Masud attacks on the road, initiated the peace process, a retired Commander of XI Corps told me some years later. 'They said, "support us, and we will bring Nek to the table and get him to deliver." The suggestion was appealing, but Safdar should have been mindful of who he was dealing with. He just thought, vaguely, that if the tribes agreed all would be well. So he ploughed on, for the glory of the Army. It was all understandable, but it was a great mistake.'

Operation Shakai Valley

By June 2004 reports were reaching GHQ, through the ISI and the Americans, that six or seven hundred militants – including a great many Uzbeks and Chechens and some Arabs, as well as local fighters – were massing in the Shakai Valley area. This was Ahmadzai Wazir territory. The size of the force was alarming. The militants were becoming more confident. They continued to attack isolated FC and Army posts, in audacious and often successful forays.

The operation was launched on 10 June 2004 and targeted a group of about ten properties that were believed to be the headquarters of the militants. It was conceived on a huge scale. Pervez Musharraf revealed in his autobiography that 10,000 regular Army troops were involved as well as Frontier Corps and SSG personnel. 'The SOTF of the SSG and an infantry brigade of 11 Corps were the backbone of the operation,' according to Faisal Alavi.

'This was an area that not even the Frontier Corps had ever entered. General Yusuf [the Vice Chief of Army Staff] was in favour of ... the SSG landing bang on the Uzbek HQ,' Major General Alavi reported. 'He asked us if we could do it. I told him we could but that we should rely on surprise.' The militants would not be expecting an attack on this scale. 'I asked for a distraction. I said that XI Corps should enter the mouth of the valley as we landed by helicopter at the other end and move to link up with us. This was agreed. XI Corps was tasked to enter the valley at first light.'

Earlier, images had been shown to the Pakistan Air Force and they had been told to bomb the ten or so houses in a line. The SSG was to be supported by helicopter gunships.

'Lt Gen. Safdar was against a heli landing on the target area, fearing that the casualties would be high even if a single helicopter was shot down. But he was overruled by the Vice Chief,' Alavi said later. Relations between Alavi and Safdar, the Commander of XI Corps, had been strained before this operation. Afterwards, in General Alavi's telling, the quarrels burst wide open.

> About an hour after first light, on the morning of 10 June 2004, Mirage jets armed with PGMs [precision-guided munitions] struck and reduced compound rooms to rubble. The operation could not start earlier because the Mirages needed clear visibility. Artillery then pounded the area and once it lifted after 10 minutes, gunship-launched rockets continued to pound the buildings. A brigade of 9 Division [from XI Corps] moved into the mouth of the Shakai Valley, as planned...
>
> After this bombardment the SSG Special Operations Task Force landed by helicopter. Never in the history of the Pakistan Army had so many helicopters been used in any operation. The helicopters numbered seventeen, mostly Mi 17s and a few Pumas backed by the much-wanted Cobras.
>
> A couple of the fighters (mostly Uzbek) were killed, the rest sent scurrying into the mountains. Three helicopters sustained bullet hits. One of the pilots panicked and flew back with all his SSG personnel, who to their utter disappointment did not participate in the operation at all. The knoll next to the landing zone had an anti-aircraft gun well emplaced to take on the landing helicopters. Fortunately none of the 76 rounds fired hit any helicopter.
>
> The SSG climbed the knoll, under fire. As they reached the ridge they found red-hot cases lying around but the militants had fled under SSG fire.
>
> By this time the infantry were moving through the valley towards the SSG. I told Brigadier Nazareth, the commander of the SOTF, to search the suspected militants' houses. He reported that fire was still coming from the buildings, so I asked for more air strikes. Every house had now been hit with 500 or 1,000lbs of PGM.
>
> Again I told Brigadier Nazareth to search the houses. He said it was still very difficult since it was now getting dark. He wanted to get dug in for the night, in a defensive position.
>
> I was very disappointed with Nazareth. Twice I had told him to search and twice he had complained that fire was coming from the houses. Even after the buildings had been bombed he was more concerned about getting settled for the night.

> I was in the Operations Room at GHQ [in Rawalpindi] and the Vice Chief, the CGS and DGMO were all getting the same feeling.
>
> I went to Tariq Majid [the CGS] and said that I should be given permission to set off early to see what was going on.
>
> CGS said that the commander of XI Corps had called and reported that the SSG were doing nothing in this operation except sitting in a hideout passing false information. So my request was granted.
>
> General Niaz Khattak, GOC 9 Division, landed on the ridge, which is still known as SOTF Ridge. He spoke to Brigadier Nazareth and gave him a pat on the back. But he then reported back to Commander XI Corps that the SSG was doing nothing. Why?

Alavi later explained that General Khattak had been annoyed to find that the SSG seemed better supplied than his own troops.

> Khattak had landed in Wana and had seen another helicopter taking off to resupply the SSG with American mineral water and MRE [meals ready to eat, US Army rations]. He cribbed that the infantry was drinking filthy water from the *nullahs* while the Special Forces were enjoying mineral water and US rations during operations. But the SOTF had been sent out for one day without any food and so the CIA guys at Wana came to our rescue.
>
> I had tasked the SSG officer in charge of the guards for the CIA and asked him to get some food for the SSG, even if he had to go to the bazaar to buy it. He called back to say that the Americans had given him some of their ration packs and I complimented him on doing a good job.
>
> The next morning I landed on the ridge and everything became clear. The SOTF had cleared all the houses and found nobody there. There was an MI officer with the SOTF and he verified that there had been firing during the night.
>
> So what Khattak called a hideout was actually a temporary defence they had taken up when the Uzbeks had attacked them during the night. The fighting had been bloody. We took two casualties, including a corporal who lost an eye. But there was no way to evacuate him before first light.
>
> While I was there the Uzbeks attacked one part of the cordon so – as usual – our lot all opened up.
>
> So I went off to see what was going on. I got in the helicopter, with Brigadier Nazareth screaming, 'Wait! Let me send some security.' I went on and as I landed I saw SSG personnel running after me.

As I went into one of the buildings I could smell dead bodies under the rubble. I saw what was left of a room that had been hit by 1,000lb of explosive. It was reduced to rubble. The kitchen, next door, had survived. In the corner a hen was sitting on her eggs. I picked her up and examined her eggs. They were intact! I put her back on her nest.

I found a nice copper used for washing. It was certainly not local but I thought it might be Afghan or Uzbek. I took it away with me.

So by now my ideas about Brigadier Nazareth were clear. The SOTF had come under fire but had succeeded in clearing the houses. The soldiers who came with me moved confidently. It was clear that they had entered the buildings earlier.

The soldiers were complaining about mosquito bites as well as the shortage of food and so on. Lots of the SSG had gone in, Rambo-style, in T-shirts. After that I stressed the importance of mosquito repellent, three-day rations and long sleeves.

The man with the eye injury was evacuated to Rawalpindi Military Hospital. I went to see him while he was there. He complained that two of the doctors there had made fun of him for fighting the Taliban so he was worried about the medical care he would receive. He told me their names. They were majors, undergoing specialised eye training. I lodged a heavy complaint and an enquiry was launched. They were being court-martialled when I left the Army.

The Army was able to seize a tremendous haul of weapons and ammunition from the building, televisions, laptops, tape recorders, discs and tapes as well as equipment for manufacturing IEDs [improvised explosive devices]. The operation seemed to be a great success although few dead bodies were found. They leave no bodies. The militants always carry their dead away. I respect them for that, as soldiers.

Although no bodies were found, the ISI reported twenty-six funerals the following day.

The strains between the SSG and XI Corps were growing. General Alavi believed that Lt General Safdar was jealous of the SSG's success. 'Safdar was stirring things up,' he later said, bluntly.

The next day at the debrief conference General Yusuf began talking about the SSG problems. He said, 'Alavi, there's a lot of talk about the SSG not doing too well in some places.'

I said, 'Yes, and the trouble is that the talk is being instigated by the

> Commander XI Corps himself. It is very difficult for us to work with XI Corps if they constantly cast aspersions on us.'
>
> General Yusuf said, 'Yes. I know that.' Then, looking at General Tariq Majid [CGS], he said, 'I suggest you talk to General Safdar... no, on second thoughts I'll do it myself.'

General Alavi told me that the anti-SSG stories continued.

'I met General Zubair, who had served in the SSG but was by then Engineer in Chief of the Pakistan Army. He told me that Safdar had told him that the engineers had done well that day. "And the SSG?" Zubair asked. "The SSG lies too much" Safdar replied.

Alavi was furious that Safdar was blackening the reputation of the SSG. He had heard similar stories before. He felt that the Corps Commander was allowing his ego to interfere with the conduct of operations. He was convinced that Lieutenant General Safdar reported the seizure of the same weaponry more than once. 'Later there was a report of another 12.7 anti-aircraft seized. Safdar tried to report that this was a second weapon.'

Operation Shakai showed how strong the militants had become. 'With American help we were learning more about the[ir] capabilities. We saw Arab, Uzbek, Tajik and Pashtu nets all spring up as Operation Shakai Valley began. This indicated that the fighters had a proper military set-up with a command and control structure. They really were a very well-organised private army.'

Within days of this operation, on 18 June 2004, Nek Mohammad was killed in a US Predator strike. He was giving an interview to a journalist, over his satellite phone, at the moment of his death.

Since 2004, the US has used unmanned aerial vehicles, remotely controlled from Nevada, to bomb jihadists in Pakistan. There is no doubt that the vast majority of victims are actually civilians. The Government of Pakistan has condemned these attacks.

Operation Tande Obo

2004, Faisal Alavi again:

> This time the information had been obtained by the Military Intelligence through an informer and the Pashtun MI officer had also driven past the area a few times to be sure. The target was just a simple compound having

> a few rooms but the report was that there was a lot of suspicious activity that took place here. The *nullah* entered the area from Afghanistan and it had a jeepable track in its bed and vehicles from Afghanistan would come and stop at this compound which as per the information had been hired by some foreigners from the locals at a phenomenal price.

Tande obo means 'cold water' in Pushto. Cold water flowed in the *nullah* on the bank of which stood the target compound. For this operation, in a remote area in the mountains a couple of kilometres from the Afghan border, SSG and other troops again landed by helicopter. The target house stood on the edge of a *nullah*, so some helicopters landed in the *nullahs*, some in the mountains above, effectively surrounding the house. About twelve Mi 17s from Rawalpindi carried the SOTF that day and the landing was, as usual, just a few minutes after first light.

> As they landed the troops ran to form the cordon effectively, as three of the pilots had not dropped their personnel at the correct spot, which could seriously jeopardise the timely formation of the cordon, which was imperative. A fleeing youth from the complex was challenged to stop by some SSG personnel. On his ignoring their calls, he was shot in the leg. He turned out to be an Arab who could speak Pushto. Meanwhile fire erupted from the compound and the brush surrounding it. The youth was told to call out to his friends and to tell them to surrender. The teenager replied that he could not speak their language. The SSG returned the fire and kept moving forward towards the compound using the typical fire and move technique. One Tajik was killed while firing from inside the brush and then the house appeared to have been abandoned, and it was unclear where the fire was coming from. But the fire kept coming. Five SSG personnel had bullet hits either in their arms or legs. Their bulletproof jackets kept their vitals safe. About four SSG personnel got direct hits in the chest. The bullets ricocheted, proving the effectiveness of the newly issued American bulletproof vests. The SSG commander, Brigadier Nazareth, responded with all weapons at his disposal in the direction he thought the fire was coming from. They must have fired in the right direction as the next day the predator reported five dead bodies being retrieved and buried by villagers. A lot of arsenal, training material, ammunition and explosive was found here, most of which was blown up by the SSG as it could not be carried back. The SSG had no dead, but

> many with bullet wounds, including a captain who had taken a bullet in each arm.
>
> During interrogation of prisoners after this operation, it emerged that Adur Rehman Libbi, or 'the Libyan', the dreaded terrorist high on the US wanted list, had left the area in a Hilux vehicle with his bodyguards just fifteen minutes before the SSG arrived. He evaded capture for quite some time thereafter, only to be nabbed by the intelligence agencies in the settled area of Mardan, in the NWFP, later in 2007. He was handed over to the Americans.

Almost every week the Army was finding proof of the presence of foreign fighters in Pakistan. The vast majority appeared to be Uzbeks but many nationalities were now there, hounded out of Afghanistan by the Americans after the Tora Bora action.

The SSG was performing well at this time. Most of the Army's notable successes involved the SSG. Lt General Safdar, Corps Commander in Peshawar, felt that operations could be carried out more effectively if the SSG was under his command.

8

The War Goes On

In the spring of 2005 the Army moved into North Waziristan.

The SSG was being strengthened to cope with the demands of constant operations in the Tribal Areas. Two battalions, 4 Commando and 5 Commando, and 11 Special Service Brigade HQ, were raised in 2005–6.

Deogar

In the first few days of March 2005 American satellite imagery revealed the presence of a well-trained and equipped group of foreign militants in a compound known to be owned by Afghans at Deogar, a small hamlet just two kilometres from the border.

General Alavi told me later:

> A company from 4 Commando, strengthened with elements from 2 Commando, was the backbone of this operation. Although a fighting-strength company should consist of 120 men, few in the SSG number more than 60. So it is standard practice to pull companies together for an operation. The troops parked their vehicles in a small gorge near an FC post, the last on the road from Sad Gai to Deogar.
>
> Commander 11 Special Service Brigade accompanied the force. So did Lieutenant Colonel Tariq Raja, Commanding Officer 4 Commando Battalion. Karrar Company was earmarked as the reserve to act as a backup force and was waiting not far away.

A young lance naik who has since left the Army recalled the operation:

> We walked through the night, sixteen kilometres in stormy weather, in cold and rain, carrying RPGs, LMGs [light machine guns], grenades and explosives. But the weather aided us immensely. In the SSG we always used to say that 'bad weather is the friend of Special Forces and

> of guerrillas'. We picked our way along the *nullah* leading to the target area. A major from the ISI who was familiar with the target was with us.

The soldiers did not complain about the discomfort of the cold and wet; they were just relieved that they did not run into any local people and that no dogs barked as they went past. But visibility was poor – the troops had no night vision goggles – and towards the end of the march the men took the wrong direction, moving about three hundred yards up the wrong hill towards a small village. But they had GPS and managed to get themselves back on the right track and locate the compound. Disturbed by the sounds of movement, men carrying torches came out of the compound to check what was going on. They peered around, but – as the soldiers held their breath – they seemed satisfied that all they had heard was wind and rain and went back indoors. It was still dark as the SSG fanned out around the compound. A car came towards them from the direction of the village further up the hill. The soldiers stopped the car, and when they were told that one of the passengers was a woman in labour (a tale that was becoming familiar to the Army operating in the Tribal Areas) they told the driver to head back to the village. But shots had now been fired and people now came out from every house and hamlet in the area, switching on lights in order to see what was going on. Again, men with lighted torches came out from the target compound, alert and anxious about what was going on. The soldiers froze, not daring to blink.

Then Major Ahsan, the company commander, softly asked a Pashto-speaking SSG colleague to call out to the people in the compound through a loudspeaker. 'Come towards us! We want to speak to you! We are the Pakistan Army.'

There was no response. The soldiers waited.

The SSG lance naik continued his story: 'As dawn was just about to break a sergeant serving with the ISI, a Pathan (from another area) called out on a loudspeaker: "Come out! All of you! We are the Pakistan Army. We won't fire if you come out. We want to talk to you."

'Still there was no reaction from the compound'.

Again Major Ahsan asked his Pashto-speaking SSG local man to try to call the fighters out.

> This time there was a reaction. The main door of the compound opened, three men came out and shouted '*Allahu-Akbar*', said a few other things

> and ran back inside, bolting the door. They were speaking a strange language, difficult to understand apart from '*Allahu-Akbar*' and some references to jihad. But we understood that we had been challenged to a fight.
>
> Having delivered this apparently bellicose statement the militants took cover. Since they had refused to come out the Army had little choice but to assault the compound. The SSG, after pounding the complex with some RPG-7s, attempted an entry but were beaten back by immense fire from inside.

The SSG soldiers were aware of tribesmen watching the action from houses dotted around on the hilltops and as the fighting intensified – 'it was virtually hand-to-hand fighting now' – two mortars were fired at the compound from the Afghan direction.

Meanwhile some of the SSG men captured a woman in a house in the same compound. She told them that there were several other women in the compound, one of whom had been wounded in the leg and needed to be evacuated. She agreed to help the Army to get into the building.

The lance naik described what happened next: 'With the woman leading the way, Major Ahsan and a combat team entered the house. They cleared the first room – an ammunition dump – but as they were moving on four men suddenly popped up behind them in the gallery of the second room. After an exchange of fire three dropped their weapons, and an SSG soldier managed to wrest his rifle away from the fourth.

Three of the fighters dropped their weapons, the lance naik explained, because the woman was the wife of the Pakistani tribal leader who owned the house. They could not risk killing the wife of their host.

The battle at the compound had raged for between three and four hours. Two militants were killed, but the SSG men suffered nothing worse than grazes and wounds from grenade splinters.

'On the other side of the compound, seven men were spotted running in the *nullah* next to the main house, trying to flee. One, carrying the machine gun, was killed by a sniper, all the others [were] captured by the men forming the cordon. (The dead man turned to be a Chechen, the others foreigners from various countries.)'

After the fighting was over, according to the lance naik, the SSG men suddenly realised just how precarious their position was. They could now see tribesmen all around them on the hills, far more than they had been aware of during the battle. There was no way to tell how hostile they might be, and they now had to cover the sixteen kilometres back to their vehicles taking with them their prisoners (including the owner of the compound, a neighbour and a man who had been there to repaint the property) and the loads of weapons and ammunition they had found. Karrar Company was ordered to link up, which it managed, despite the bad terrain and bad weather which had turned all tracks muddy and unnavigable. The Army tasked the Frontier Corps with picqueting the route back, which was swiftly done, and the SSG moved back with its prisoners, the militant dead and all the weaponry and explosives.

Of the ten prisoners, one was from the Cherat area and two or three of them were Urdu speakers from Karachi. The others, all foreigners, included an Albanian (the first European militant to have been captured in Pakistan), a Tajik, a Sudanese, and a Chechen. They had had no common language and it never became clear quite how the terrorist compound had functioned. The night's haul included RPGs, AK 47s, a 75 RR gun, lots of explosives, timers and switches for explosive devices. The compound had been an explosives factory, and all those captured were explosives experts who made bombs and IEDs for the militants.

Operation Mana Valley

General Alavi sent me, by email, his account of another significant operation, involving elements of three SSG battalions, that took place soon afterwards in the Mana Valley in North Waziristan.

> The Mana Valley operation was based on MI information, through an informer, that a large number of Uzbek militants were living in the valley itself and in the surrounding forests. The informer wanted to go back to Mana Valley at once so that he was not missed as he knew what happened to suspected spies in Waziristan. The MI Directorate, however, did not allow him and he remained confined to their safe house till the operation took off. The actual operation took place on 13 March 2005.
>
> The forests were covered in snow, and the SSG could find no evidence that anyone was lurking there, despite carrying out aerial reconnaissance, off and on. But the MI's agent insisted that the foreigners were in the forests. A Piffer battalion from XI Corps was stationed in the area. The plan was that they would help form the inner cordon when the operation was launched and the SSG landed by helicopters. The operation kept

> getting delayed for weeks due to bad weather. XI Corps would be informed at the last moment, once the SSG took off, in order to maintain secrecy. However, a few days before the operation was launched, the commanding officer of the Piffer Battalion, also ex SSG, rang up his twin brother, who was serving as commanding officer 3 Commando Battalion, and asked him ... when was the SSG coming. Such breaches of information were commonplace as nobody up and down the ladder wanted anything to go wrong. The zero error syndrome was at work. This information was only supposed to be known to the Corps Commander, Lt Gen Safdar, and his Chief of Staff but invariably where the SSG was involved with XI Corps, the information that the SSG was coming would be passed down much earlier, in most cases to make sure XI Corps troops fared as well as the SSG, if not better. That is how the SSG viewed these leakages.
>
> On the appointed day ... a vast armada of helicopters landed [the] SSG around Mana Valley. The FF battalion was up and awake at first light to join in and help out with the cordon as this was a vast 12 kilometres Valley. The brigade headquarters of XI Corps was also in the Valley and the exuberant Brigadier supervised his troops and coordinated with the SSG very well. The SSG imposed a curfew and started searching all the houses from the East and West of the valley simultaneously. It was a colossal task. Over 250 houses were searched thoroughly. No foreigners were found but plenty of rockets, explosive, mines, machineguns, grenades and all kinds of ammunition was found hidden in a number of houses and was loaded onto helicopters for Rawalpindi. The persons inhabiting the houses arrested and their women set free as per tribal custom. The SSG flew back.
>
> A week later the informer who was a local was shot dead in Mana Valley, once he returned back home. On the other hand, the arrested persons were set free by the Military Intelligence after a couple of weeks after the customary interrogation and de-briefs. Apparently, that was done to prevent overcrowding in their cells but it indicated that the Intelligence Agencies had no clear disposal strategy for such arrested or captured persons and the ones guilty of lesser crimes were capable of extracting a complete pardon from the Agencies, themselves.

General Alavi's anger that informers were not protected was echoed by other responsible people in the Army. His fury that militants captured during operations were being let off was also a recurrent complaint.

'My troops risk their lives to get these people, we turn them over to the MI and they are back in the hills a couple of weeks later,' a Lieutenant General who was involved in these operations complained some years later.

After the deals with the tribes the local militants became far more powerful, openly describing themselves as Taliban.

The Taliban were imposing an ever fiercer reign of terror. Music and television were banned. In 2005 sixty tribesmen in Waziristan were murdered as American spies, their bodies strung on lampposts. Ahmed Rashid describes in *Descent into Chaos* how the Taliban ritualised their threats, enhancing the terror: 'To a tribal elder marked to be killed they sent a needle with a long thread and one thousand rupees ($16). The money was for him to buy his shroud and the needle to sew it with.'

Pakistan continued to find itself the victim of American infighting. Rivalries between the CIA and Centcom that had surfaced early in the Afghan war were still causing difficulties for Pakistan three years later. The CIA was supporting the Pakistan Army's operations in the Tribal Areas, particularly with intelligence, and was providing training to the SSG. A senior Army officer, who had held planning and command jobs since the war began, talked about the situation late in 2005.

'Whenever US soldiers were killed in Afghanistan, Centcom came under pressure. But why were they killed? Because the Afghan government had no control over the country. After conducting an operation the troops (whether US or Afghan) would return to their bases, leaving the area insecure. The Afghan government and Centcom would shoulder the blame. President Karzai would resort to blaming Pakistan for harbouring al Qaeda and Taliban fighters. Then the CIA would come under domestic pressure. 'You work with Pakistan, why is this happening?' Karzai's accusations were the CIA's only defence. So Centcom blamed the CIA for the mess in Afghanistan and the CIA blamed Pakistan. Deliberate leaks ensured that the media picked up on the line that Pakistan was being at best ineffective and at worst was actively assisting al Qaeda and Taliban.

The 2005 Earthquake

The holy month of *Ramazan* in 2005 (1426 in the Islamic calendar) began on 6 October (in the NWFP, local clerics glimpsed the crescent moon one day earlier, so fasting began on the 5th). The annual routine of prayer and fasting was underway again. Across the country families ate before dawn, and not again until sunset.

For the Army, it was business as usual. On Saturday 8 October new lieutenant generals were being inducted in a ceremony at Aiwan-i-Sedr, the official residence of the President. Among them were Masood Aslam, who was to become Inspector General Training and Evaluation in GHQ, and Hamid Khan, who was to replace Safdar Hussain as commander of XI Corps in Peshawar. By the time the ceremony started at 10.00 in the morning, news was arriving that a serious earthquake had struck the mountainous north of the country and was being felt across a huge swathe of Pakistan. A tower block in Islamabad had collapsed and reports of devastation in other places began to trickle in. As the morning drew on it became clear that this was the worst natural disaster Pakistan had ever faced. The quake, centred on Muzaffarabad in Azad Kashmir, devastated an area of twelve thousand square miles. Within twenty-four hours almost one hundred and fifty aftershocks were registered, across much of Pakistan, a thousand by the end of the month. The tremors were felt throughout much of the NWFP and Punjab, and as far away as Karachi.

'When the earthquake came it was like Judgement Day,' a villager in the NWFP told a Reuters correspondent (*Dawn* newspaper, 10 October 2005). He thought it was the end of the world, as buildings were flattened all around him. His wife and son were killed as their home collapsed and his fourteen-year-old daughter died in his arms as they eventually reached the gates of Mansehra Hospital, forty-six kilometres away. The mountains were torn apart, and whole towns flattened. Over seventy thousand people died that day, as many again were seriously injured and three and a half million were left homeless. Half of the victims were children, buried in the rubble that had been their schools. Adults, many of them resting to conserve their strength during the long fast, were crushed in their homes.

Reaching earthquake victims in the inaccessible mountainous regions and rescuing survivors was an immediate priority for the military. Over the coming months this stretched the Army's capabilities at a time when it was, in any case, struggling to respond adequately to the militant threat. It also gave extremist groups an opportunity to strengthen their support. The groups, who had effective structures but no cumbersome logistics to slow them down, were able to reach some stricken communities before the Army could get to them. *Jamaat-ud-Dawa*, the political wing of *Lashkar-e-Taiba*, was notably effective at this time. Its name means something like 'Invitation Group', or 'Calling Group', in the sense of calling people to Islam, an allusion to a verse in the Koran: 'Invite (all) to the Way of thy Lord with wisdom and beautiful preaching; and argue with them in ways that are best and most gracious: for thy Lord knows best, who have strayed from His Path, and who receive guidance.' (An-Nahl: 125)

2006 January–June Offensive

Lt Gen. Hamid Khan, the new Corps Commander in Peshawar, had been Inspector General of the Frontier Corps from 2003 to 2004, so he knew exactly what he was taking on in his new job.

> When I came here nothing was new to me. The local people kept in contact with me while I was at NDU [National Defense University]. I knew the militants and could get quite a lot through to them… My aim was to get the right tribesmen on our side, so that they would support us. There wasn't any fighting going on when I arrived in October 2005. I was setting up new control posts, to choke the militants' movement, and these posts were attacked. For example, I set up a post at Khaso Khel, near Mir Ali, in December 2006 and it was attacked in January.

Six Frontier Corps soldiers were reported killed in this action. This was not an isolated incident: checkpoints and posts were constantly being attacked, and day after day soldiers were being wounded or killed. 'So we unleashed a series of precision strikes … You have to know when to send a tough signal. It is important to be firm, but you must not get into a cycle of violence. If you belittle the local people, or are too oppressive, antagonism towards the Army will grow.' General Hamid insisted that military action had to be effective and targeted.

'From January to June 2006 we had a real offensive. There were more than 500 local militants and foreigners killed. We lost between fifty and sixty people during this period.

'We destroyed three major ammunition dumps. By June the militants were out of stores and ammunition and began to make contact with us.' This, General Hamid said, was the way it should be. 'The Army can only create the environment to help the politicians to succeed. The proper strategy has to be in place in this kind of situation. There have to be military operations, then the politicians can work from a position of strength, and then you have to follow through with development works.'

> In July the militants went for a unilateral ceasefire. Their representatives were running around everywhere, asking for operations to be stopped. They approached me. I was working towards an unconditional surrender. As part of this, the President was in Peshawar and a *jirga* approached him and asked him to give the *jirga* a chance. I tried to prevent this. But Orakzai rushed it all through. The political situation should have been better and the deal binding. We introduced checkposts and patrols and slowed down the operations.

General Hamid reported that the toughest operation in his time as Corps Commander was clearing Miramshah of militants. This was in March 2006.

Operation Saidgai March 2006

> The target of this operation was a compound in Danday Saidgai, a small border town about ten miles north of Miramshah that was believed to be housing lots of foreigners. Cobra gunships attacked the buildings and then the SSG landed. The operation was planned and executed by me, with the SOTF under my command. We were moving away from large-scale operations by this time towards swift, surgical strikes. The plan was to insert the SOTF quickly and then exit quickly. No cordon was put in place. I was always against cordons. The soldiers get caught up in the battle and it is then difficult to extricate them.
>
> A Mi 17 helicopter carrying the commander of the SOTF along with his troops was hit by an RPG 7, but the pilot managed to lift the crippled aircraft and take it back to Miramshah.

The militants' revenge attacks on Miramshah lasted for about a week. On 2 March they were reported to have taken over the bazaar, and the following morning they forced the security guards out of the Pakistan Telecommunications Ltd telephone exchange – although it had been shut down in order to interrupt the militants' communications – and took control of the building. They were openly patrolling the streets, and on 4 March they forced shopkeepers to close their shops. The North Waziristan Scouts Fort in Miramshah was attacked the next day.

General Hamid Khan continued his account:

> I knew through intercepts that the militants were going to attack the HQ in Miramshah. 'Lure them in,' I said. If our men came under attack they should use it as an opportunity. The militants would be in the open, and we'd find them. We reportedly killed more than four hundred in the fighting. After this they vacated the city, taking whatever they could with them.
>
> Then, from March to September 2006 we imposed a curfew and we were able to declare Miramshah a weapons-free zone. After this the militants began seeking a ceasefire and this led to the September ceasefire. This was tough. If we had failed to defeat them then it would have been the end of the military presence there. If they had even partially taken over it would have been disastrous for us.
>
> This operation changed the tide. The militants were given a real beating and the movement of weapons and ammunition was stopped'.

But the violence continued.

Shatghalai Narai 4 April 2006

General Hamid Khan described a raid on the Shatghalai Narai post, perched above the road from Datta Khel to Shawal. The post was attacked by militants, most of them connected to Hafiz Gul Bahadur.

> The Post was raided while the militants were withdrawing. I had asked the FC to lay ambushes on all approaches and the enemy walked right into them. We were able to kill or arrest many of those who had raided the post. One was carrying the head of one of our soldiers.
>
> Some of Baitullah's men came to me. I had found out that it was his men who had carried out the raid. They said, 'We did not know that it would be a raid on the Army.'
>
> So I said to them, 'Bring me the head of the man who tricked you.'
>
> They agreed to do this if I released their prisoners.
>
> 'No way,' I said.
>
> Beheading soldiers was standard practice. This was un-Islamic and

> untribal. It was something the Uzbeks, Chechens and Arabs brought to our part of the world.
>
> Baitullah would not hand over the alleged trickster.
>
> Later, in the run-up to the deal, President Musharraf said to me, 'Come on, Hamid, for the sake of the greater cause...'
>
> The prisoners were still in the lock-up in Miramshah but my permission, as Corps Commander, was needed in order to release them'.

In May 2006 the retired Lieutenant General Ali Jan Orakzai was appointed Governor of the North West Frontier Province.

In September he struck a deal, at a Grand Jirga in Miramshah, with the Utmanzai Wazirs. Maulana Gul Bahadur Khan and Maulana Sadiq Noor, key Taliban commanders in North Waziristan, were party to this deal. Jalaluddin Haqqani and Tahir Yuldashev were also present when it was signed. Under this agreement, known as the Waziristan Accord, the Taliban pledged to eject foreign fighters, prevent cross-border attacks into Afghanistan, stop running camps in the FATA and end efforts to run a parallel system of government. The government of Pakistan, in return, undertook to pull its troops back, end attacks on the Taliban, return seized weapons and pay reparation.

'Until September 2006 we had operations virtually every day,' General Hamid Khan said. One would lead to another, often to several more.

'Orakzai persuaded General Musharraf that all the trouble would stop and there would be no problems if his deal was done. Pakistan was already coming under American pressure. Our Western allies were confused. On the whole they did not like this but it was our strategy at the time. In fact the deal only helped the militants'.

After South Waziristan the militants shifted to North Waziristan and then on to Bajaur and Swat. But trouble continued in South Waziristan. In March 2007 there was a dangerous incident near Shin Warsak.

Shin Warsak Ridge March 2007

Lieutenant General Hamid Khan again:

> In February [2007] the brother of a *malik* was killed. The tribes agreed to help, then backed off. So I got hold of more people who had operated in Afghanistan during the Soviet war. They joined us and helped to identify where the foreigners were. But when we had identified the ridge near

Wana the locals again backed off. I knew that the locals would leave me in the lead.

The enemy was firing rockets at us so we replied with artillery. This was the first attempt to take the ridge.

The first attempt to take the ridge failed. So we tried again. Three or four days later we approached from another direction and eventually succeeded. More than two hundred militants were killed in the operation, others managed to escape.

But we managed to rid the Wazir area of South Waziristan of foreigners.

All the local houses were occupied. The main strength of the local Talibs was these people. Hard-line Talibs fled. I asked the local *maliks* to help. I said, 'There is a vacuum.' The *maliks* began to reassert their power. But the foreigners slaughtered anyone they hated.

The whole operation lasted twenty days.

The Red Mosque

Extremist violence was now reaching into the heart of Pakistan's capital city. The Lal Masjid, or Red Mosque (so called because of its red walls), said to be the oldest mosque in Islamabad, was threatening the stability of the city. Its leaders, brothers called Abdul Aziz and Abdul Rashid Ghazi, were not only calling for shariah law but imposing their version of it on parts of the capital. Gangs of armed militants from the mosque and the madrassahs it controlled threatened shops selling Western films, and menaced unveiled women. Women from the mosque, wielding batons, roamed Islamabad kidnapping women they considered to be prostitutes. Activists from the Lal Masjid, protesting against the demolition of an illegally constructed mosque, occupied a children's library. The government had been growing ever more concerned about the activities of the Lal Masjid vigilantes, and – after several months of attempting to negotiate with the leaders, President Musharraf gave orders for troops to surround and then assault the mosque. When the Lal Masjid was finally stormed in July 2007 ten soldiers were killed, and about a hundred militants. Abdul Rashid died; his brother was arrested trying to escape dressed as a woman. The government had little choice but to storm the mosque, but the episode was exploited by the anti-government forces.

After the Lal Masjid episode the militants stepped up their attacks. *Dawn* reported on 23 July that 194 people had been killed in suicide attacks during the previous twenty-two days. Suicide bombing became part of the Pakistani landscape after 9/11, and particularly after the government siege of the Red Mosque. Soldiers, police, politicians and Shia mosques are favoured targets; frequently the perpetrators are Taliban-trained teenagers.

Pamphlets distributed in Miramshah at the end of July warned that suicide bombs would bring soldiers 'the gift of death'. 'We know that you have become America's slave and are serving infidel Musharraf and have become a traitor to your religion for food, clothes and shelter.'

In North Waziristan the militants launched intense assaults on check-posts and ambushed convoys. In the last few days of July and in August there were attacks virtually every day, especially around Miramshah and Mir Ali. The Pakistan Army was losing control of territory, but Governor Orakzai was determined to try to preserve the Waziristan Accord. In August the violence in North Waziristan diminished, but in South Waziristan the Army was faced with the worst episode yet in its struggle against the militants.

Lieutenant General Masood Aslam, who had just succeeded Lieutenant General Hamid Khan as Corps Commander, described what happened:

> A logistical convoy from 7 Baloch was headed for the Laddha Fort, a Frontier Corps base near Makeen (in South Waziristan) on 30 August [2007]. The convoy was headed by about forty men, heavily armed but travelling in light vehicles. Four or five kilometres behind was a group of about sixty soldiers, followed by the main body of the convoy, in eight or ten vehicles. They were followed by another thirty to forty troops in light vehicles. The Frontier Corps had been tasked to picket the route.
>
> As they moved through a narrow defile towards the fort the lead element found that the road was half blocked with rocks. They sent word to the column behind them that the road was impassable, and the whole convoy stopped moving. Very shortly afterwards the advance party communicated that explosives would be needed to move the rocks.
>
> At this stage, we learned later, four or five local men appeared, offering to help clear the road. A couple more sauntered up. Suddenly, as they saw forty or fifty men gathering in the mountains above them, the soldiers realised their predicament. The troops saw no alternative but to obey, when ordered to lay down their weapons and surrender. Armed men were now to be seen on the mountains for the whole length of the convoy.
>
> It was about midday by this time. I had known that the convoy was

going to the Laddha Fort, and the Governor had also known. General Orakzai had been convinced that, in the light of the agreements with the tribes, there would be no interference. We had arranged that helicopter cover would be available if it should be needed. We had Cobra and Bell helicopters in Wana that day, ready to be called upon. In the early morning the sky looked good, but by midday there was rain, and we were told that the helicopters could not fly.

The column should have been able to defend itself. It should have moved up to the heights. It didn't.

And it emerged that the FC had only mounted five or six pickets. They said that the villagers had asked them not to picket the whole road properly, because there were women around.

The CO should have taken the situation in hand when he arrived on the scene; he should have realised that his troops were in hostile territory. The troops should have been able to hold out until help arrived. In this case, no one would have been blamed.

As it was…

The general shrugged.

The last party in the convoy held a bridge that they were about to cross, and then pulled back to Brigade HQ in Shagai. They reported everything that had happened.

General Orakzai began negotiating with the tribes, and the tribes began moving the goalposts. Finally, they produced a list of twenty-five names. These men, they said, were being held by the government. Until they were released, our soldiers would be held prisoner. Orakzai took the list, and would not share it with the rest of us.

XI Corps began preparing a military operation to rescue the soldiers. GHQ said that we could not do this without endangering our own soldiers. My argument was that if we did nothing the militants would start killing our men, as they had threatened, five on the first day and then more. If we moved in, they would start killing – to deter us – and they would then kill more. But then, they would stop the slaughter in order to keep a bargaining chip. I agreed with GHQ's assessment that it would be difficult, and I knew that we might not succeed. But I thought we should do it.

However, caution prevailed, and General Orakzai continued to negotiate. I heard it said at the time that 'we should give them [the militants] the moon. Whatever they ask for, we should give. We'll revoke everything later.' This thinking prevailed. Alam Khattak [Major General, IGFC] and I disagreed with it. We argued that we would lose the moral ground if we broke our word just because the Army was in a squeeze. We both thought that we should deal straight. Where the Army is involved, especially domestically, we need to be seen to be in the right.

But the other side prevailed. Orakzai managed to persuade the President to agree to the release of the militants on the list. But he could only find twenty of them. Five simply did not exist. So Orakzai told the militants that they could ask for the release of another five men. Our soldiers were then freed. Only two had died. But, among the five new names produced by the militants were some Afghan Taliban. President Musharraf – backed by the intelligence services – refused to sanction their release. Orakzai came to me and asked for help. 'Come on,' he said, 'you agreed.'

'No,' I said, 'I did not agree. I had nothing to do with it. I never saw the list. Do what you want but don't involve me.'

North Waziristan was by now fairly peaceful. After I was still ashamed that my men had been taken prisoner. I wanted to restore the Army's honour by teaching Baitullah Mehsud a lesson. He should have been asking us for peace.

Orakzai could not get the men released.

In mid-December he resigned. This was his way of telling Baitullah that he had played it straight, to persuade the tribes that he had behaved honourably. Otherwise, Baitullah would have gone after Orakzai. He would have been a marked man.

Orakzai never wanted to discuss what he was doing with the Army, with the bureaucrats or with politicians. Nobody could control him.

Operation Rah-e-Haq November 2007–Dec 2007

As the Army was handling the crisis over the kidnap of 7 Baloch, during the autumn of 2007, it was also having to launch a major operation to tackle a growing menace in another area.

Swat had been a princely state during the British era and it remained semi-independent until 1969, when (along with the other princely states of Dir and Chitral) it was absorbed into Pakistan. Jehanzeb, the last hereditary ruler, was an enlightened autocrat who built schools, roads and medical facilities and encouraged economic development. Crucially, he also dispensed swift justice. After the state became part of Pakistan, Swatis were left without a functioning judicial system (see Chapter 3).

A protest movement, the *Tehrik-e-Nifaz-e-Shariat-e-Mohammadi* (Movement for the Enforcement of Islamic Law, TNSM) had been calling for the introduction of shariah law since the early 1990s. In 1995 the Army had been called in to restore order, and Benazir Bhutto's government agreed to the introduction of an element of shariah law. The leader of the TNSM was Maulana Sufi Muhammad, formerly of the *Jamaat Islami*. In 2002 Sufi Muhammad was jailed for sending thousands of volunteers to fight with the Taliban in Afghanistan, and his son-in-law, Maulana Fazlullah, became head of the TNSM. The movement was outlawed, but it flourished nevertheless. Fazlullah, along with other militant leaders, exploited the 2005 earthquake. Islamist groups were able to get help to some stricken areas before the Army managed to reach them, and then to portray the disaster as divine punishment for Pakistan's godless ways. By 2006 'Mullah Radio', as Fazlullah was now known, was running an illegal FM radio channel broadcasting hellfire sermons denouncing modernity and its vices (including CDs, television, computers and polio vaccinations) and advocating the forcible promotion of virtue. The maulana was reputed to have a great following among housewives, who were said to be selling their jewellery and sending. him their savings, to fund his campaigns.

After the Lal Masjid siege Fazlullah led an open revolt in Swat. In a broadcast in July he declared jihad against Pervez Musharraf's government and the Army.

The *Muttahida Majlis-e-Amal* (MMA), a party formed out of a group of six religious organisations, had been in control of the NWFP provincial government since 2002, and effectively sanctioned the TNSM's activities. By late October Fazlullah controlled much of Swat.

17 Division, now under the command of Major General Naseer Janjua, was sent into Swat to clear the district of Mullah Fazlullah's forces. Cordon-and-search operations swept through the valley and – with the exception of Peochar Valley – Swat was cleared by mid-December 2007.

Fazlullah and a large number of his fighters had escaped to the mountains. He would return all too soon, as Army officers who were involved with Swat knew.

That autumn, though, there was plenty to think about other than Swat.

The militants were demonstrating that they could hit back at the Army, even in its own home town of Rawalpindi. On the morning of 3 September two suicide bombers attacked - almost simultaneously - military and intelligence targets: a bus carrying intelligence personnel and the Royal Artillery Bazaar, an area that people heading to GHQ would be likely to be walking or driving through. About thirty people were killed and dozens wounded in the two attacks. The targeting of the Intelligence Agencies was clearly intended to warn the Army, and anyone tempted to help the Army, that the Taliban had sources within the military. The bus was, however, a soft target: any local person might well have known who was on board and where they were going.

Ten days later, on 13 September, a teenage suicide bomber blew himself in the soldiers' canteen of the SSG base at Tarbela, killing twenty-two soldiers. Tarbela was a major SSG base, with the Special Operations Task Force (SOTF), Karrar Company (anti-terrorist unit), Zarrar (a unit designated for major anti-hijacking, hostage rescue and other such operations, primarily in urban areas) and aviation assets. The loss of the soldiers shocked the Army, and the idea that militants could penetrate Special Forces facilities appalled them. The soldiers who were targeted belonged to Karrar Company, which had been deployed in the Lal Masjid Operation. These were elite troops, trained by the CIA, platoon by platoon, in the US. It emerged later that local construction work had caused security regulations around the base to be relaxed.

Political dramas and terrorist attacks vied for newspaper headlines that autumn and winter. Neither seemed to bode well for the country, but ordinary people carried on with their lives, becoming inured to the violence.

27 December 2007 was different. Benazir Bhutto, who had returned home a few months before, was assassinated at a political rally in Rawalpindi. No one who was in Pakistan that day will ever forget it. What staggered me most was that people were not talking. In the bazaars and in my hotel there was silence.

No one has been convicted of the murder of Benazir Bhutto. In Pakistan, wild allegations of every sort have been made, feeding pet conspiracy theories or making political capital out of the horror.

The government of Pakistan believed that Baitullah Mehsud was responsible for ordering the killing. On 18 January 2008 the *Washington*

Post carried a report that the CIA 'has concluded that... [allies of Baitullah] were responsible for [the murder] and that they also stand behind a new wave of violence threatening the country's stability, the agency's director, Michael V. Hayden, said in an interview.'

Operation Tristar 16–28 January 2008

Baitullah Mehsud was becoming ever more openly insolent towards the government. In December he was appointed head of the newly formed *Tehrik-e-Taliban*, the Movement of the Taliban in Pakistan. Maulana Fazlullah was one of a number of militant leaders who joined him in this.

In January 2008 two key South Waziristan forts, Sararogha (Frontier Corps) near Jandola and Laddha (Army and Frontier Corps) near Makeen were besieged by Baitullah's men. Logistics convoys were unable to reach the men, who began to run short of supplies, especially of fresh water. Forts in Sarawakai and Splitoi were also attacked.

In mid-January Sararogha Fort fell to Baitullah's men. A force estimated at about five hundred men finally stormed the fort on the night of 15–16 January. In a well-planned action they breached the walls with explosives before pouring into the fort. According to the Corps Commander, Lieutenant General Masood Aslam, two FC soldiers were killed, three escaped and about thirty surrendered.

The fort was razed to the ground.

Operation Tristar was the Army's response to the disaster. XI Corps had developed the plans some time before. The operation involved a three-pronged attack, targeting Baitullah's network.

14 Division provided the main thrust – codenamed Zalzala – with two brigades moving east from Dera Ismail Khan to Jandola. A brigade from 7 Division moved north from Razmak through the Makin Valley to Laddha, while a brigade from 9 Division moved through the Shakhai Valley towards Laddha. These two were mainly diversionary movements, intended to threaten and draw out the Mehsuds.

7 Baloch, which had performed so poorly when ambushed in August, was given the chance to redeem its reputation in Operation Tristar. The unit – under a new CO – acquitted itself honourably, reaching Kotkai, home of Qari Hussain, by 28 January. He was one of Baitullah's key lieutenants, controlling the area between Kotkai and Spinka Razoi.

To the annoyance of senior officers involved, Operation Tristar was halted when troops reached Kotkai. 'We had not moved as far as we wanted.' Lt Gen. Masood Aslam recalled later. 'We needed to extricate our men. We did not have the resources to take Baitullah on properly. All we could do was teach him a lesson. We were able to show him it was the Army that set the terms. The operation was a success. But we should have pressed our advantage home.' Major General Tariq Khan, then commanding 14 Division, was still more outspoken in his anger that the operation was halted.

On 5 February a helicopter crash killed Major General Javed Sultan, the greatly respected GOC 7 Division, two brigade commanders, a lieutenant colonel and three young officers. The losses stunned the Army. So many deaths in a single incident was devastating, and the loss of these key figures hampered operations in South Waziristan. 'The pilot should never have flown,' an influential major general said later. 'They often take risks with short hops. With longer flights they are more careful. And it is tough for senior officers to fly if a young pilot is eager to do it. We knew the weather was bad, but the pilot wanted to do it. Also, of course, they were flouting the Standard Operating Procedures. There should never have been so many senior officers in one aircraft.'

In a brief two-week operation in June 2008 the Army cleared the Khyber Agency. Attacks on NATO convoys taking supplies to coalition forces in Afghanistan were growing in intensity. So the Army engaged in this operation to clear the area.

In July 2008 the Army was in action again in Swat, with the second phase of Operation Rah-e-Haq.

On 21 May 2008 a deal had been done with Maulana Fazlullah's followers in Swat. The agreement did not look very stable; only hours before the deal was signed a policeman was murdered and two girls' schools were set on fire. As a result of this deal Fazlullah swept back in and exacted his revenge on people he suspected of having supported the Army operations.

'Announcing successes, as in Swat, has been a very great mistake,' a senior officer commented later. 'The people of Swat complained that the Army had been too cautious and that it was not in control of the situation. The militants struck close to Army camps but the troops did not come out to challenge them'. In the second phase of the operation the Army had brought in more forces.

In August Major General Tariq Khan was appointed Inspector General of the Frontier Corps, replacing Major General Alam Khattak.

Operation Sherdil September 2008

'In August 2008 the Bajaur Agency was becoming unwieldy,' Lieutenant General Masood Aslam told me. 'We had been wanting to extend the security perimeter around Peshawar, to ensure the safety of the city and to put an end to attacks on NATO convoys traveling to Afghanistan. But Bajaur flared up first.'

Frontier Corps soldiers moved into Bajaur early in August to set up a border post to control the movement of foreign and Pakistani militants across the border. They were ambushed by several hundred Taliban fighters and a savage three-day battle ensued. The Army had known that there were militants, local men and foreigners in the agency, but they were taken aback by the ferocity of this attack.

Operation Sherdil (Lionheart) was launched, to regain control of Bajaur. As the Frontier Corps and Army fought on they were staggered to discover the militants dug into a network of tunnels and underground defences. These were well constructed and clearly specially built, and the militants' resistance was highly professional. The Pakistan Army was ruthless in the battle for Bajaur. Major General Tariq Khan was in command, with regular Army troops subordinated to him. He was determined, he told me, that the militants should be dealt with properly. He was concerned, as others in the Army had been, that too many deals had been done that had given militant leaders a useful breathing space to regroup. Aerial bombing, tanks, artillery and bulldozers flattened the town of Loesam. When I visited, nothing remained above knee height.

At the end of February 2009 a ceasefire was declared in Bajaur.

Operation Rah-e-Rast May 2009

It was obvious that the Army had failed to clear Swat, and in the early summer of 2009 a second attempt was made. In the first week of May the operation was launched. Again, the action was tough. Helicopter gunships, fighter jets and artillery were used.

Two million people were estimated to have been driven from their homes by the fighting in Swat. By 28 June Mingora was secured, after government troops had cleared the town street by street. By 15 July the thousands of internally displaced persons were beginning to return, and by 14 August all were back home, according to XI Corps.

In the spring of 2009 something remarkable happened. Public opinion suddenly swung behind the Pakistan Army more forcefully than ever before. A video surfaced showing a girl being beaten by the Taliban in Swat. It was shocking, but I did not think that it added much to what we knew of the brutality of the militants. There were already bits of footage floating around the internet showing real atrocities, unspeakably brutal murders that were filmed as they were carried out. But the film of the girl's flogging struck a raw nerve. Everyone talked about it: people who had been prepared to see the Taliban as unsophisticated countrymen carrying on the fight against the latest Western invaders of Afghanistan, and understandably targeting the government of Pakistan as an ally of the US, were brought up sharp. The mood of the people had changed, and now, for the first time, everyone seemed to see the militants as the enemies of ordinary Pakistanis.

At about the same time, the media began to give much more coverage to the hardships that the Army was going through. Television channels started to report soldiers' deaths in human terms. The stories of the men who had lost their lives in the struggle against terrorism were told, and images of funerals were shown.

Operations continue still in South Waziristan, and the Army is expected to extend the fight into North Waziristan soon.

9

The Death of Faisal Alavi

On 19 November 2008 Major General Amir Faisal Alavi, the former commander of Pakistan's Special Forces, was brutally murdered. He had told me that he feared this might happen, and he had told me what to do if he was killed.

I first met Faisal Alavi in 2005. He was riding high in those days. Lauded as the gallant leader of a number of recent operations, he was the first general officer to command Pakistan's Special Forces (SF). He was running the Special Services Group (SSG) for the second time; he had commanded it as a brigadier, and then, when the post was upgraded, he was brought back as GOC. During the few months that I had been working with the Pakistan Army I had heard his name repeatedly. Young officers – people who had never served with him – proudly talked about the dashing general, telling of his exploits. There was a 'Wait-until-you-meet-General-Alavi!' sense in the air that spring. He was known nationally for having jumped with his men during a parachuting display on 23 March, Pakistan Day, a feat unheard of for a general officer. President Musharraf publicly embraced him after he sailed smoothly to the ground, a gesture that was interpreted by many as evidence that Alavi was a favourite of the Head of State. Quite apart from the President's goodwill, it was clear that Alavi was an asset to the Army. At a time when many in the Army were still worried about the operations in the Tribal Areas, his flamboyant confidence boosted waverers' morale.

Faisal Alavi crashed into my view on 13 April 2005, bounding out of his office at Cherat, the mountain headquarters of the SSG. He was a big, dark man with enormous eyes, exuding energy and life. The trip to Cherat was my first brush with Pakistan's Special Forces and I was struck that day that the general officer commanding the SSG was so like SF people in other countries and other continents. In 1991 I had written about the Soviet Army Special Forces: 'The officers reveal an almost theatrical self-awareness and an easy assumption of their superiority.' I had also noted that they laughed more, and louder, than the rest of the

Army. This could have been said about General Alavi, sweeping dramatically around his mountain eyrie.

During our first conversation in his office at Cherat it was clear that his was a generous and brave spirit. Other Army officers, faced with a foreign writer whom they have never met before, vacillate, evade or at least pick their words carefully. Alavi simply smiled and talked, words and emotions – humour and kindness and excitement – tumbling out as he talked about himself, his men and SSG operations. He told me then that he had been born British in Kenya, of Punjabi parents (with a dash of Kashmiri blood), and that his older brother had fought against the Mau Mau with the Kenyan Police. His affection for Britain was touching; his love for the land of his fathers even more striking. Determined from early childhood to join the Pakistan Army he had defied his father's plan to educate him in England and persuaded the family to send him to Abbottabad Public School and thence to the Pakistan Military Academy. It was characteristic that he sailed through the intensely competitive selection procedure without realising that to join the military Academy he would need Pakistani citizenship. When this emerged the young Faisal did what seemed obvious: he appealed to the country's leader, Zulfiqar Ali Bhutto.

Cherat was an old British hill station, a summer retreat from Peshawar. From 1861 onwards it was used as a sanatorium for soldiers, Alavi told me. Apart from the hospital the British built bungalows, a post office and a church. They left their dead – including young mothers and children – in a sheltered cemetery. The general clearly loved Cherat. He talked of the British building the place in the nineteenth century when every single thing had to be brought up by mule train. He knew the mountain well – he had been running up and down it, carrying a load of thirty pounds or more, ever since he first joined the SSG – and he understood how difficult it must have been to build the road. It was steep and the sign welcoming visitors to the SSG, 'Well you made it', felt appropriate. Another board carried the slogan 'The Proud the Few'. Alavi's pride in the SSG was clear. During that first encounter the names of the great men of the Special Forces came tumbling out: especially the father of the SSG, Major General Aboobaker Osman Mitha, and the legendary Brigadier TM (Tariq Mehmood), hero of the 1965 and 1971 wars. Alavi showed me around the SSG Museum, telling the stories of these and other men who still inspired the Special Forces. He pointed out – as if I had not already known it – that the President had served in the Special Forces. It was due to him that the SSG had been strengthened from the equivalent of a brigade to division size.

After lunch, a tour of the base and a demonstration of SSG training, General Alavi invited me to drive down to Attock Fort with him. We bounced down the hill in his jeep, with a Makrani soldier from the coast of Balochistan, a member of a very dark-skinned community that was thought to be African in origin. It was not clear how these people got there, Alavi said, but they had been living in the area for hundreds of years. They were probably the descendants of slaves brought over by Arabs who were trading in Balochistan and Sindh. No one knew for sure because there were no records. But the interesting thing, the general said, was that there were traces of Swahili in their dialect. He had heard words and phrases that he recognised clearly from his own east African childhood. The Makranis made good soldiers: he had found them to be committed and dependable. General Alavi told me, as we travelled, of a related community who were – among other things – guardians of a shrine where huge crocodiles lived in a pond fed by an underground stream and were so revered that they were buried like human beings when they died. I was intrigued by the story he was telling, of the huge chief crocodile who was garlanded during an annual festival, but I noticed that – despite the fun of the sacred crocodiles – the general was really more interested in the plight of the Makranis and the racism they endured. I had rarely heard anyone in Pakistan talk about the country's minorities.

The sandstone Attock Fort, built by the Emperor Akbar in the sixteenth century, was an SSG facility that included, among other things, an Army-controlled prison. It was a historically important Mughal building but, above all, it was a military base. The Army can make anywhere its home and I was struck, as we climbed around the Emperor's sprawling ramparts, by the way that this magnificent monument, with its sinister past, was an Army base like any other. The order and discipline of the military, with all its banality, took precedence over the historical legacy.

I had driven past the fort several times before. It is an unmissable landmark, towering about the Grand Trunk Road near the strange spot where the Indus and Kabul meet, but do not mingle. They flow, together yet distinct (the Kabul muddy brown and the Indus blue) before joining forces to water Punjab and Sindh. In the nineteenth century the British threw a sturdy iron bridge across the Indus hereabouts. General Alavi asked me, that afternoon, whether I had noticed old signs forbidding photography on the bridge. A lot of the regulations governing military and civilian life in Pakistan, he commented, predated independence. Both excessive bureaucracy and obsessive concerns about security were part of the legacy of empire. He had great admiration for the British, Alavi said. Despite all that was wrong with the empire they had two characteristics that redeemed them in his eyes: 'They believe in justice and they are loyal to their friends.' This was a thought that he was to repeat several times over the next few years.

Nawaz Sharif had been imprisoned in Attock Fort after his ill-considered attempt to sack the Army Chief (Pervez Musharraf) led to his removal, Alavi told me. Grinning, he said that, as head of the SSG, he had been the former Prime Minister's jailer and had interviewed Nawaz and his brother Shahbaz when they were first brought to the fort. He asked which of them was older. 'If I were the elder we wouldn't be here,' Shahbaz told the general, through gritted teeth. Shahbaz's conduct in Attock Fort had been reasonable, Alavi said, but Nawaz had cut a very poor figure. He was greedy, the most gluttonous person Alavi had ever seen. He demanded that all his food – and it was a lot – should be sent in from a restaurant he liked. After a while, Alavi said, he began to lose patience with the fuss about Nawaz's food and with his craven whining. Nawaz was convinced – among other things – that he was going to be poisoned. 'So I called for him and said that I really could not guarantee the safety of food that was delivered from outside. He immediately saw the point and agreed to eat what our cooks produced.'

We drank strong, sweet tea sitting in the open air at Attock with a group of SSG officers. General Alavi talked on, and it grew dark as we sat there.

He was still talking when he and his attractive and long-suffering wife came to dinner in London on 22 June that year. The Alavis were at that time passing through London on their way home after a trip to the US during which the general talked at length to his American counterparts. By the end of the evening a garden-full of Londoners were totally won over to the cause of Pakistan and its Army. The anthropologist Jonathan King was there, and was gratified that Alavi had clearly read his Indian Civil Service great-grandfather's rather neglected work on the Orakzai country and clans. An Iraqi academic was intrigued by his openness. She thought Alavi unusually candid for a soldier. Anthony Ramsay, a Scottish friend, told the general that his uncle had founded Britain's SAS. Alavi was interested, but I noticed that he paid even more attention when Anthony talked about his son's experience fighting in Iraq. Only the neighbours were unhappy about that noisy evening.

In July Alavi was back in England, this time to talk to the SAS in Hereford. He told me that he had initiated the visit. Although the SAS had worked with the SSG during the years of the Soviet war in Afghanistan, there had been little real contact since then. A small team had visited Cherat in 2004, but it had not led to the sort of support that Alavi was seeking. He was keen to revive the SSG's relationship with the British Special Forces because he was convinced that the British had much to teach about handling terrorists. He wanted help from the SAS with training – particularly for reconnaissance operations – and he wanted to reinforce requests that Pakistan had already made for help with equipment. But Alavi's encounter with the SAS was not entirely easy. Britain (like the US) believed that Pakistan was not doing enough to tackle the militants in the Tribal Areas who were endangering Coalition troops in Afghanistan. Lieutenant Colonel Richard Williams, who was then commanding 22 SAS, was Major General Alavi's host in Hereford and later described the situation at that time. 'The Americans were at their wits' end. They were throwing lots of money at Pakistan Special Forces people, who took the cash but delivered nothing. The US passed intelligence to the Pakistanis but they did nothing, or they did too little, too late. Everybody, on both sides of the Atlantic, was trying to work out how to get things done.'

Anger towards Pakistan was building up, and Alavi was confronted, in the mess at Hereford, with allegations that his own Army had been colluding with the enemy. His conduct under fire won him respect.

General Alavi 'was brutally frank about the situation', Richard Williams said. He 'was a straight-talking soldier and some pretty robust conversations took place in the mess. He wanted kit, skills and training from the UK. But he was asked, bluntly, why the Pakistan Army should be given all this help if nothing came of it in terms of getting the al Qaeda leadership.'

Alavi's response was candid, the SAS commander said. 'He knew that Pakistan was not pulling its weight in the war on terror. He told us that a considerable section of Pakistani society was sympathetic to the Taliban, and that this affected the ISI and the military.

'There was a dampening effect, he said, between Army orders issued by the Chief and their execution. Alavi believed that a great many officers were concerned about the impact that tough military action would have. People were concerned about the safety of their families. MI and ISI officers were diluting General Musharraf's orders. He advised us to build better bridges to the ISI and the MI, so that there were personal relationships to rely on.' Although Alavi was not telling the SAS officers anything that they did not already know, they found his honesty reassuring. It was not they who would decide whether or not the SSG could be given the equipment and support that Alavi was asking for, but the officers who met him in Hereford certainly wanted to continue the relationship with him. Apart from anything else, 'the discussions with Alavi were constructive in terms of enabling us to understand the difficulties within Pakistan', Richard Williams reported. 'Faisal Alavi knew that Pakistan was not pulling its weight in the war on terror and that the country's intelligence institutions were not doing right by the country.'

The British recognised a kindred spirit. '[He] had a devil-may-care attitude. He was one of the buccaneering, incredibly brave minority who take risks,' Williams said later. 'I remember him wandering round at Hereford, obviously feeling very much at home.'

After Hereford he spent a few days in London, staying with his sister Nadira Naipaul in South Kensington. He told me, during that time, that his visit to Hereford had been a success. It seemed to him that the SAS was on his side and that its help would be crucial. He needed to demonstrate to GHQ that the SSG was becoming a world-class counter-terrorist force. As it was, he said, the human material was second to none, but they lacked proper equipment. The SSG needed kit, and it also needed support from the UK to boost confidence. He told me, as he had told Richard Williams, that there were people in the Army who did not believe that the militants could be beaten. Alavi was convinced that the threat could be dealt with and he believed that the Special Forces had to play a major role in this. He had to overcome opposition from some in the Army who were risk averse, and from others who were resentful of the SSG. Luckily, he said, President Musharraf understood all this and would always support the SSG. Alavi was full of praise for the President. He admired his grasp of every issue that crossed his desk, his courage in pursuing policies that he believed right even when they were unpopular, and his judgement. With the President's backing, Alavi was confident that he would win the argument and the Army would defeat the militants; things were going his way. He seemed to think he was bulletproof.

On 18 August 2005, a few weeks later, I returned to Pakistan, arriving in the early hours of the morning. It was already hot when I checked into the Marriott Hotel in Islamabad. I picked up a newspaper as I went to my room. Lying back in air-conditioned comfort – waiting for my luggage to arrive – I skimmed through it.

> Maj Gen Faisal Alvi retired on disciplinary grounds
> By our correspondent
> RAWALPINDI: Major General Amir Faisal Alvi [*sic*] of Special Services Group (SSG) has been retired from service. A spokesman of ISPR confirming the news said that the officer has been retired on disciplinary grounds for conduct unbecoming. To a question whether Major General Alvi was involved in financial irregularities or differences on operation in Tribal Areas the spokesman categorically denied both.

There was no explanation, no speculation, just this curt note of damnation. It was too early then to telephone anyone, but later I called friends in the Army and the media. None had any idea what had happened – although they were all aware of the scandal – and all of them seemed to feel that it would be a bad idea to delve into the mystery. I realised, over the next day or so, that nobody in the Army even wanted to hear Alavi's name. When I asked Colonel Baseer, in ISPR, what had happened he simply shrugged. 'We don't know either', he said. 'It's a mystery.' I scoured every newspaper I could find, and began digging out telephone numbers for people who might know more.

Late in the morning of the second day General Alavi telephoned. He said that he would come to see me, and would explain everything, but that it might take him a day or two to get to the Marriott. Two or three days later he finally turned up, looking dishevelled. He told me that it had been hard for him to shake off the Military Intelligence operatives who trailed him everywhere. He had had to send his own car and driver out, making it look as though he was in the car, and then leave in another vehicle, lying in the back – covered with a blanket – so that he was not seen. His story was bewildering. It was less than a month since his trip to Hereford, and now, suddenly, he was a pariah.

The general sat on my desk chair and began to tell his story. He said that the people in the Army who opposed his approach to handling the terrorists had conspired against him. In particular, he said, he had crossed swords over the conduct of operations with two highly placed generals who occupied crucially important positions. He was convinced they had constructed a plot to persuade President Musharraf that he was disloyal. But only a few weeks before he had been convinced of the President's support. One of these generals had been unnerved by the losses that the Army had taken in early operations against the Taliban. He had opposed Alavi's belief that better-planning and execution was the answer and thought the answer was to buy off militant leaders. Alavi complained that another general, Lt General Safdar, had been given ISI funds that were intended for controlling the Tribal Areas as hush-money, and had agreed a deal with the militant leader Baitullah Mehsud whereby – in return for a large sum of money – Mahsud's three thousand armed fighters would not attack the Army. Following policy from above endorsed by President Musharraf, Safdar came to a similar agreement with Nek Mohammad who reneged on the agreement. Alavi believed these deals achieved nothing for Pakistan or for its allies in the war against terror. Alavi had made known his anger that these warlords were free to roam around, openly recruiting, because some in the Army dared not tackle them. He had a running battle with Safdar, who wanted the Special Forces to be brought under his operational command. Alavi was swimming against the tide as the senior echelon was happy to agree to this; for Faisal Alavi it was vitally important that they should remain directly subordinate to CGS, even though General Tariq Majid was hostile.

Alavi's enemies had been effective, he said sadly. He had had an affair with a divorced woman – 'the Pathan bitch' as he referred to her now – and he admitted that he had been indiscreet about it. The infatuation was over; he had discovered that she was also close to other people in the Army. But he had retained some affection for her and had agreed to help her when she appealed to him to save her from harassment by a senior general. All this had happened before his trip to Hereford. As he was fighting in England, persuading the SAS that the Pakistan Army could take on the militants properly, and could win, the very men who opposed this approach were causing his undoing. He had discovered, since the debacle, that this had been part of a Byzantine plot, cooked up by his enemies, to lure him into talking about them on the telephone. In one of many taped conversations, as the messy intrigue played itself out, Alavi was goaded into making remarks that – taken out of context – sounded disloyal to General Musharraf. He had walked head first into the trap. The President, who by Alavi's own admission had repeatedly protected him, understandably lost patience. Alavi was sacked, ignominiously, from the SSG. He seemed utterly bewildered by the disaster, aghast that his enemies had at last managed to poison General Musharraf's mind against him. If only he could see him, Alavi kept insisting, the Boss would realise that he had never wavered in his loyalty. In the days and weeks after the initial blow General Alavi made his position worse. The Vice Chief of Army Staff, General Ahsan Saleem Hyat, advised him to accept being posted out of the SSG with a good grace. Initially, it seemed that he might perhaps be able to serve out his time as a major general, if he kept a low profile and accepted whatever the Army offered him. He liked and trusted the kind, softly spoken Vice Chief, but he was outraged by the injustice of his sacking – as he saw it – and determined to fight. He had no intention of going quietly. He raged, publicly and privately, at the men who had orchestrated his downfall. It took some time for him to realise that the President's wrath had been raised, and that there would be no way back into his favour for quite a while.

Although the President had been hurt by Alavi's apparent betrayal, and refused to see him, it was made clear to others, at least, that he retained some regard for Alavi. A retired three-star told me what happened at the first Corps Commanders Conference after the sacking. The drama was still fresh, and there had been much speculation – and some schadenfreude – about what had happened. At the beginning of the meeting the President reported that he had received a belated birthday card. He handed the card, showing a man flattened by a truck, round the table. The message inside said that the sender had been having troubles and was sorry the greetings were late.

'From Faisal Alavi' was all the President said. His message was clear. Alavi might have been sacked and disgraced but he still enjoyed some protection from his old boss. 'It was as if he was sending a warning to leave off, where Alavi was concerned.' Alavi's panache, even when he was facing catastrophe, was undeniable.

Alavi wanted to fight. The tapes that had been played to the Boss had ruined him. But, he said, he had also been taping telephone conversations, and he insisted that – if he could present his evidence – it would become clear that one of his persecutors – possibly both of them – had been having an affair with the same Pathan girl. He also believed that his tapes – and other material – would prove that key players had been lying about operations in the Tribal Areas.

As Alavi was roaring his anger at anyone who would listen, Military Intelligence operatives not only kept him under close and intrusive surveillance, but they questioned his servants and visitors, not always politely. The MI knew that Alavi had material that would rock the Army and ruin the careers of two very ambitious generals. The DG MI was probably aware that his men had not managed to lay their hands on everything. It was a dangerous game for a man as straightforward as Faisal Alavi. He was an honest soldier, unused to intrigue. And this was not, for him, a game. He had been dishonoured, he felt, by cowardly men. He used to say repeatedly, in the months after his sacking, that he would rather go down in a hail of bullets than endure his shame while his enemies flourished.

He was devastated by ISPR's statement that he had 'been retired on disciplinary grounds for conduct unbecoming'. He thought that the Vice Chief had undertaken that no such thing should be said.

The catastrophe was not only personal. The general's wife and daughters also felt themselves disgraced by the scandal. Alavi suffered lacerating reproaches from the family, or from some of them. He was comforted at this time, he told me, by his younger daughter Aleena, who stood by him throughout. She was loyal and kind, and could always, even in his worst days, make him laugh. A visit from Nadira, the sister nearest to him in age, cheered him up later that summer. She spurred him on, making him go out, see people and hold his head up high. Her company reminded him again of the fun they had had as children in Africa. An important friend in the family was Ruby, who was his niece although they were about the same age. Alavi had loved her since they were children, and would go to see Ruby and her husband (retired general Ehtisham Zamir) whenever he could.

Above all, though, it was Farida, the sister he had always been able to rely on, who sustained him. Farida was the widow of Air Marshal Shabbir Hussain Syed (*Sitara-e-Jurat*), a pilot and a hero of the 1965 war who ended his career as Vice Chief of Air Staff. She had seen brave men taking risks and ambitious men reaching for the stars before; she probably understood more of her brother's life than anyone else. The world – the President, the Army, friends, colleagues and relations – might abandon him but Farida never faltered. 'At the worst time I just used to go and slump on Farida's sofa,' he told me later. 'She never questioned me.'

Over the next few weeks and months Faisal Alavi learnt a lot about the men with whom he had served. Several of his own subordinates – officers and men alike – had borne false witness against him, he said. Some, he thought, had been pressured into cooperating with his enemies. Others had been eager to help. His own ADC, whom he had trusted implicitly, was not among them Only a few weeks earlier this young man had been wanting to get close to his family, Alavi told me. Old acquaintances shunned him. General officers who had been friendly when he had been successful now avoided his eye. But others were kind. In his darkest days after the sacking Alavi used to see a deputy Director-General of the ISI when they were both out jogging. He was touched that this man always made a point of altering his pace in order to jog alongside him. This man, a major general, told Alavi that he had discussed his case with very senior officers. They agreed that he had been unfairly treated. Others were supportive too. Some, in key operational positions, had not been close friends but now indicated support. Any gesture of friendliness, or even of decency, meant a lot at this time.

In February 2006 Alavi sent me an email:

> I've been thru 6 months of hell. Even after my retirement, I was harassed beyond limits, which made me c the ugly side of r establishment. But thruout this period, I remained bold and upright and took everything like a man and did not 'break', the way they normally want a guy 2. Anyway, after 6 months, I told them that I would b cancelling my Leave Pending Release and getting the hell out of the Army into the civil world. That's how I got out… I became a victim of 'palace intrigue' in which the other side managed to damage me substantially thru a well planned conspiracy and it cost me my uniform. The thought … makes me v bitter but then I thought that there was no use cryin over spilled milk and 2 get on with my life and make the best of it. I do have the confidence that i can succeed in any field I venture in, due to my pushing and industrious nature, so I decided finally to take up this job as the country head of this telecomm company... But I now find myself happy

> and contented as the job is as per my previous 'bullshit rank and status.' Difference is I am leading a v competent and highly educated team here, whereas I led semi-educated trained killers earlier. I like the difference. I try 2 b more civil here by avoiding swear words, a loud voice and an ominous demeanour. It's difficult though.

Life was looking up for Alavi. He and his family had moved to a house in Bahria Town, a newly developed area between Islamabad and Rawalpindi. His niece Ruby and her husband Ehtisham lived virtually opposite, and other friends were not far away. But – as his email revealed – he was still brooding on what had happened the previous August. He also missed Army life. Despite the joke about 'killers' he had loved his soldiers and still hoped for some sort of rapprochement with the Army.

On 10 April Alavi reported cheering news:

'I've recently had some positive overtures coming from the Army. I was invited by the Vice Chief 2 attend his sons' Walima ceremony yesterday, which I did, as I had a feeling this kind of thing would come one day.... It was a good thing I went... as it sent some real healthy signals 2 all the other Generals who were there, most of whom were flabbergasted 2 c me.'

As time passed Alavi saw many of his former comrades. General Ashfaq Kayani (DG ISI) seemed to be sympathetic and other three-stars were friendly. It was clear to Alavi that the hostility towards him was coming from the General Staff and the MI Directorate. Although many were sympathetic, no one was willing – or able – to give Alavi the help he wanted. He toyed with the idea of finding a job that used his military experience. In due course he applied to the UN and to private security companies in England. But his heart remained with the Pakistan Army.

'Sometimes I wish I'd gone 2 UK 2 pursue my studies there and then obviously, I would have settled there, the way my Dad wanted me 2 do. But I guess I always wanted to join the Army and that also 2 fight the Indians and that mindset brought me here. Hence, no regrets, despite this unceremonious end to my career.

And so life went on. But Alavi never stopped agonizing over his sacking. He was bitter that the Army refused to give him the retirement benefits that he had been promised, and this became more of an issue as domestic pressures mounted. In December 2006 his elder daughter married, but the marriage soon broke down. Alavi was furious that the scandal surrounding his departure from the Army was brought up in the divorce case. The divorce also added to his financial concerns.

Despite these worries, 2007 was a good year for Alavi. His second career was going well and he was becoming very sociable once again. Every day he met friends for lunch or in the evening, relishing jokes and gup, the endless gossip that Pakistan runs on. During one such lunch Alavi received a phone call that stunned him. He was being asked to take charge of Nawaz Sharif's personal security when he returned to Pakistan that autumn. An old acquaintance called Nasir, a retired colonel, who worked for the same company as Alavi, was the link. His brother Mushtaq, another former Army officer (who had gone into the police and risen very high), now worked closely with the former Prime Minister. Alavi rocked with mirth at the idea that his abject prisoner was now asking him for physical protection. It was not only out of fidelity to Musharraf that Alavi turned the job down. (But Nawaz was clearly serious about the idea. Nine months later, in June 2008, Mushtaq discovered that Alavi was in Lahore and turned up, announcing that he had fixed a meeting for the following morning. Again, Alavi told him to 'take a hike'.) Nawaz's instinct was, in this case, good. The general was infinitely loyal to those he respected, superiors or not. Former soldiers – from his own regiment and from the SSG – called on him often. They were no longer coming to commiserate, as they had in the darkest days, but to pay their respects or ask for advice or for help finding jobs when they retired from the Army. Sometimes they brought presents. One evening during *Ramazan* I saw Alavi arriving late for a big *Iftar* (breaking of fast) party. 'One of my soldiers came to the office and gave me a gun that they had seized a few days ago during an operation' he explained. 'He thought it was interesting and had never seen one like it, so he decided that I would like it'.

Alavi was greatly relieved by the announcement in September 2007 that President Musharraf had appointed General Ashfaq Kayani (rather than General Tariq Majid, who was the other contender) as the Vice Chief of Army Staff. Whoever became Vice Chief would (God willing) become Chief in due course.

Alavi respected General Kayani and thought he would be good for the Army.

His personal relationship with Kayani had always been good, if not particularly close. And he had dreaded the idea that General Tariq Majid, who had implicitly supported appeasement of the Taliban by backing Safdar, might succeed Musharraf. Tariq Majid was appointed Chairman of the Joint Chiefs of Staff, a four-star post but one that carried little real power.

General Ehsan ul-Haq, the outgoing Chairman, duly left his official residence (a prominent building, which had once been General Zia's home), a couple of minutes' walk from Army House, where the Chief lived. General Tariq Majid's wife got to work redecorating the house for her family. Shortly afterwards, the house was attacked by a suicide bomber. Neither the general nor any of his family was hurt, but seven people were killed (including the attacker and three policemen who were manning a checkpost in the road outside) and eleven wounded. As we discussed the tragedy, a day or so later, Alavi insisted that this could have been retribution for the Army's attack on the Lal Masjid (the mosque that became a hotbed of terrorism) in July 2007. General Tariq Majid (at that time Commander of X Corps, based in Rawalpindi), had been in charge of the military operation, although all key decisions were taken by President Musharraf. 'At least I am out of the line of fire,' Alavi commented. He was completely confident that he was no longer much of a target for the militants, although he had been high on – if not top of – their list when he was GOC SSG.

In October 2007 Alavi was finally able to have the discussion he had longed for with President Musharraf.

> Once I entered the Camp Office and was directed to the waiting room, all the SSG guys present started filing in one after the other to meet and hug me. I asked them about Tariq 'TOKA', the boss's close gunman, and was told that he was on duty at home. However, minutes later, he also appeared on the scene after coming to know I was there. He confided to me that all would now be fine as he was sure of it…
>
> My time came. I walked in. The boss was in his uniform and on seeing me got up, moved a few steps towards me, first shook my hand and then hugged me. 'Come, come sit,' he said. Once I parked my bum comfortably in the chair in front of his desk he asked me about the family. Then he asked me about my job and I gave him a briefing on the problems multi-national companies were facing in Pakistan.
>
> Thereafter, he came to the point and said, 'Well, Alavi, let's just forget the past and renew our friendship.' Just forget whatever happened and

> let's move on was what he followed up with… I told him that I had always been loyal 2 him, was loyal 2 him even after my retirement and remained loyal 2 him even today but I had heard that aspersions had been cast on my loyalty to him by others. He told me that was not the case and he had been hurt by hearing that my wife had been talking against him. I told him I had also heard about that and it was utter lies that had been communicated to him. He said, 'OK, forget it, forget it!'

Alavi persisted and told Musharaf the background to the rivalries in the Army and how they'd been used against him. The Prime Minister told him to make up with his bitter rivals. Alavi continued:

> He said he knew how I felt but I should try and overcome these hard feelings towards them … And then the boss said most probably [he] was hurt bcos of what I had said and he had personally heard the tape. That GAVE ME THE OPPORTUNITY TO CLEAR MYSELF. And then I exactly told him the correct version of my conversation with that Pathan bitch and apprised him how my conversation had been given a concocted interpretation by these guys and that they had been involved with her. 'OK, OK! Let's forget the whole thing!' he said again, now we need to move on. Despite all this, he said, it would be great on my part to make up with these two characters. I told him I had no problems in doing that as I was already moving forward with my life.
>
> Meanwhile, the ADC interrupted us for the 2nd time and told him that the PM had arrived. I then told him I'd excuse myself. He got up and again hugged me and we shook hands warmly. While shaking hands I told him, 'Well, you are also going thru some tough times nowadays. All I can advise you is to remain resolute!' He chuckled at that and said we'd get to see each other again and I moved my African ass out of his office.
>
> The ADC saw me out and the moment I stepped out, there were my darling SSG guys whom I'd not met waiting to see me and again I went thru a complete huggin parade b4 jumping into my car and moving out of the Camp Office feeling light, happy and exhilarated.

2008 was a year of political turmoil for Pakistan. The general election in February – less than two months after the assassination of Benazir Bhutto – brought the PPP to power, in a coalition with Nawaz Sharif's PML-N.

In August 2008 Pervez Musharraf resigned as President, handing over to Benazir's widower, Asif Zardari. For Alavi, the year was coloured by domestic turmoil as the wrangling over his daughter's divorce, and arguments about the custody of her child, dragged on. He found the business upsetting, demanding (he had to go to Washington to handle the lawyers there) and expensive. Throughout everything, the horror of his dismissal from the Army was never far from his thoughts. Although he had made his peace with General Musharraf – and Alavi assumed that there would be further meetings – he still longed for some public sign that he had served his country well and left the service with honour.

We met for lunch one day at Talking Fish, his favourite restaurant. It was hot – although it was October – despite two fans rattling away in the back room where we were sitting. The general pushed his plate of qeema away uneaten and smoked half a dozen cigarettes as he talked. He was full of fun, as always, rattling off stories and jokes and gossip in between taking calls on his mobile phones. The restaurant was empty. Since the attack on an Italian restaurant earlier that year many Pakistanis, and most of the foreign community, had decided that such places were unsafe.

'Read this,' he said, handing me a copy of a three-page letter he had written to the Chief of Army Staff.

He lit yet another cigarette, the last in the packet, as I scanned the letter.

'Don't send it,' I told the General, folding the letter and handing it back to him.

'I knew you would talk me out of it, so I've already sent it. But', he said, handing the letter back to me, 'I want you to keep this and publish it if anything happens to me.'

Alavi had written to General Kayani, now the Chief of the Army Staff, asking for an enquiry into the circumstances leading to his sacking. Now, three years on, he said that he wanted justice and he wanted his honour restored.

In the penultimate paragraph of his letter, he wrote of his hope that an enquiry would lead to 'disciplinary action … against these General officers, who grossly misused their office … in order to settle personal scores/animosities which resulted in a General Officer being despatched on retirement, in a manner worse than an OR i.e. overnight, without even a charge sheet. This is a retirement UNPRECEDENTED in the history of the Pakistan Army. The entire purpose of this plot by these

General officers was to hide their own involvement in a matter they knew, I was privy to ... I will not reveal further details here but before an enquiry, I will furnish all relevant proof/information, which is readily available with me.'

'You are a fool to have sent this,' I said, grimly aware that – if he was right about what had happened in 2005 – his enemies of three years ago were still serving and would see the letter as a casus belli. 'You have now been given almost all your statutory benefits. You have a good job in the commercial sector. Why not leave all this alone? Why are you doing this now?'

He explained that if he did not act now he would be unable to seek redress later for the crime that he believed had been committed against him. The Army would conclude that he had accepted the situation.

Whenever he talked about the events of 2005 he returned to the question of honour.

'I want justice. And I want my honour restored. And you know what? I give a damn [sic] what they do to me now. They did their worst three years ago.'

He was serious, staring angrily as he remembered the debacle. And then the moment was gone. He ran a hand across his face, in a characteristic downward sweeping gesture, and turned the conversation to nonsense.

A few days later we talked about his safety. He agreed that it would be prudent, for the time being, to avoid mountain roads, too much partying and driving late at night. Alavi decided that he would travel with his driver as much as possible. He hoped that the Army would give him something of what he needed. But he believed that the letter to the Chief of Army Staff might also prove to be his death warrant. He saw this letter as something dangerous, and possession of it as dangerous too. He asked me, during another meeting, where I had put it, and was concerned when I told him that it was in the drawer of the desk in my room at the Serena Hotel.

'Put it in the safe.'

It struck me as very odd that Alavi, who had shown so little fear when – as he had told me – he had been being hounded by the MI after his sacking, was so concerned about the whereabouts of the letter.

Life went on. Faisal Alavi had a telecommunications company to run, I a book to write. During one meeting he told me that was sending his uniform to the SSG Museum. In another he told me that he had been in touch with Lieutenant General Masood Aslam, the Commander of XI Corps in Peshawar, to petition the Army to provide a Christian chaplain at an Army base under XI Corps' jurisdiction. It was odd to think of a Christian community in such a remote place, and interesting that they had sought Alavi's help.

On the evening of Saturday 15 November we met again at Talking Fish. I had just returned from Bajaur and was heading off to Waziristan the following day. He wanted to know everything about my trip: who, when, where? The debriefing was thorough. In return he had a week's worth of stories to tell, jokes to pass on. He was full of plans, important family arrangements as well as ideas about friends he wanted to see.

I asked whether there was any news from GHQ. He shook his head. He had known what the stakes were when he sent the letter.

'It hasn't worked. They'll shoot me.' And then, as usual, he changed gear.

I was at Wana in South Waziristan staying with 9 Division when I heard the news.

That morning I had flown to Landai Nur, a nearby post manned by 9 Punjab, an impressive unit. The officers and men seemed to be pulling together, handling difficult terrain and difficult tribesmen with the usual Army humour and resilience. It was a clear, cold morning in the mountains and I was grateful to be with the Army, seeing it at its best, deployed in a testing environment.

At about 18.00 I returned to my quarters in the Divisional HQ, Javed Sultan Camp. The HQ consists almost entirely of prefabricated containers, including the visitor accommodation. Sitting down to pull off my boots I switched on the television.

'RETIRED MAJOR GENERAL FAISAL ALAVI AND HIS DRIVER SHOT DEAD ON THE WAY TO WORK.'

It took me a moment to understand the television breaking news strapline.

I pulled my boots on again and walked round to the Divisional Commander's house, where I had had dinner the night before with a small group of officers. It was very odd to call unannounced on a senior officer, but the General was kind. He had been resting, but came quickly into his sitting room when he was told that I had arrived. He had not heard the news about Alavi, but he switched on his television and saw that the strapline was still running.

I asked the Divisional Commander to help me to get back to Islamabad as soon as possible. Lieutenant General Masood Aslam was visiting the Division the following day, and he kindly said I should be allowed to go to Islamabad on one of the day's flights. I was grateful; there are often, it seems to me, more people hoping to get on these flights than there is room. As it happened, we only got as far as Dera Ismail Khan. The weather was turning bad, and the pilot was unwilling to fly further. Again the Army helped. Major General Athar Abbas, the Director General of ISPR, helped to arrange for me to drive from DI Khan to Islamabad the following morning. I went with a young officer from Military Intelligence, a nice man as I remember. I arrived back at my hotel with barely time to change, after a short night and a long drive before going to the graveyard.

The story of the murder of the SSG Chief was front-page news in Pakistan the morning after it happened, and most of the press followed it up the following day.

> According to witnesses, General Alvi's vehicle was intercepted ... by two youths on a motorcycle and a Mitsubishi Pajero SUV. Acting in a deliberate fashion, the assailants, one youth from the motorcycle and two men from the SUV, opened fire simultaneously, making sure that Alvi was dead before leaving. The whole operation took roughly 30 seconds. According to police, 9mm pistols were used in the attack, with the General struck by bullets eight times, his driver six times. (*The News*, 20 November).

Accounts of the shooting varied. Some talked of two motorcyclists. Most reported that the path of Alavi's car had been blocked by the Pajero. All agreed that the slaughter had been efficient. The general had been murdered only yards away from his own front door.

I heard later that Ruby, his lifelong friend, found him. She too lived a short distance from the place of the murder.

The scene at the Army graveyard in Rawalpindi that day was grim. Soldiers and officers had come from all over the country to bury Faisal Alavi. The SSG was well represented, and so was 26 Cavalry. Their grief was palpable. I saw a three-star general, a hard-headed man, wandering around as if he was lost.

Many of the women from Faisal's family were at the graveyard, to the consternation of the Army, which was organising the funeral. Women do not normally follow the coffin to the grave in Pakistan. A place was found for us, in the end, apart from the men. Pretty Alia, Alavi's sister from Lahore, was there and so were all his favourite nieces. Steadfast Farida stood straight, pale, unblinking. As she watched her brother being borne to his last home she spoke:

'They do these things better in the Pakistan Air Force, you know.'

Ruby was there too, of course. I did not recognise her at first, she was so undone by the horror.

Alavi was lowered into his grave by soldiers, buried with military honours. Wreaths were laid on behalf of the Chief of Army Staff and most of the country's military leadership.

But friends and family members were taken aback to be told by serving and retired officers and soldiers, including members of the SSG, that the killing was not the work of militants. 'This was the Army,' a number of people report having been told that day. Over the next few days I heard the same comment in Army circles. It seemed that everybody believed that Faisal had been murdered exactly as he had anticipated.

After Alavi's murder I stayed in Pakistan for a couple of weeks. I assumed that I, and anyone who was in regular contact with him, would be questioned by the authorities investigating the case. I was pleased by the news that the ISI was to be in charge of the investigation. They, I thought, would be thorough and scrupulous. But no one contacted me. I gathered from Alavi's sisters and nieces that only cursory interviews were held even with them. His friends were not, as far as I could discover, interviewed by anyone.

So I returned home to London and did as Alavi had asked me to do. I published an article in the *Sunday Times*, using his letter, reporting that the General had feared that his enemies in the Army would kill him.

My position was not then and is not now, that two men specifically named in Alavi's letter had had him killed. I do not know what happened that day in Bahria Town. My position is that Alavi had believed that the two might have him eliminated, and that it was my duty to him to make that clear, as he had wanted.

The reaction to my article was understandably somewhat harsh. I knew that all the people who had been so kind to me, for so long, would be shocked by what seemed like a betrayal. The irony of my position, I thought, was that I would normally have defended anyone in the Army against any allegations of plots or violence. In any case, Alavi was not 'murdered by the Army'. He thought that two men in the Army might have him killed, which is a very different matter.

After his death I talked to people in England who had known Alavi. He made friends wherever he went either at home or abroad. Lord Guthrie, former Chief of Defence Staff in the UK, remembers him warmly: 'I liked him. He was clearly a very professional soldier and he struck me as someone who would really move things along.'

Then I spoke to Richard Williams, Alavi's old friend from Hereford. He was saddened by the story, but said that he could see what had motivated him to write to General Kayani. He understood Alavi's longing for the *Hilal-i-Imtiaz*:

> It is interesting that he wanted [that]. Every soldier, in the moment before death, craves to be recognised. Powerful things, medals. It seems reasonable to me that he staked everything on his honour. The idea that it is better to be dead than dishonoured does run deep in soldiers.
>
> It's a sad story. I can see it.

Colonel Williams continued, in a salute to Alavi:

> There is often a clash between the SF [Special Forces] personality and the Army institution, since special Forces are a very different breed from the rest of the Army. You are used to commanding men who won't do something unless they think it's a good idea. Faisal Alavi was the sort of SF officer who is often at war with his bosses in the Army. Confident, no respecter of persons. Just by being himself, being so colourful, he'd have made enemies.

In March 2009 it was reported in the Pakistan *Daily Times* that a retired major, Haroon Rashid, who had been picked up by the police in connection with a kidnapping case, had confessed to the murder of Faisal Alavi. He and two accomplices had been arrested for Alavi's murder. As months passed, more information emerged. Major Haroon, it was reported, was a confederate of the notorious Ilyas Kashmiri, a veteran of the Soviet war in Afghanistan and the Kashmir conflict, and now said to be a senior al Qaeda member (probably killed on 3 June 2011). Through

Ilyas Kashmiri the killers were connected to David Headley, a Pakistani American charged with involvement in the Mumbai bombings.

Since the killing, and the arrest of Major Haroon, I have spent a great deal of time pondering all these things. I do not know who killed, or commissioned the killing of, Major General Alavi. It may be a sad coincidence that while Alavi prepared for assault by his personal enemies he was, in fact, targeted by others.

Major Haroon was acquitted in 2010. I was told by Alavi's family that he walked out of jail in the early summer of 2011. I have no confirmation of this.

Alavi had a reputation as a fearsome soldier. A fellow cavalry officer was once telling me that he had never really liked him. But – he said – 'if I was going into battle he's the one man I'd want alongside me'. I heard the same, again and again, from detractors as well as admirers. So, I asked Alavi once what had made him brave. 'The first thing is that you don't stop to think. You just plough on.'

And? Anything else?

'I never thought they'd get me.'

10

Conclusion

The Pakistan Army may be flawed but it is the best we've got. Despite its failings it works better than anything else in Pakistan. The politicians are still venal, the liberal intelligentsia callous about the hardships faced by ordinary people. The civilian elites seem to have no interest in making things function. I used to call on President Musharraf from time to time, both at the Camp Office (his base in Rawalpindi as Chief of Army Staff) and at Aiwan-i-Sedr (the President's official residence in Islamabad). The routine was the same at both places. A time for the meeting would be set. Checkposts and guards on the gate had a list of people with appointments. Visitors were greeted and shown into a waiting room where there might be two other people waiting to see the President. There were never more than two people unless a delegation was visiting the President.

After President Musharraf resigned I called on his successor. I liked Mr Zardari; he was original and funny, and unassuming. But the set-up at Aiwan-i-Sedr was shambolic. Neither the checkposts nor the guards had my name, but I gathered that they didn't really have the names of any visitors. The policemen and guards were frazzled, shouting, waving their arms, running around yelling into radios. Inside Aiwan-i-Sedr, there was havoc. The waiting room had become a bazaar, hordes sitting, standing, talking, arguing and laughing. They poured out into the corridor, talking into mobile phones (in theory handed over at the entrance). No one seemed to know who was scheduled to see the President next, but nor did they much mind. Everyone seemed to take it for granted that they would spend hours hanging around, waiting. There was a party atmosphere, and a feeling that simply being inside the Presidency was a pleasure.

Later, I talked about all this to a friend who was not well-disposed to the Army at that time. 'Of course that's how it is,' she said. 'Civilian governments can't do anything'. I still do not understand why this should be the case, but it is an accepted fact, in Pakistan, that the Army functions better than the civilian sector, and the fact that so many believe this so forcefully makes it true.

The Pakistan Army is not riddled with extremism. Pakistani society is becoming more pious, and the Army necessarily reflects the country. The Army prays more and drinks less than it did a generation ago. It is not, however, full of violent jihadis. There have been publicly documented cases of soldiers and officers being radicalised, and others that have not been publicly revealed, but there is no real evidence that this is widespread. The Army goes to a great deal of trouble to ensure that soldiers and officers are given sound Islamic teaching. It is highly unlikely that significant numbers of Army personnel would be actively involved in terrorism. The Pakistan Army, with its strong British roots, is institutionally powerful – the soldiers identify with the Army and derive their self-respect from being part of it – and like any regular Army it abhors disorder. Soldiers and officers do not want to attack the state and spread chaos. Many believe that the country and the Army will continue to become more religious with the passage of time: there's no need to take up arms to make this happen.

I am not suggesting that all is well with the Army. Morale was shattered by the Abbottabad affair. The Army feels publicly humiliated, and it needs to find a way to regain public confidence. The Army can cope with danger and hardship, but needs the trust of the nation. Recovering this trust will take time.

There is another difficulty with the Pakistan Army. Officers, even fairly senior people, are disposed to believe wild conspiracy theories. Thousands of able and sophisticated military people truly believe that the West wants to dismember Pakistan, for example. Still more believe that the United States wants to invade Iran. Hardly any believe that Osama bin Laden masterminded the 9/11 attacks.

Genuine fear of the United States and other countries underlies a great deal of Pakistani thinking, in the Army as well as outside.

Pakistan is frightened of India.

Pakistan is frightened by the deteriorating security situation inside its borders.

Pakistan is frightened by American threats, explicit and not (its people see threats where none have been made).

Pakistan is frightened by the Coalition presence in Afghanistan, and by the effect it is having on the region, and frightened too of the prospect that the Allies are going to leave, abandoning Pakistan yet again as its neighbour falls apart.

Pakistan is annoyed that after a decade of this war, the Western powers still fail to acknowledge that the country cannot always be driven by their needs, at the expense of its own.

In the end, Afghanistan does not matter very much to the British public. The Coalition will pull out fairly soon. The worst that can happen, if Afghanistan slides entirely out of control, is another attack on the scale of 9/11. This would not change very much.

The fate of Pakistan, on the other hand, matters greatly to the United Kingdom and the United States, and this fate lies, to a considerable extent, in the hands of the Army.

Appendix I

Operation Nepal and the Men of Steel

'Operation Nepal and the Men of Steel' is the story told by a journalist of a tank regiment of the Pakistan Army in the 1965 war in the Sialkot Sector. It is a story of boldness, courage and fog of war. In this case the fog of war helped the 25th Cavalry fulfil its mission. As destiny would have it I was the Adjutant of that tank regiment, the 25th Cavalry (25 Cav). What is related here is through the eyes of a young captain who was manning the regimental command post of 25 Cav throughout that short but intense war. For brevity a lot of inessential details have been left out.

The area of operations of 25 Cav was to the south-east of the city of Sialkot and centred on Chawinda, a small rural town not more than 30 km from the border, incidentally Sialkot was less than 20 km from the border. 25 Cav for the duration of the war was under the command of the 24 Infantry Brigade.

A warm September morning found 25 Cav, refuelling and resting in a small clump on the northern edge of Pasrur, a town about 15 km south of Chawinda, after a futile forced march the night before towards Narowal, a town south-east of Pasrur, and back. The same night the enemy had launched its main offensive in the area of Charwa, a village barely 30 km north-east of Chawinda. The Indians found some light opposition and our engineers laying mines. The core of the enemy offensive was an armoured division. While protecting its flanks, again using armour and mechanised forces, the Indian advance was led by the 16th Cavalry.

24 Brigade HQ found the Indian attack when the enemy had already covered over 20 km inside Pakistan and were knocking on the doors of Chawinda. At that point in time there was thin air between the leading Indian elements and Pasrur. 25 Cav was ordered to stop the Indian advance in the general direction of Chawinda. Not much else was know about the strength of the Indian force, except that they were advancing with tanks. With this scanty information, the commanding officer of 25

Cav decided to move with all the three squadrons abreast: C Squadron on the left, B Squadron in the centre following the main Pasrur, Chawinda, Phillora, Charwa axis and A Squadron on the right in the direction of the villages of Dugri and Matta. After crossing Chawinda, the regiment met its first opposition. B Squadron ran into 16 Cav, A squadron fought with 17 Poona Horse. All three squadrons of 25 Cav, almost in an 'advance to contact' mode, came head on with three units (battalion size) of the Indian force.

To the good fortune of 25 Cav, the Pakistan Air Force attacked the advancing Indian tanks at almost the same time that we ran into the enemy. We lost a number of tanks but the Indians lost many more. Our bold, almost reckless action forced the Indians to recoil back and lose ground which they had easily won hours earlier. An element of B squadron managed to penetrate deep inside the Indian front and reached the village of Maharajke, from where it was chased back by the Indians back to the village of Gadgor, where elements of B and C Squadrons had finally converged around sunset. In the meantime I in my command vehicle had caught up with the leading elements of my regiment and established the command post in Phillora. In the excitement of our advance I travelled to Gadgor and crawled all over an Indian Centurion which we had shot and captured hours earlier. Operational documents retrieved from that tank made us aware of the magnitude of the Indian thrust and 'Operation Nepal', the code name of this thrust. Not bad for an armoured regiment (tank battalion). Had we known what we were up against, an armoured division plus an infantry division, we would have been far more careful and had the Indians known that it was only a tank battalion which blocked their way to Pasrur and Sialkot, they would have been more bold. Such is the fog of war. That day two of the three squadron commanders of 25 Cav were wounded and evacuated and we lost a number of men and many tanks.

25 Cav continued to hold the line of Gadgor for another three/four days till the time they were withdrawn to Pasrur for rest and refit and we were replaced by fresh troops including an armoured regiment. But R and R was not for the men of 25 Cav. Barely had the regiment reached back to Pasrur than the Indian attacked the new troops holding the line of Gadgor and pushed them back almost to the outskirts of Chawinda, with heavy casualties.

The next morning, 25 Cav was ordered once again to move out of Pasrur post haste and stop the Indians. Because of attrition the regiment had now been reorganised into two squadrons. Once again 25Cav stopped the Indians but in the meantime the Indians had managed to come right up to Chawinda, where 25 Cav as the backbone of 24 Infantry Brigade held the line till the end of the war.

Besides the daily fighting, the Indians launched a number of attacks to break the Chawinda defence but failed. I particularly remember two such attacks. One was a massive infantry attack on the night of probably the 14th or 15th of September followed by a classic armour attack, probably the next day. Both days were a touch and go affair but we won both days though with heavy casualties for both sides. Thus on at least two occasions 25 Cav helped forestall two major military reverses for Pakistan. I do not want to downgrade the role of other armour, infantry and the artillery units who fought alongside 25 Cavalry but the fact is that the role of 25 Cavalry was central in avoiding a major military reversal for Pakistan. The role of 25 Cav has been acknowledged both nationally and internationally and earned them the title of Men of Steel who brought Operation Nepal to a grinding halt on day one of the Indian offensive.

Mahmud Ali Durrani

Appendix II: Armoured Regiments of the Pakistan Army

The President's Body Guard: Faith, Unity and Discipline
Raised 1773
Prominent officers:
LG Sahibzada Yaqub Khan
Col Sher Khan
Col Shahid Ali Khan

4 Cavalry: The Valiant Fourth
Raised 1956
Prominent officers:
LC Azmat Khan (prev. 11)
LG Tariq Khan (son of Col Azmat Khan of 11 Cav, later 12)
Brigadier Tariq Jilani

5 Horse Probyn's Horse: Ich Dien
Raised 1857
Prominent officers:
General Gul Hassan
LG Shah Rafi Alam (prev. 12)
MG Saeed-uz-Zaman Janjua (later Ambassador to Burma)
Brig. Isfandiyar Pataudi
Notes:

- 'Probyn Sahibki Regiment' as the *jawans* call it.
- The richest regiment in the Army, with astonishing silver.
- Officers traditionally from rich or very well-connected families. Anyone from a different background would simply not fit in.
- The old criticism that it was full of the sons of general officers, and therefore never deployed in the most dangerous operations, was probably unfair.

6 Lancers Duke of Connaught's Own
Raised 1857
Prominent officers:
Brigadier Ingall,
General Zia ul-Haq (prev. 13, later 10 and 22)
Lt General Sahibzada Yaqub Khan (prev. 11)
MG Zaffar Abbas (DG ANTF)
Brigadier Haroon (8 Arm Brig)
Notes:
Officers characteristically friendly, relaxed. A disciplined regiment that has produced distinguished sportsmen.

7 Lancers
Raised 1991

8 Cavalry
Raised 1991

9 Horse
Raised 1991

10 Cavalry Guides Cavalry
(FF)
Raised 1846
Prominent Officers:
General Zia ul-Haq (later 22)
LG Zarrar Azeem
MG Mahmud Durrani (later 25)
MG Saeedullah Khan (later? 56)
Notes:
Old, Anglophile. Zia did not fit in.

11 Cavalry Prince Albert Victor's Own Kabul to Kandahar
(FF) Raised 1849
Prominent officers:
General K. M. Arif
Lt General Sahibzada Yaqub Khan (later 6)
Lt General Hamid Khan

LG Khurshid Ali Khan (later Gov. NWFP)
Brig Effendi (later 6)
Col Azmat Khan
Notes:

- Good war record in 1965 and 1971.
- Sometimes teased by other regiments… 'Kabul to Kandahar is all you know'.

12 Cavalry Sam Browne's
(FF) Raised 1955
Prominent officers:
Lt Gen Shah Rafi Alam (later 5) (d)
MG Jamshed Khan (d) f(DGMO)
MG Mahmud Najeeb Khan
LG Tariq Khan (prev 4)
Major Salar Malik (Sandhurst)
Notes:

- Reconnaissance regiment.
- Combines some of the grandeur of the old cavalry regiments with the agility and vigour of the more recently raised.
- Outstanding sporting record.

13 Lancers Spearhead
Raised 1817
Prominent officers:
General Jehangir Karamat
Gen. Zia ul-Haq (later 6, 10 and 22)
LG Zarar Azeem (prev 10)
MG Nadim Ijaz
Brig Saad
Brig Derek Joseph
Col Haroon Abbas
Capt Ejaz Alam Khan [shaheed 71]
Notes:

- The oldest and truly the grandest regiment, described by Brigadier Z. Alam Khan as '*qanooni*'.
- 13 L officers have an air of reserve. They are generally quiet and never allow their excellence to appear other than effortless. Their humour

is ironic.

- Almost wiped out in 1971 at Bara Pind in the Sialkot Sector.

14 Lancers Ghazi Squadron
Raised 1993

15 Lancers
Raised 1955
Prominent officers:
Lt Gen Farrukh Khan (f C11 Corps)
Brig Akram Hussain Syed (?)

16 Horse
Raised 1993

17 Lancers
Raised 1998

18 Horse
Raised 1994

19 Lancers Tiwana Lancers
Raised 1858
Prominent officers:
Lt Gen Alam Jan Mahsud
Lt Gen Hamid Gul
Lt Gen Syed Arif Hassan
LG Ahsan Azhar Hayat
LG Sikander Afzal
Brig Hashim
Notes:

- In 'JCO's Lancers' the JCOs are said by the rest of the armoured corps to be brighter than the officers.
- This is the 'factory for generals', the regiment that has produced more general officers than any other, supposedly by ensuring that no one is ever given a less-than-glowing report.
- The 19 L network (wryly described as 'philanthropy' by others) is formidable.

- You can spot 19 L officers by their supreme confidence. Outgoing and hospitable, they are also sometimes described as flashy and arrogant.
- For all the sniping they attract, they also have a distinguished record.
- The regiment also produces excellent sportsmen.
- A very rich regiment.

20 Lancers *Haidri*
Raised 1956
Prominent officers:
General Shamim Alam Khan (later 24, 28)
Lt Gen Mohammad Akram (f C4 Corps/QMG)

21 Horse
Raised 1990

22 Cavalry Death or Glory
Raised 1962
Prominent officers:
Zia-ul-Haq (prev. 13, 6 and 10. CO 1966–68)
Brig Talat Saeed

23 Cavalry
(FF) Raised 1962
Prominent officers:
LG Salauddin Tirmizi (C2 Corps, now MNA)
MG Farooq
MG Resham Ejaz

24 Cavalry The Chargers
(FF) Raised 1962
Prominent officers:
General Shamim Alam Khan (prev. 20, later 28)
LG Javed Alam
Notes:
24 Cavalry has a reputation for going the extra mile, for doing more than is asked of it. But as well as working hard, it parties hard. Arguably the most sociable regiment in the Army, with a big clique of retired officers in Karachi.

25 Cavalry Men of Steel
Raised 1962
Prominent officers:
MG Mahmud Durrani
Brig Javed Nasir
LC Mansoor (current CO)
Notes:
The regiment that stopped an armoured division, 25 Cav's performance in 1965 was the stuff of legend.

26 Cavalry The Mustangs
Raised 1968
Prominent officers:
MG Syed Ali Hamid
MG Faisal Alavi
Col Sher Khan (later PB)
Notes:

- The Mustangs have famously known how to party ever since the regiment was raised by Lt Col Akram Hussain Syed.
- Large number of Pathan officers.
- 26 Cav JCOs noticeably confident and competent. The regt has long given them greater independence than others and this has paid off.

27 Cavalry Steeds of War
Raised 1965
Prominent officers:
MG Athar Abbas
MG Iftikhar Malik
Brig Imran Malik

28 Cavalry Chhamb
Raised 1969
Reconnaissance regiment
Prominent officers:
General Shamim Alam Khan (prev 20,24)
Brigadier Iftikhar Opel
Brigadier Abdul Hamid Dogar (CO during 71 war)

29 Cavalry
Raised 1968

30 Cavalry Bold Till Death
Raised 1966
MG Ghulam Ahmad ('GA')
MG Rahmat Khan

31 Cavalry
Raised 1966

32 Cavalry
Raised 1964
Prominent officers:
MG Tahir Siddiqui
Notes:
32 Cav is famously brilliant at pulling everything together at the last minute, although senior officers are frequently stressed before that happens.

33 Cavalry Fortune's with the Bold
Raised 1971
Prominent officers:
General Ahsan Saleem Hayat (later 42)

38 Cavalry Desert Hawks
Raised 1971
Prominent officers:
Brig Zahir Alam Khan
LG Waheed Arshad
MG Hussain Mehdi (f DG Pak Rangers Punjab)
MG Mustapha Khan (f ISI)

39 Cavalry
Raised 1971

40 Horse (Sindh) (Sindh Regt Group)
Raised 1987

41 Horse
(FF) Raised 1987

42 Lancers (Punjab Regt Group)
Raised 1988
Prominent officers:
General Ahsan Saleem Hyat (prev 33)

51 Lancers
Raised 1971

52 Cavalry
Raised 1972

53 Cavalry
Raised 1972
Prominent officers:
MG Khalid Naeem

54 Cavalry The Fifty-Fourth
Raised 1974

56 Cavalry
Raised 1985
Prominent officers:
MG Abid (1 Arm Div)
MG Saeedullah Khan (prev. 10)

57 Cavalry
Raised 1985
58 Cavalry
Raised 1985
Prominent officers:
LG Tariq Khan (??)

21 Independent Armoured Squadron
Raised 1985

Appendix III: Pakistan Army Corps

I Corps, Mangla
Armour-heavy 'strike' corps intended to conduct counter-offensive operations within Pakistan or to strike into Indian territory.

II Corps Multan
Armour-heavy 'strike' corps. Function as above.

IV Corps
Lahore infantry-heavy holding corps intended to counter Indian attacks in its immediate area.

V Corps
Karachi Infantry-heavy holding corps intended to defend Sindh against any thrust by India. India would probably try to cut Karachi off from the rest of the country. Also responsible for defending against sea-borne landings.

X Corps
Rawalpindi Infantry-heavy holding corps intended to defend the Line of Control and counter-attack within Punjab. In charge of Force Command, Northern Area, responsible for the mountainous region, including Siachen Glacier.

XI Corps
Peshawar infantry-heavy holding corps intended to defend the northern border with Afghanistan, but would reinforce the east in the event of war with India.

XII Corps
Quetta infantry-heavy holding corps intended to defend the southern Afghanistan and Iran borders, but would reinforce the east in the event of war with India.

XXX Corps
Gujranwala infantry-heavy holding corps intended to counter Indian attacks in its immediate area.

XXXI Corps
Bahawlpur mixed infantry-armour corps intended to counter Indian attacks in its immediate area.

These are the wartime roles assigned to the Pakistan Army's nine corps. The counter-insurgency operations of the last decade have clearly altered the Army's perspective. Divisions have been shifted into the Tribal Areas and the Army's training programmes have been overhauled to reflect its current role.

But – given the historical context – the Pakistan Army is inevitably focused on India.

The border with India falls into four sections:

i. International Border: 1,200 km long. Between Indian states of Punjab, Rajasthan and Gujarat from the Pakistan provinces of Punjab and Sindh. Uncontested.
ii. Working Boundary: 200 km long. Between Pakistan and Indian-occupied Jammu. Not recognised by Pakistan.
iii. Line of Control: 600 km long. Between Pakistan-administered Kashmir ('Azad Kashmir') and Indian-held Kashmir. De facto border, but not recognised as permanent by either side.
iv. Line of Effective Control: 65 km long. Runs north from the Line of Control, and is the current position of Pakistan and Indian Army troops at the Siachen Glacier.

Index